Philanthropy in Nineteenth-Century Ireland

In this series:

Philanthropy in Nineteenth-Century Ireland

Laurence M. Geary & Oonagh Walsh
EDITORS

FOUR COURTS PRESS

Set in 10 on 12.5 point Bembo for
FOUR COURTS PRESS LTD
7 Malpas Street, Dublin 8, Ireland
www.fourcourtspress.ie
and in North America for
FOUR COURTS PRESS
c/o ISBS, 920 N.E. 58th Avenue, Suite 300, Portland, OR 97213.

A catalogue record for this title
is available from the British Library.

ISBN 978-1-84682-350-3

Printed in England
by Antony Rowe Ltd, Chippenham, Wilts.

Contents

Abbreviations

AU	Audit Office
CLSF	Charitable Loan Fund Society
CRF	Convict Reference Files
CSORP	Chief Secretary's Office Registered Papers
DADC	Dublin Artisans' Dwellings Company
DMS	Dublin Musical Society
HC	House of Commons sessional papers
IDC	4% Industrial Dwellings Company
ISPCC	Irish Society for the Prevention of Cruelty to Children
LFB	Loan Fund Board
LFS	Loan Fund Society
NAI	National Archives of Ireland
NGI	National Gallery of Ireland
NLI	National Library of Ireland
NSPCC	National Society for the Prevention of Cruelty to Children
NUI	National University of Ireland
PRONI	Public Records Office of Northern Ireland
RA	Royal Academy of Arts
RCPI	Royal College of Physicians Ireland Archives
RHA	Royal Hibernian Academy
RIAU	Royal Irish Art Union
RII	Royal Irish Institute
SPCP	Society for Promoting the Comforts of the Poor
SSNCI	Society for the Study of Nineteenth-Century Ireland
TCD	Trinity College Dublin
TNA	The National Archives
TSB	Trustee Savings Bank
UCD	University College Dublin

Contributors

SARAH-ANNE BUCKLEY lectures in the Department of History, NUI, Galway. Her monograph, *The cruelty man: child welfare, the NSPCC and the State in Ireland, 1889–1956*, was published by Manchester University Press in 2013.

MEL COUSINS has written extensively on the history of poverty and poor relief in Ireland and Europe. His most recent book is *Poor relief in Ireland, 1851–1914* (Bern, 2011). He is a research associate at the School of Social Work and Social Policy at Trinity College, Dublin.

JOHN WILSON FOSTER is emeritus professor of English at the University of British Columbia and honorary research fellow at the Institute of Irish Studies, Queens' University Belfast. His most recent book is *Pilgrims of the air* (London, 2014).

LAURENCE M. GEARY is senior lecturer in history at University College Cork, where he teaches modern Irish history. He has published extensively on the social, political and medical history of nineteenth-century Ireland, and on the history of the Irish in Australia.

LINDA KING is a lecturer in design history at the Institute of Art, Design and Technology (IADT), Dublin. She has published widely on Irish design, including the co-edited volume (with Elaine Sisson) *Ireland, design and visual culture: negotiating modernity, 1922–1992* (Cork, 2011).

JOANNE McENTEE received a PhD in history in 2013 from NUI, Galway, for research entitled 'The state and the landed estate: order and shifting power relations in Ireland, 1815–1891'.

PHILIP McEVANSONEYA is a lecturer in the history of art at Trinity College, Dublin. He has published widely on Irish and British topics and is currently working on aspects of Irish antiquarianism.

KEVIN McKENNA completed his PhD, 'Power, resistance, and ritual: paternalism on the Clonbrock estates, 1826–1908', at NUI, Maynooth, in 2011, and has since published a number of chapters in edited volumes based on his doctoral research.

EOIN McLAUGHLIN is a lecturer in environmental economics at the University of St Andrews.

CONOR McNAMARA has worked at the University of Notre Dame, Keough-Naughton Centre for Irish Studies, where he was commissioned to produce *Easter 1916: a research guide* (Dublin, 2015). He was formerly an archivist in the Manuscripts

Department of the National Library of Ireland where he catalogued the Mahon Papers, one of the largest collections of estate papers held by the state.

MARY PIERSE, a former IRCHSS research fellow, compiled *Irish feminisms, 1810–1930 (I–V)* (London, 2009). She has published widely on George Moore and *fin-de-siècle* literature, and is a board member at the National Centre for Franco-Irish Studies.

OONAGH WALSH is professor of gender studies at Glasgow Caledonian University. She has published on a range of areas in modern Irish history, including Protestant women's social, political and cultural experiences, the development of the asylum system in the west of Ireland, and twentieth-century obstetrics.

Acknowledgments

The editors gratefully acknowledge the financial assistance towards this publication that we received from the Publications Fund of the College of Arts, Celtic Studies and Social Sciences, University College Cork, and also from the Publications Fund of the National University of Ireland.

We also wish to acknowledge the support of the Programme for Research in Third Level Institutions, through which the conference at which these papers were presented was funded.

We appreciate the forbearance and professionalism of Martin Fanning and the entire production team at Four Courts Press.

Introduction

LAURENCE M. GEARY AND OONAGH WALSH

Poverty and its relief have always gone hand in hand. For as long as society has recognized the needy, it has also had a wide variety of philanthropic organizations designed
to feed, clothe, and improve the lot of the poor. From the first organized instances
of fellow-feeling and responsibility, as expressed in the tradition of alms-giving in the
early Islamic world, and the creation of alms-houses in Europe from the tenth
century onwards, a sense of duty for the less fortunate characterizes human society.[1]
But it was the rapid social development wrought by the Industrial Revolution, and
the creation of more complex urban as well as rural societies, that signalled dramatic
developments in the world of philanthropy. The nineteenth century may truly be
described as the century of philanthropy, as across Europe voluntary organizations
developed without precedent, and addressed an overwhelming range of needs. The
emergence of a class system inevitably produced an underclass, and included those
who were marginalized from birth through poverty and congenital disability, or
became so as a result of economic upheaval, illness or old age. New categories of
workers and the introduction of a waged economy threw non-productive members
of society into sharp relief, and voluntary groups sprang up to assist injured workmen,
orphans, distressed gentlewomen, widows, the handicapped, the elderly of both sexes,
and religious converts abandoned by their families. All categories, at every stage of
the life cycle, were represented.

Scholarly interest in philanthropy in the western world was part of the general
academic engagement with non-canonical histories, born of the 'history from below'
movement of the 1960s and 70s. Individual institutional histories had, of course,
always celebrated anniversaries and centenaries, but the new studies used the archives
of various institutions to contextualize the involvement of, for example, women
workers, or organized religion, in the alleviation of poverty.[2] The field expanded
rapidly to include work on the role of philanthropy in Empire, and to emphasize the
centrality of class as an organizing principle in most Victorian and Edwardian relief
systems. The relationships between philanthropic administrators and those they
supported were increasingly analysed, and the complex interactions between 'giver'
and 'recipient' were examined to offer deeper understandings of social, gender and
political relations.[3]

1 Individuals had a religious obligation to help the needy, ensuring that the fulfilment of
this duty benefited both parties. Thierry Kochuyt, 'God, gifts and poor people: on charity
in Islam', *Social Compass*, 56:1 (Mar. 2009), pp 98–116. 2 The early work of Frank
Prochaska had an enormous influence upon the development of this field. *Women and
philanthropy in nineteenth-century England* (Oxford, 1980). 3 The large-scale involvement of

This volume includes studies of a range of efforts to improve the lot of the poor in nineteenth-century Ireland, and extends the range of analysis in the field of philanthropy studies. This is evident in the general move by contributors away from an emphasis upon the role of women as philanthropists, which has tended to domi-nate Irish work to date. The pioneering work of Maria Luddy precipitated two decades of fruitful research into philanthropy and charity in Ireland, which had focused particularly on the voluntary efforts of women.[4] The work reflected a growing interest in women's history in Ireland, and also the reality that a substantial proportion of the archives relating to organized activities by groups of Irishwomen involved philanthropic work.[5] The work undertaken by nuns in nursing and educa-tion, which, for the most part, was voluntary and broadly philanthropic, represented some of the earliest professional advances for women.[6] Moreover, the fullest records were those left by the middle classes, creating an inherent bias towards the unpaid work of educated, literate women.[7]

This volume concerns itself with the exercise of philanthropy, rather than the world of charity, although some essays (on estate philanthropy in particular) contain elements of both. Charity refers for the most part to one-off or very specific dona-tions in cash or kind, to address an immediate crisis. Thus, for example, when Lord Longford's agent bestowed clothing and funds on his tenants, he was alleviating acute starvation and deprivation. But when he then offered passage money, or made loans for improvements to dwellings, or to increase his tenants' livestock holdings, he was a philanthropist in the truest sense, providing persons with the tools for self-

middle-class women in philanthropy ensures that research into their activities continues. Recent works by scholars including Gabrielle Mearns, 'Appropriate fields of action: nineteenth-century representations of the female philanthropist and the parochial sphere' (PhD, University of Warwick, 2012) demonstrates the continuing interest in the association between philanthropy and perceptions of appropriate roles for women.   4 Maria Luddy, *Women and philanthropy in nineteenth-century Ireland* (Cambridge, 1995). Other works have focused upon specific philanthropic fields, or on the associations between philanthropy and female professional advance. Siobhan Nelson, *Say little, do much: nursing, nuns, and hospitals in the nineteenth century* (Philadelphia, 2001); Caroline Skehill, 'An examination of the transition from philanthropy to professional social work in Ireland', *Research on Social Work Practice*, 10:6 (2000), pp 688–704. Recent works have examined the role of the professed religious in philanthropy at home and abroad, including John Belchem, 'Priests, publicans and the Irish poor: ethnic enterprise and migrant networks in mid-nineteenth-century Liverpool', *Immigrants & Minorities*, 23:2–3 (2005), pp 207–31.   5 Margaret Preston, *Charitable words: women, philanthropy and the language of charity in nineteenth-century Dublin* (Westport, CT, 2004); Oonagh Walsh, *Anglican women in Dublin: philanthropy, politics and education in the early twentieth century* (Dublin, 2004).   6 Maria Luddy, 'Religion, philanthropy and the State in late eighteenth and early nineteenth-century Ireland' in Hugh Cunningham and Joanna Innes (eds), *Charity, philanthropy and reform: from the 1690s to 1850* (Basingstoke, 1998), pp 148–67.   7 The work of scholars such as Martha Vicinus helped to consolidate an early focus upon the use of voluntary work as a means of expanding middle-class women's spheres. *Independent women: work and community for single women, 1850–1920* (Chicago, 1988).

improvement. Similarly, the efforts of the Guinness Trust to offer high standards of accommodation to their workers were made in the hope that it would result in a general rise in the broader quality of life. Not all philanthropy addressed material needs, however. The opening of the Royal Hibernian Academy exhibition in Dublin to less affluent visitors reflected a consciousness of the importance of intellectual stimulation for society generally, an example of municipal obligation that became increasingly important towards the end of the nineteenth century. The growth of Mechanics Institutes and Carnegie Libraries also facilitated the autodidact, and held out the prospect of self-improvement for all.

Of course, many of the initiatives examined in the chapters of this volume also had significant benefits for the apparently benevolent philanthropist. On the most obvious level, encouraging tenants on unprofitable holdings to emigrate had signifi-cant attractions for landowners: the surrendered land could be offered to more reliable families, or turned to greater profit through grazing or large-scale cultivation. In addition to the aristocratic obligation to succour the poor, all philanthropists gained satisfaction from the fulfilment of their Christian duty, an element faithfully stressed in every call for donations by charitable organizations. Furthermore, on the evidence of much of the research in this volume, the State was often a beneficiary of philanthropic largesse, albeit less obviously and more tangentially than needy indi-vidual recipients. Philanthropic intervention enabled the State to save funds that would otherwise have been expended on the support of asylums and workhouses, or through the public health costs of inadequate housing or education. It is an often neglected element in philanthropy studies, where the benefits of charity are more often sought in the advantages to organizers or recipients. But the rapid decline of estate philanthropy, as demonstrated on the Clonbrock estate with the advent of the poor law in the late 1830s, is a clear example of the manner in which private charity filled a need more appropriately the responsibility of the modern State. Similarly, the competition between Protestant and Catholic institutions for the care of the intel-lectually disabled ensured that the State did not have to support individuals who would be a life-long burden.

The contributions in this volume are based partly on presentations made at the annual conference of the Society for the Study of Nineteenth-Century Ireland (SSNCI), which was held at University College Cork in 2010, and partly upon specially commissioned articles, and the volume includes work by emerging scholars as well as established academics. Taken as a whole, the book reveals new emphases in the field: in contrast to a great deal of earlier writing, there is little on the role of reli-gion in philanthropy, nor on the mainstream Christian impetus behind many charitable organizations. It represents a broadening of the field from the first works on fallen women, mainstream Church organizations with conversionist or prosely-tizing impulses, to the education and medical missionaries, at home and abroad in the service of Empire. The theme of 'philanthropy' allows for a wide range of approaches to the topic, including State and voluntary philanthropy; poor relief; formal and informal systems of assistance on landed estates; housing schemes for the poor, and subsidized exhibitions for the education of the working classes. It reflects the varied nature of charitable relief in nineteenth-century Ireland, and the contrast between nineteenth-century attitudes towards the important role philanthropy played in Irish society and the twenty-first century faith in State-sponsored relief. The book as a whole reflects the manner in which academic studies of philanthropy have developed. These chapters largely eschew religion as an organizing principle, and religious constraints as an analytical tool, with the exception of the chapter on intellectual disability. Religious obligation underpins most, if not all, of the philanthropic initiatives examined here (most emerge from an individual or collective awareness of Christian duty), but few have an explicitly religious agenda such as conversion or church attendance. In that sense, it is a snapshot of both trends in scholarship and of the influence of large-scale research projects undertaken in Ireland in recent years. One suspects that it is no coincidence that this volume includes three papers on estate philanthropy: the 'Landed Estates' project at NUI Galway, as well as the programme of research in local history at NUI Maynooth, have at the very least raised awareness of the social history value of Irish estate papers.[8]

The volume opens with an examination of philanthropic endeavour in Ireland prior to the establishment of the poor law, which rapidly replaced existing systems of voluntary support for the poor. Mel Cousins' 'Philanthropy and poor relief before the poor law, 1801–30' scrutinizes the often-fluid nature of public and private funding in this period, and examines the interaction between the rather miserly public provision newly available to Ireland, with the subjective and erratic system of private provision that had prevailed to the end of the eighteenth century. Despite its limitations, Cousins identifies the start of a State acceptance of responsibility for the poor, which marks an important moment of transition in Ireland towards democracy. The chapter reveals a convoluted system of separate sources of support, often with competing ideologies and ambitions. However, an increasing State involvement in the care of the needy may be seen in the work of the House of Industry, as well as the tentative emergence of a national system of support. This is consolidated by the establishment of the poor law in 1838, which, despite its shortcomings during the Famine, was a step towards a modern State in which government recognized its social responsibilities, and a minimal entitlement of its citizens to survival.

Chapter two retains the early nineteenth-century focus, and provides an analysis of one of the first significant conceptualizations of poverty and its possible alleviation. Laurence M. Geary's ' "The best relief the poor can receive is from themselves": the Society for Promoting the Comforts of the Poor' engages with early attempts to encourage self-help among the poorest in Ireland. Drawing upon similar associations in England and Germany, the SPCP in Ireland articulated an ambitious faith in the broader possibilities of philanthropy. Their foundational premise suggests a liberal attitude towards the poor that is unusual in this period. The organizers resolutely refused to attribute any moral implication to poverty, nor did they subscribe to a

---

8 See: landedestates.nuigalway.ie/LandedEstates/jsp/ for full details of this project.

belief system that accepted 'the poor ye shall always have with you'. Rather, the organization stressed that there was no moral failure in poverty, nor virtue in wealth, but that individuals at either end of the economic scale could lead equally valid and valuable lives. The Society placed significant emphasis upon the dignity of the individual. This was to be achieved by assisting the poor to improve their lot if they wished, but equally to permit them to raise their living standards without significantly altering their social status. Their promotion of Friendly Societies was intended to foster a sense of community as well as individual responsibility, and to elide the divisions between rich and poor, while accepting the reality of economic disadvantage.

Eoin McLaughlin's 'Charitable loan fund societies in Ireland, *c.*1820–1914' is a topical examination of surprisingly large-scale lending to the poor in nineteenth-century Ireland. Intended to assist the 'industrious poor' towards greater prosperity through unsecured small loans, the scheme grew to an extraordinary degree in the century's early decades, lending the equivalent of €283 million by 1845. It began as a consequence of the purely philanthropic impulse to collect funds for Famine relief in the 1820s, but grew into a profitable enterprise, a precursor of many modern charities that are, in fact, highly profitable businesses. Surplus funds were to be loaned to impoverished individuals who could be trusted to invest them in practical schemes for economic self-improvement, and offered a practical alternative to the monolithic Bank of Ireland, which was singularly uninterested in the limited banking affairs of the poor. The CLFS offered rare opportunities towards substantial self-improvement, at low rates of interest for loans, and relatively high for savings, and for the first decades operated successfully. But an increasing tendency to ignore their own regulations, combined with reckless lending to ineligible customers and illegal and often exploitative loan terms, ensured that the CLFS had ceased to be philanthropic bodies in the true sense of the word by the century's end.

Section Two of the volume focuses upon the philanthropy of the landed gentry, to their rural estate tenants, and their urban workers. It opens with Conor McNamara's '"The monster misery of Ireland": landlord paternalism and the 1822 famine in the West', an examination of the manner in which the 1822 Famine precipitated an extremely vulnerable class into utter destitution. The essay serves as a useful reminder of the fact that the Great Famine of mid-century had many precursors, and that many landlords were well practised in seasonal and periodic philanthropy. However, the response to the 1822 disaster suggests that traditional quasi-feudal attitudes were beginning to change: McNamara indicates how some landlords seized the opportunity of the crisis to offer conditional philanthropy, which allowed them to rid themselves of permanently dependent tenants, and take advantage of the increasingly sophisticated international transport system to ensure that they would not eventually return. It is an interesting example of the negotiated nature of philanthropy on landed estates, which is very different in character from a more distant urban charity. Despite the economic disparity between recipient and donor, there was mutual understanding of the unwritten rules of dependence and

responsibility, and the negotiations between tenants and agents indicate the importance of personal knowledge of character and circumstances in mediating
philanthropy.

Kevin Mc Kenna's 'Charity, paternalism and power on the Clonbrock Estates,
County Galway, 1834–44' continues the theme of pre-Famine landlord responsibility,
and examines the impact of the poor law on the traditional landlord-tenant relationship. The crucial decade that followed the introduction of the poor law saw a
permanent erosion of well-established patterns of estate philanthropy, where tenants
appealed for assistance with the expectation of success, and landlords, however reluctantly, recognized their obligations to a people who teetered permanently on the
brink of economic disaster. The introduction of the poor law, however, fundamentally altered expectations: landlords such as Clonbrock in Galway, who had accepted
their paternalistic duty to their tenants, now looked to the State to assume that traditional role. Despite a lengthy period of adjustment, when tenants still turned to their
landlords for a variety of support, the philanthropic relationship had changed irrevo-
cably. The creation of the poor law, and the financial burden it placed upon landlords,
eroded long traditions of unregulated philanthropy in Ireland, and it remained to be
seen if the new system would represent an improvement for either party.

The third contribution on the theme of landlord philanthropy expands the study
to include an engagement with the issue of elite relief activity and its broader significance. Drawing upon the models used to interrogate similar activity in England,
Joanne McEntee's 'Pecuniary assistance for poverty and emigration: the politics of
landed estate management and philanthropy in mid-nineteenth-century Ireland'
seeks to explore the significance of philanthropic activity as a means of maintaining
social order. It also confirms the persistence of estate philanthropy after the introduction of the poor law, despite a determined effort on the part of landlords to place
responsibility for the poor firmly with the State. This study of the Shirley Estate in
County Monaghan and the Farnham Estate in County Cavan indicates the sophisticated levels of negotiation that took place between landlords and tenants, and the
enduring sense of obligation that both sides recognized as an essential element in the
landlord-tenant relationship. These three chapters raise questions regarding the
nature of philanthropy itself: when relief is an integral element in the landlord-tenant
relationship, and the parameters of charitable responsibility are openly accepted by
each partner, is the extension of funds or support in kind actually charitable, or part
of a sophisticated social contract?

The final contribution in this section extends the range of landed philanthropy
in both chronological and regional terms. Linda King's '"Guinness is good for you":
experiments in workers' housing and public amenities by the Guinness Brewery and
Guinness/Iveagh Trust, 1872–1915' addresses the substantial role played by the
Guinness family in the provision of high-quality housing for the Dublin poor. The
financial commitment was enormous – the equivalent of almost €81 million in
contemporary terms – and the project was one of the most ambitious philanthropic
interventions in nineteenth-century Ireland. King examines the precedents upon

which the Guinness/Iveagh schemes drew, and the articulated belief that model housing schemes would not merely offer a decent standard of accommodation for suitable tenants, but would act as exemplars for ideal urban communities, where tenants recognized their social and moral responsibilities to each other as well as to their benefactors. These obligations were reinforced in the early years by a system of surveillance and inspection by agents acting for the Trust, something that was an intermittent cause of resentment among the residents. But this is not to say that the schemes operated as straightforward mechanisms of control, in which a resentful workforce reluctantly agreed to the imposition of rules in order to keep their homes. The developments were remarkably progressive and liberal in their design, and provided an exceptionally high standard of living in a city with appalling infant mortality rates, and universally recognized poor public health provisions. Demand was high, ensuring that a crucial secondary prerogative was met: the occupants enjoyed better health, and were more productive workers in Guinness' industries, than were their counterparts in other Dublin industries.

Our third section addresses the roles of women and children as both philanthropic agents and subjects. Oonagh Walsh's '"A person of the second order": the plight of the intellectually disabled in nineteenth-century Ireland' opens with an examination of the manner in which the Intellectually Disabled became a specific focus for philanthropists in the second half of the nineteenth century. This group emerged as worthy objects of support for a number of reasons: they became more visible in an increasingly literate society, where a premium was placed upon the ability to undertake productive, paid employment. They were also viewed with increasing concern by the medical profession, and by the State, which in the early decades of the eugenics movement worried about the weakening effect the feeble-minded in particular might have upon future generations. There was also, of course, a genuine and well-founded anxiety about their vulnerability to exploitation and abuse, especially in urban areas, and a recognition that they required specialist intervention. But perhaps the key element in driving care for the Intellectually Disabled was religious philanthropic rivalry. When Dr Stewart's Institution was founded in Dublin in 1869, it provoked an immediate response from the Catholic Church, which feared that these wholly innocent individuals would become unwitting converts to Protestantism. The entry of the Daughters of Charity to their field of care established a conceptualization of the cohort that persisted for over one hundred years, and saw a virtual monopoly of Catholic provision for this group for the same period of time. Moreover, as the following chapter also indicates, the care of vulnerable children in Ireland was conceived in institutional terms, with a virtual absence of the sheltered communities and boarding-out systems that developed in England and Scotland in particular.

Sarah-Anne Buckley's '"Saver of the children": the National Society for the Prevention of Cruelty to Children in Ireland, 1889–1921' continues the theme of philanthropy and children, but examines a rather different cohort, those who came to the attention of the newly established NSPCC for reasons of neglect or abuse. The early years of the Society confirms the increasing importance granted to childhood in late nineteenth-century Irish society, and a recognition that an older acceptance of high mortality rates, chronic ill-health, and the neglect and even active abuse of offspring was no longer viable. But as Buckley's chapter indicates, the philanthropists who drove the establishment of the Society, and their supporters, often approached the children as potentially criminal, dangerous, or even in some way complicit in their often appalling circumstances. Class presumption played an important role in determining the outcome of investigations, and the early inspectors (who were middle class) proved perhaps all too willing to remove children from families to industrial schools, and mothers to inebriate homes, without seeking to question the underlying economic, political and gender problems that created such difficult circumstances. Indeed, Ireland's ultimately destructive dependence upon industrial and reform schools may be seen to have its origins in organizations such as the NSPCC, which, while undoubtedly exerting a positive influence in terms of its attention to the quality of children's lives, also set a philanthropic precedent of institutional care that arguably had a detrimental effect on the lives of many.

Middle-class women had been at the forefront of philanthropic endeavour from the early nineteenth-century, and represented an enormous unpaid workforce throughout Britain and Ireland. Their efforts have often been dismissed as inquisitive interference, but Mary Pierse's 'From lace making to social activism: the resourcefulness of campaigning women philanthropists' discusses two crucial aspects of female charitable effort that significantly advanced women's positions in nineteenth-century Ireland. Women campaigners such as Susan Lloyd made strategic use of philanthropic work to advance women's political positions, and gather the vital political experience that was needed to justify women's formal participation on public boards. But they also significantly advanced the economic position of women, by re-establishing dormant industries, including lace making, which had an exclusively female workforce. Theirs was an early example of the importance of 'self-help' that underpinned other philanthropic efforts, but the results were more successful, because they produced significant and direct economic benefits. Like the modern micro-finance schemes in the developing world, these women philanthropists understood the importance of equipping women in deprived communities with the means of economic advancement, knowing that they would use the funds to support families and reap a much broader advantage than through the employment of men. The philanthropists pragmatically accepted the realities of class, while stressing the opportunities available to ambitious and focused female workers for significant economic improvement.

Our final section, on cultural philanthropy, broadens the conception of what constitutes 'doing good' on an organized voluntary basis. Not all philanthropic initiatives addressed material wants, or sought to ensure that the working classes or agricultural labourers remained firmly in their appropriate socio-economic groups. As Philip McEvansoneya's 'Cultural philanthropy in mid-nineteenth-century Ireland' shows, there were also voluntary initiatives that recognized intellectual needs, and made high art available to all and not merely the elite. Like Mary Pierse's chapter, however, the impulse was not without benefit to the philanthropists. The Royal Hibernian Academy had seen a catastrophic decline in visitor numbers to its annual exhibition, and was facing a substantial deficit. The decision was made to 'democratize' the consumption of high art, by ensuring that the general public could afford to view the paintings. The large-scale attendance of members of the 'operative classes' as a result of the first experimental cut-price entry charges was a tremendous success, resulting in a sharp increase in visitors, and providing an essential revenue boost for the RHA. The enthusiasm with which the initiative was greeted ensured that the strategy was repeated, and was indeed turned to even greater philanthropic ends, when an exhibition of old masters was arranged by the Royal Irish Art Union in 1847 in order to raise funds for famine relief. The RIAU had itself been in decline, but seized the opportunity to respond to the horrors of the Great Famine, and also to reassert its own cultural significance in the face of declining public interest in its activities. Thus philanthropy served two distinct purposes, the broadening of access to high culture, and the survival of prestigious, though poorly resourced, institutions. This chapter raises another intriguing element of philanthropic work: some of the prime beneficiaries of the reduced entry fees to artistic exhibitions were not the awed working-classes, but the more affluent and financially shrewd middle-classes. They had formerly paid their shilling entry but now prudently waited for the bargain penny days, apparently indifferent to the social cachet of viewing paintings alongside the wealthier members of Dublin society. It is an early instance of an issue that bedevilled and bemused many charitable organizations, the fact that the most vigorous applicants for relief were often those with some resources.

Our volume concludes with John Wilson Foster's 'Doing good and being bad in Victorian Ireland: some literary and evolutionary perspectives'. Reading the philanthropic relationship not as a straightforward transaction between poor and privileged, but as a constantly evolving expression of Anglo-Irish relations, the chapter examines the means through which philanthropic efforts informed the works of travellers, clerics and commentators, and contributed to a consolidation of ethnic stereotypes. The range of representation was considerable, from the shiftless peasant, through the grasping gombeen man, to the fading aristocracy, and informed literary representations of Ireland from the sixteenth to the twentieth centuries. The novels reflect the moral judgements made by philanthropists of their subjects, and offered an imaginative space within which authors (especially women writers) challenged gender, class and religious conventions. Startling critiques of 'good works' were often embedded in late nineteenth-century female-authored novels, with the saintly do-gooders articulating radical critiques of philanthropy itself, as well as of those who received it. Foster identifies a broadly gendered division between the authors who challenged philanthropic motivations (often female) and those who read poverty, and the Irish who endured it, in socio-biological terms (often male). Deprivation and its causes thus produced creative writing that incorporated influences as diverse as royal commissions, pulpit politics, and Darwin's *Origin of species,* to produce literature that expressed the often unguarded dislike and suspicion of both sides of the philanthropic relationship. As the chapters in this volume indicate, the kindest of philanthropic gestures often masked less obvious social, economic and political objectives.

Philanthropy and poor relief
before the poor law, 1801–30

MEL COUSINS

INTRODUCTION

This chapter examines poor relief in the period before the introduction of the poor law (*c.*1800–30), emphasizing the philanthropic aspects and highlighting issues such as the 'mixed economy' of poor relief at the time.[1] It also considers the impact of the introduction of the poor law in 1838 which, as suggested by many contemporary commentators on the poor law, does seem to have altered patterns of private philanthropy. The chapter draws on the Royal Commission on the Poor in Ireland (the Whately Commission) reports and evidence from sources such as the census to describe philanthropic practices. The focus here is on relief in cash and kind to the poor[2] and on the more regular forms of relief rather than on philanthropic responses to the rather frequent crises of the period.[3]

In the first part of this chapter, we examine the structure of philanthropic support, distinguishing by the type of provider of relief (statutory, civic, church and private) and the source of funding (Exchequer, grand jury, local and private). The second part examines the main statutory and civic bodies: the houses of industry, foundling hospitals and mendicity societies, providing some estimate of the scope of relief provided. Part three turns to religious and private charity. Here it is much more difficult currently to make any hard estimates of the extent and scope of relief. This section focuses on providing some impressionistic evidence of patterns of relief (and how they interrelated with the more formal sources of relief discussed in part 2) and in identifying sources which would allow a more detailed picture to be developed.

---

1 On the mixed economy of relief, see, for example, Alan J. Kidd, *State, society and the poor in nineteenth-century England* (London, 1999). 2 The scope of relief would be greater if we were to take into acount the extent to which systems of medical relief operated, in part, as relief for the sick poor: see, generally, Laurence M. Geary, *Medicine and charity in Ireland, 1781–1851* (Dublin, 2004). 3 Subsistence crises occurred in 1800–1, 1817–19, 1821 and 1831. The worst were in 1800–1 and 1817–19, which led to an estimated 40,000–60,000 excess deaths (Cormac Ó Gráda, *Ireland: a new economic history* (Oxford, 1994), p. 73). The cholera epidemic of 1832 led to an estimated death toll of 50,000. In these periods, additional supports were provided both by the State and through philanthropic means. The latter involved both the establishment of specific funds to support the poor (both in Ireland and in Great Britain) and more local action by landowners and others to create employment and provide poor relief. See, for example, Craig Bailey, 'Micro-credit, misappropriation and morality: British responses to Irish distress, 1822–31', *Continuity and Change*, 21:3 (2006), pp 455–74.

Part 4 examines the impact of the poor law on pre-Famine patterns of relief and part 5 concludes with a discussion of the key issues.

THE STRUCTURE OF PHILANTHROPIC SUPPORT

Unlike the rest of the United Kingdom, Ireland in 1801 did not have a national poor law. Even allowing for the permissive nature of the Scottish poor law and the fact that the English poor law was arguably a national framework for local and regional systems of poor relief,[4] this left Ireland in a significantly different position to the rest of the United Kingdom. However, the lack of a national system of relief was, in fact, common to most European countries at the time.

Like the pattern in other European countries, support for the poor depended on a range of different sources. However, one cannot make a simple distinction between public and private support in the period in question. One approach in trying to understand the complicated network of supports is to examine it under two different headings: first, the type of provider of support, and, second, the source of funding. In table 1, we set out four categories of provider by their status:

1) bodies established or recognized in law
2) civic bodies – bodies formally established but not by statute
3) church bodies
4) private individuals

We also identify four sources of support:

1) Exchequer funding
2) grand jury funding
3) other compulsory (or quasi-compulsory) local funding[5]
4) support provided voluntarily by private individuals.

As can be seen, statutory bodies funded by the Exchequer were the exception with only the Dublin House of Industry and the Foundling Hospital (which were, in reality, national bodies) structured in this way. The main method of the provision of 'public' support was through permissive legislation allowing local grand juries to maintain different types of institution (houses of industry, dispensaries, etc.), which were also supported by private donations – although in most cases the support levied by the grand juries dwarfed the private support. Charitable bodies (including the

---

4 See Steven A. King, *Poverty and welfare in England, 1700–1850: a regional perspective* (Manchester, 2000).   5 Including the coal tax which largely funded the Cork Foundling Hospital, and the house tax which funded (in part) the Dublin Foundling Hospital to 1822, and funding levied by church vestries.

Table 1

	Statutory	**Civic**	**Church**	**Private**
Exchequer	Dublin House of Industry Dublin Foundling Hospital	[Dublin Mendicity Association]		
Grand jury	Most other houses of industry Dispensaries			
Other local	Cork Foundling Hospital [Dublin Foundling Hospital]		Support for foundlings Church poor lists Orphanages	
Private	Belfast Charitable Society [Houses of Industry] [Dispensaries][6]	Mendicity Associations Charitable bodies		Direct support

(Institution in [] indicate a minority source of funding)

mendicity associations discussed below) were generally supported only by private donations, although the Dublin Mendicity Association received some public or quasi-public assistance.[7] Local parishes provided support for foundlings and to the poor more generally through the provision of relief via vestry collection and/or voluntary church collections and charity sermons.[8] In addition, at least in the major cities, Catholic organizations and those of other denominations – both religious and lay – provided support through the provision of institutions such as orphanages, widows' homes, houses of refuge and infirmaries.[9] Finally, private support was extensive, ranging from support provided by the landlords to intra-community support.

6 Funding for dispensaries was shared between grand jury and local voluntary support. Subscriptions had first to be raised by the dispensaries before grand jury funds were awarded, and the ratio was specified by legislation. **7** See Audrey Woods, *Dublin outsiders: a history of the Mendicity Institution* (Dublin, 1988), chapter 5. **8** David Dickson, 'In search of the old Irish poor law' in Rosalind Mitchison and Peter Roebuck (eds), *Economy and society in Scotland and Ireland, 1500–1939* (Edinburgh, 1988), pp 149–59. **9** For Dublin, see Cormac Begadon, 'Laity and clergy in the Catholic renewal of Dublin *c.*1750–1830' (PhD, NUI Maynooth (2009), chapter 2), although the main focus of the supports provided seems to have been educational rather than poor relief per se. As Begadon points out, the growth in such institutions reflects the growing status of the Catholic middle class (a point also emphasized by Anthony Blake in his contemporary account: *Thoughts on the Catholic question,* Dublin and London, 1828).

STATUTORY AND CIVIC BODIES

HOUSES OF INDUSTRY

Houses of industry had been established in Dublin and Cork in the early eighteenth century and permissive legislation had been adopted in 1772 allowing for the establishment of such houses on a nationwide basis but only eight were in operation by 1830.[10] The legislation was adopted with the dual purpose of (i) giving 'countenance and assistance' to the poor 'disabled by old age or infirmities to earn their living', and (ii) restraining and punishing those 'able to support themselves by labour or industry' who 'yet choose to live in idleness by begging'.[11]

The Dublin House of Industry was by far the largest institution and operated, in practice, as a national rather than purely local institution.[12] It was established in 1773, replacing an earlier institution that became the Dublin Foundling Hospital. The objects of the initial institution included general support to 'helpless' men and women; the incarceration of men committed as vagabonds and sturdy beggars, and 'idle strolling and disorderly women'; and support to deserted and fatherless children.[13] Although it was initially intended that the house would be supported locally, it quickly relied on a parliamentary grant which reached almost £50,000 by 1810.[14] Clearly concerned at the rising costs, a report on charitable institutions in Dublin (including the House of Industry) was commissioned by the Irish government in 1809. This found that the main principle of the House of Industry was 'indiscriminate and free admission accompanied with the liberty of unrestrained egress'.[15] The authors saw this approach as an 'insurmountable impediment' to improving young people or improving adults' habits of industry but it was one which could not be 'abruptly relinquished'.[16] However, it is not clear that significant action was taken on

10 Mel Cousins, 'The Irish Parliament and relief of the poor: the 1772 legislation establishing houses of industry', *Eighteenth-Century Ireland*, 28 (2013), pp 95–115. 11 11&12 Geo. III, c. 30, 'An act for badging such poor as shall be found unable to support themselves by labour, and otherwise providing for them, and for refraining such as shall be found able to support themselves by labour or industry from begging'. 12 Of the 6,145 persons admitted in 1807, 3,075 were from outside Dublin: John D. Latouche, William Disney and George Renny, *A report upon certain charitable establishments in the City of Dublin which receive aid from parliament* (Dublin, 1809), pp 36–7. 13 House of Industry and Foundling Hospital, Dublin. *Accounts of the period when first established; their object, and how supported* (Dublin, 1828), p. 176. 14 On the Dublin House of Industry around 1800, see Thomas Bernard, 'Extracts from an account of the late improvements, in the House of Industry, at Dublin' in *The Reports of the Society for Bettering the Condition and Increasing the Comforts of the Poor* (London, 1798), pp 99–107. 15 Latouche, Disney and Renny, *A report upon certain charitable establishments in the City of Dublin*, p. 36. 16 All three were senior figures in Dublin philanthropy. Latouche was a director of La Touche Bank, and a vice-president of Dublin Chamber of Commerce; Disney was a barrister, a member of the general board of health and a commissioner of education, 1806–12; Renny was a medical doctor and served in an official capacity with several public institutions in Dublin, including the Cork St fever hospital.

foot of the report and Exchequer funding remained high. In 1816, Robert Peel (Irish chief secretary, 1812–18) wrote to the governors who, despite the level of funding, argued that they had insufficient funding to meet the demand.[17] Peel recommended that admissions be limited and that the admission of 'vagrant and refractory beggars' should cease entirely. It appears that the latter recommendation was adopted and continued in effect, despite the efforts of the Dublin Mendicity Association to have this function restored to the House.[18]

At the end of the French wars, from 1815, public funding declined, so that by the 1820s only £20,000–£21,000 per annum was being provided. A further report was commissioned (from the same authors as the 1809 report) in 1820. They recommended that the House of Industry should serve a local rather than national demand and proposed a number of economies, including a reduction in the paid governors from five to one and a reduction in staffing.[19] However, it would appear that many of the inmates continued to be drawn from outside Dublin and any reforms that did take place do not appear to have improved the conditions of the paupers. Alexis de Tocqueville, in his tour of Ireland in 1830, visited the house of industry and was not complimentary about the conditions he found.[20]

Most of the houses of industry outside Dublin were established in the late eighteenth century and although a number were established in the early 1800s (including Clonmel, (1811), Kilkenny (1814) and Wexford (1816)), these tended to be smaller and their establishment appears to have been part of a long campaign dating back to the eighteenth century. These houses of industry received much lower levels of funding than Dublin (from about £200 per annum in Kilkenny to £4,500 in Cork) and also supported fewer inmates (from 1–200 in small houses like Clonmel and Waterford) though, if contemporary data are to be believed, the Cork house supported about as many paupers as the much better funded Dublin institution.

The Belfast institutions defy easy categorization. Although referred to as the 'house of industry', the Belfast institution of that name was not established under law and was not supported by the grand jury. Nor was it similar in function to many of the other 'catch-all' institutions and it is perhaps best treated as a mendicity society[21] and is categorized as such below.[22] The Belfast Charitable Society or Poor House (established in 1771 and given a statutory basis in 1774) is closer to the southern

---

17 Robert Peel to governors of the House of Industry, 14 Sept. 1816 in *Report of the commissioners appointed by the Lord Lieutenant of Ireland to inspect the House of Industry...*, HC 1820 (84) viii. 1. **18** *Report of Dublin Mendicity Association* (Dublin, 1833), p. 11. **19** *Report of the commissioners appointed by the Lord Lieutenant of Ireland to inspect the House of Industry...*, HC 1820 (84) 8. 1. **20** Emmet J. Larkin (ed.), *Alexis de Tocqueville's journey in Ireland, July–August 1835* (Washington, 1990), p. 24. Henry Inglis was rather more positive stating that it was 'altogether as fine an institution of the kind as I have anywhere seen': Henry Inglis, *Ireland in 1834* (London, 1835), p. 18. **21** See 'Rules and regulations for the House of Industry', *The Belfast Monthly Magazine*, 4:21 (30 Apr. 1810), pp 261–9. **22** The same approach is taken with the smaller Newtownards 'house of industry' which again was not a statutory house nor supported by the grand jury.

houses of industry in function and is treated here as a house of industry.[23] However, unlike the southern institutions it was not supported by the grand jury (or Parliament) and relied generally on charitable support.

FOUNDLING HOSPITALS AND SUPPORT FOR DESERTED CHILDREN

Foundling hospitals existed in Dublin and Cork.[24] The Dublin institution, originally established in 1703, was by far the largest. Following a major scandal concerning abnormally high child mortality in 1797, the Dublin Foundling Hospital was reorganized. Children were sent to the institution from all over Ireland and were then normally put out to nurse up to the age of seven or eight. Despite this reform, the Dublin institution had annual admissions of about 1,500 to 2,000 in the 1810s and Exchequer funding reaching £32,500 in 1820. Initially the Hospital was funded, in part, by a Dublin house tax but this was altered in 1822, with a view to spreading the burden on the basis that it was unfair that Dublin residents fund what was a national service. Parishes were then required to pay a sum of £5 for each child sent to the hospital. This had a major impact on admissions, which dropped to about 500 annually.

However, standards remained unacceptably low even by the standards of the time. A major investigation by the Commissioners of the Irish Education Inquiry in 1826 found that of the 52,150 children admitted from 1796 to 1826, no less than 41,524 were recorded as dead.[25] The Commissioners refused to believe these figures and suggested that about 10,000 children recorded as dead were probably still alive and with their nurses.[26] Despite this rather optimistic assumption, the Commissioners tactfully concluded that 'at no period since its commencement have the results realized in the Foundling Hospital of Dublin been fully satisfactory to those concerned in its management ...'[27] The Commissioners investigated the impact of the 1822 funding reform, being concerned that it might have led to an increase in infanticide, but could find no indication that this had been the result.

An 1829 House of Commons Select Committee, chaired by Chief Secretary Lord Francis Leveson Gower, took a rather less sanguine view of the operation of the Hospital, based on the Commissioners' report.[28] It concluded that the Hospital 'does not appear to have satisfactorily answered either for the purpose of the preservation

23 Robert W.M. Strain, 'The history and associations of the Belfast Charitable Society', *Ulster Medical Journal*, 22:1 (1953), pp 31–60. The society running the poor house was incorporated in an amendment to the 1772 Houses of Industry Act. **24** See, generally, Joseph Robins, *The lost children: a study of charity children in Ireland, 1700–1900* (Dublin, 1980). A Galway Foundling Hospital, with eight children on the books, is recorded in the second report of the Whately Commission. *Second report of the commissioners for inquiring into the condition of the poorer classes in Ireland*, HC 1837 (68) 31.587, p. 18. **25** *Third report of the commissioners of Irish education inquiry*, HC 1826–27 (13) 8.1, at p. 5. **26** The registrar of the hospital did not agree. **27** *Third report of the commissioners of Irish education inquiry*, p. 3. **28** *Report from the select committee into Irish miscellaneous estimates ...* , HC 1829 (342) 4.127.

of human life, or for the proper education of the children admitted to it'.[29] On the basis that the reduction in admissions from 2,000 to 500 had not been shown to have had any 'mischievous or injurious effects', the Committee recommended that all further admissions to the Hospital should cease from 1830 and this was implemented with effect from 1831. This slowly led to a fall in the funding for the Hospital (as a large number of existing foundlings remained on its books). The Cork Foundling Hospital, largely funded by a local coal tax, was established in 1747. It was considerably smaller than the Dublin body, supporting about 1,300 children in the 1830s (850 at nurse). It should be noted here that support to foundlings was also provided locally through grand juries and church vestries.[30] For example, in 1827, the vestry of the Protestant parish of St Mary's in Dublin assessed a sum of £50 'to provide for deserted children'.[31]

THE RISE OF MENDICITY SOCIETIES

There was a striking growth in mendicity societies (especially in Ulster) after 1818. It seems likely that the economic impact of the end of the French wars combined with the reduction in Exchequer support to the Dublin institutions contributed to this development. Although the establishment of the Dublin Mendicity Association took place in the same year as the establishment of the London Society for the Suppression of Mendicity,[32] it is not clear that the Irish societies were greatly influenced by the ideology of the London body or, indeed, that the Irish societies themselves shared a clear philosophy, other than in the very general sense of making some effort to address poverty in their local area.[33] However, some general principles to which, it would appear, at least some of the societies tried to adhere were set out by a committee member of the Dublin Mendicity Association in the context of a review of the Dublin House of Industry.[34] This set out a number of propositions for the 'management of the poor'.

First, 'the utmost economy should be observed' in the use of funds and, second, 'the course of nature should be deviated from as little as possible'. Thus, and third, 'every means should be taken' to discourage the breaking of social ties among the poor, such as the parent-child relationship. Fourth, 'as little encouragement as possible

29 Ibid., p. 6.   **30** See, for example, ibid., appendix 4.   **31** *Parochial rates (Ireland)*, HC 1828 (241) 22. The vestry also provided for coffins for poor persons. This return provides similar details for parishes in the dioces of Dublin and Armagh. See also the more extensive returns contained in *Parochial rates (Ireland)*, HC 1828 (370) 22.   **32** Michael J.D. Roberts, 'Reshaping the gift relationship: the London Mendicity Society and the suppression of begging in England, 1818–69', *International Review of Social History*, 36 (1991), pp 201–31. **33** On the Dublin Mendicity Association, see, in particular, its annual report for 1833 which includes a detailed description of its activities: *Sixteenth report of the managing committee of the Association for the Suppression of Mendicity in Dublin for the year 1833*. See Woods, *Dublin outsiders*.   **34** *Report of the commissioners appointed by the Lord Lieutenant of Ireland to inspect the House of Industry ...* HC 1820 (84) 8, at p. 46.

should be given to relax foresight and weaken reliance on their own exertions ...'
Fifth, 'all persons relieved by public charity should be made to contribute, as far as
they can, to their own support ...' Sixth, the 'adult and healthy poor' should only be
relieved through the means of employment. Seventh, in providing relief 'reference
should be made as far as possible to the comforts enjoyed by the lowest class of *independent poor*'.[35] Eight, 'large establishments should ... be avoided as much as possible'.
Ninth, and conversely, relief should be given 'in the home and in the family'. Tenth,
'no poor person should be supported at a distance from their former residence'
where they were known and had friends. Finally, poor children should not be raised
to a situation 'beyond that in which it hath pleased God to place them'. As can be
seen, the propositions combined providentialism with economic liberalism but while
some principles – such as 'less eligibility' – corresponded with those shortly to appear
in the English Poor Law Commission's report, others – such as the preference for
outdoor relief – were entirely alien to that approach.[36]

Unsurprisingly, there was considerable variation in how the societies operated in
practice. However, it is clear that – at least numerically – the dominant form of relief
was domiciliary. In this, the societies followed the general pattern to be seen in the
rest of the United Kingdom and, indeed, throughout most of Europe. A number of
societies did establish (or link to) a poor house either in an attempt to suppress
vagrancy (Newry) or to provide support to the sick and aged (Coleraine). As implied
by the name (mendicity) societies did generally attempt to suppress begging but with
varying degrees of success. In some, the employment of beadles (or 'bang-beggars')
was claimed to have led to some success (e.g., in Lisburn) but in others the Poor
Inquiry's assistant commissioners found that the relief provided was insufficient to
allow for the suppression of mendicancy (Ballymena, Larne). The northern societies
in particular operated a 'law of settlement', requiring individuals to have lived in the
area for between three and ten years in order to qualify for assistance.[37]

The Poor Inquiry's assistant commissioners were highly critical of the management of a number of societies (in particular, Drogheda and Limerick) and the Dublin
Mendicity Institution fared no better than had the House of Industry in the eyes of
a visiting commentator. Henry Inglis, visiting the institution in 1834, described it as
a 'miserable make-shift' and stated that 'a visit to the Dublin mendicity society will
not put anybody in love with that system of voluntary charity, which, we are told by
an eminent divine, is so blessed an encourager of human sympathies'.[38]

35 Emphasis in original.   **36** S.G. and E.O.A. Checkland (eds), *The poor law report of 1834*
(London, 1974).   **37** In contrast the Dublin society required only six months residence and
even that was not strictly enforced: see *Royal commission for inquiring into the condition of the
poorer classes in Ireland: Appendix C*, HC 1836 (36) xxx, at p. 222.   **38** Inglis 'saw hundreds,
for whom no employment could be found, lying and sitting in the court, waiting for the
mess which had tempted them from their hovels, and the incertitude of mendicity –
which many however prefer; and I saw an attempt at teaching the young – who, whatever
progress they may make in head learning, cannot, I fear, make great progress in morals,
consigned, as they are, after day-light, to the care of their worthless parents; and returning to

The societies were generally run by committees elected by subscribers and list-ings in the local newspapers allow us to indentify the social class of those involved. In striking contrast to the grand jury, which was generally constituted of large landowners,[39] the mendicity societies were run by men much further down the social scale. The committee of the Armagh society in 1828, for example, largely consisted of grocers, spirit dealers, oil and colour dealers and similar merchants.[40] Gentry were strikingly absent, even if Archbishop Beresford chaired the society's annual meeting.[41] The inaugural Galway committee was dominated by Roman Catholic clergy but its lay members included a woollen draper, a kelp merchant, a surveyor and a revenue collector. Only one member appears to have been a large landowner.[42] The relatively low social standing of the committee members may, at least in part, explain why their work received so little attention at the time (and indeed subsequently) in that they were not the type of men to be invited to give evidence to a parliamentary committee or to have the ear of Archbishop Whately or his colleagues.

RELIGIOUS AND PRIVATE CHARITY

SOURCES

There is an absence of any comprehensive directory of charitable organizations in early nineteenth-century Ireland.[43] However, some data are available from sources such as the annual reports of various voluntary bodies, the Irish Catholic Directory, and (from 1844) the annual *Thom's* directories. A listing of 'charitable and benevo-lent institutions' is to be found in *Thom's* directories although the term is very broadly defined and the directories contain rather limited information. In smaller towns outside Dublin, one would have to rely on more sporadic local or regional directories, again cross-checking with sources such as *Thom's*. It should, nonetheless, be possible to carry out such studies, at least in selected regional locations which would begin the process of tracing the level of charity and philanthropy in Ireland. Such local studies might also examine the relationship between poor law policies and

the hovels in which vice and misery are so often united.' Inglis, *Ireland in 1834,* vol. 1, pp 16–18. **39** Neal Garnham, 'Elite creation in early Hanoverian Ireland: the case of the assize grand jury', *Historical Journal,* 42:3 (1999), pp 623–42. **40** *Newry Commercial Telegraph,* 8 Feb. 1828. Identification is from *Pigot's Directory* of 1824. **41** Beresford, son of George de La Poer Beresford, first marquess of Waterford, was appointed as archbishop of Armagh and therefore primate of All Ireland in 1822 (having been a bishop since 1805). He was a conservative in politics and opposed the Roman Catholic Relief Bill of 1829. **42** *Connaught Journal,* 19 July 1824. This was Lachlan MacLachlan, later elected Repeal MP for Galway borough in 1832 before being unseated on petition. MacLachlan was the only person to be a member of both the society and the Galway grand jury at the time. **43** Rosa M. Barratt, *Guide to Dublin charities* (Dublin, 1884) appears to be the first detailed listing.

voluntary activity at a local level. It seems likely that there were significant variations in the manner in which the poor law practices and voluntary activity interrelated both over space and time. The Whately Commission estimated that farmers donated between £1 and 2 million to the direct support of the poor.[44] Lord Morpeth (Irish chief secretary, 1835–41) carried out a rough-and-ready survey (in the context of the introduction of the 1837 Poor Law Bill) which suggested that the level of support was about £700,000–800,000 or perhaps £1 million, somewhat more modest but still very significant.[45]

THE WHATELY COMMISSION

The extensive investigations by the Whately Commission give some picture of the range of supports available. Extracts from the evidence to the Whately Commission give some sense of the type of supports provided in towns and rural areas (though we have no means of knowing how representative these were).[46] In Templemichael and Ballymacormic (close to Longford town), the witnesses, including Lord Longford's under-agent, explained that

> About 12 of the 200 [persons of the labouring class infirm from age] beg their bread from door to door; seven or eight are assisted to the extent of from 10s. to 15s. per annum from a collection in the Presbyterian meeting-house; from sixteen to eighteen from the collection in the Established Church, which varies from £30 to £40 annually.[47] Lord Longford allows £10 per annum for bread, and one of the Edgeworth family £5, to be distributed weekly to persons on the latter list; Lady Longford gives £40 per annum for clothing and blankets, distributed at Christmas among about 50 old persons; 15 small houses, with a garden to each of 10 perches, are given by Lord Longford rent-free to distressed families. They contain at present 14 persons of each sex past their labour. There are besides seven old persons assisted or supported by Lord Longford, with sums varying from £2 to £16 annually. About £50 per

---

44 *Royal Commission for inquiring into the condition of the poorer classes in Ireland: Appendix C – Parts 1 and 2*, HC 1836 (36), 30.   **45** *Hansard*, 36, at col. 463, 13 Feb. 1836.   **46** See also the more detailed description of supports in the main cities in the Commission's report. See also publications such as John J. McGregor, *New history of Dublin* (Dublin, 1821) which provides an account of, inter alia, Dublin charitable institutions; and the *Irish Catholic Directory* which provides an account of Catholic charities in Dublin.   **47** 'Those on the Protestant list at present are mostly under 50; many of these would never apply for charity. Those on the Presbyterian list are principally old persons, and their claims on both are determined by the degree of distress. This mode of relief is deemed more respectable than even private begging. There are at present on the Protestant list twenty heads of families, but sometimes there are four times as many applicants. The Presbyterian collection is distributed yearly or half yearly; 10s. or 15s. to each person: the number relieved being determined by the amount of the money, which is from £7 to £8 annually; the Protestant collection is from £30 to £40 annually; food is never given by the congregations.'

annum is collected in the town by occasional subscriptions, a fair proportion of which is given to cases of infirmity from age. These are the only regular funds for the relief of the aged. About 100 persons, among whom are many obtaining relief from the above sources, gain their chief support from the middling classes. The age at which the poor become incapable of supporting themselves from labour varies, according to constitution, from 50 to 55.[47a]

Later in the same evidence it was stated that the middle classes also played an important role:

> The gentry of the neighbourhood do not subscribe regularly for their [those who depend on alms] support, which is given principally by the middle classes, six or eight different families of whom contribute alternately, without any understanding among each other, to the support of the same individuals, who, through long acquaintance, have established a sort of claim upon them, and who thus subsist by private begging, which is considered more reputable than public.

However, the Longford witnesses pointed out that the primary responsibility fell on family members:

> The support of destitute persons usually devolves, as a matter of duty, upon the nearest relatives, at least as far as children, brothers and sisters. Should they refuse their aid, they are looked upon among their own equals with the greatest abhorrence.

In Longford there was no almshouse or mendicity association. In the northern town of Lisburn, however, where a mendicity society (referred to in evidence as the Charitable Society) did exist, it appears that much of the private charity was channelled though the society. Witnesses, including several officers of the society, told the commissioners that

> The collections in the Established Church amount to about £55 yearly, and of this sum about £42 yearly are given to be distributed by the Charitable Society of the town, among the poor on their list, without distinction of religion.
>
> The Presbyterian collection is partly divided among a few of their own members, and part is given by them to the Charitable Society. There are not any regular collections for the poor made in any other of the houses of worship. Two-thirds of the poor relieved by the Charitable Society are of the Roman Catholic persuasion.
>
> There is in the town a general subscription to the funds of the Charitable Society, which averages about £[ ],[48] (including £92 6s. 2d. yearly from the

---

47a *Royal commission for inquiring into the condition of the poorer classes in Ireland: Appendix A,* HC 1836 (36), 219. **48** Figure is blank in the published report.

Marquis of Hertford), arising from the higher and middle classes only, but some refuse who are well able to contribute.

No doubt similar supports were provided in cities but here there were also more formal institutions supported by lay and religious bodies such as orphanages. The *Irish Catholic Directory* indicates that in 1846 there were twenty orphan societies in Dublin catering for over 800 orphans and a further ten asylums for 'female penitents'.[49]

CENSUS DATA

The census of Ireland also provides an important source of data for the extent of voluntary activity – albeit confined to those charities providing institutional care. Beginning in 1851, the census has a listing of charitable residential institutions.[50] The censuses for 1851 and 1861 listed about 90 such institutions containing about 2,300 persons in 1851, of whom 1,700 were women but the census commissioners at the time acknowledged that this listing was not 'perfectly accurate'.[51] The 1871 Census contains a more comprehensive listing of about 120 such bodies established up to 1854. However, the total numbers accommodated rose only to 3,100, indicating that the additional institutions included in the later censuses tended to be smaller than those originally captured in 1851.

The census commissioners categorized the institutions in three categories:[52]

1) hospitals for the incurables (of which there were only two in 1851);
2) 'retreats for the deserving, the aged and the destitute', including many widows' alms houses which were numerous (73 in 1851) but often rather small in size and many of which dated back several centuries;
3) Magdalen asylums and similar institutions (such as homes for women

49 *Irish Catholic Directory*, 1846, pp 274–5, 289. Similar information is not available for other dioceses. Many (if not all) of the asylums would also appear in the Census listings discussed below.   **50** The Census originally (1851) defined these as 'hospitals and asylums for the permanent residence of the sick, aged, infirm and decrepit in Ireland' but in subsequent censuses this was expanded somewhat to 'hospitals, asylums, alms houses, penitentiaries, and other charitable institution for the permanent residence of the distressed, sick, aged or infirm in Ireland': *Census of Ireland, 1851, report on the status of disease*, p. 107 for the original definition; *Census of Ireland, 1881, general report*, HC 1882, c.3365, pp 319–21, for the expanded version. The later censuses include details as to the religion and former employment of the residents but this issue is not explored here given that this post-Famine data do not necessarily tell us much about the pre-Famine population. These listings are continued in later censuses running into the twentieth century. Of course these data must be interpreted with some caution as we do not know how many institutions may have disappeared in the pre-Famine and Famine periods.   **51** *Census of Ireland, 1851, report on the status of disease*, pp 106–7.   **52** See, *Census of Ireland, 1851, report on the status of disease*, pp 106–8; *Census of Ireland, 1871, report on the status of disease*, pp 132–6. These returns do not include 'Orphan houses and institutions of that character'.

discharged from prison) which were smaller in number and more recent in establishment.[53]

The census gives dates for the establishment of these bodies (although it is impossible to know how accurate these are).[54] Of a total of about 121 institutions established up to 1854, 56 were established before 1800, 30 in the period 1800 to 1830, 24 in the period around the establishment of the poor law (1830–45) and only 11 in the period around the Great Famine (1846–54).[55] Residential charitable institutions were most common in Leinster and Munster with relatively few such institutions in Ulster and almost none in Connacht. The southern institutions (outside Dublin) were generally in the main urban areas (i.e., Kilkenny, Cork, Limerick and Waterford cities) although they tended to be small.[56] It is perhaps unsurprising that there are few pre-1800 institutions in Ulster given the lack of any significant urban centres with Belfast in 1800 being a town of about 20,000. However, there is no sign that the significant population growth in the first half of the nineteenth century led to any major growth in such centres and some existing institutions appear to have closed (perhaps as a result of the poor law). The data generally suggest a preference for outdoor relief in Ulster.

While one might have expected some fall off in the establishment of such institutions during the period in which the establishment of a poor law was under consideration and – even more – during its implementation, in fact we see the establishment of a significant number of institutions in the period 1830–45, with over half being established after 1838. The Famine period, however, does seem to have had some chilling effect on the establishment of long-term institutions, with resources, perhaps, being directed towards immediate famine relief.[57] The period after the Famine shows quite a regional contrast with little development in southern Ireland outside Dublin and strong growth in Ulster, mainly in Belfast and surrounding towns in the period from the mid-1850s and, peaking somewhat later, in Dublin.

IMPACT OF THE POOR LAW

As Peter Gray has discussed in detail, following a period of discussion and debate, a poor law was introduced in Ireland in 1838 and was, in effect, more-or-less nation-wide by the eve of the Great Famine.[58] This followed a period of lengthy and

53 In 1851, there were seventeen such bodies accommodating 450 women.   **54** There is some variation in the dates given in different censuses and where this occurs the earlier date is used here.   **55** We have included data up to 1854 so as to look at the impact of the Famine on the establishment of such institutions. The analysis is based on the more complete listing of 1871.   **56** At least if the post-Famine data are an accurate reflection of the size of the institution in the earlier period.   **57** See, for example, Helen E. Hatton, *The largest amount of good: Quaker relief in Ireland, 1654–1921* (Montreal, 1993).   **58** Peter Gray, *The making of the Irish poor law, 1815–43* (Manchester, 2009).

intensive debate. The opponents of a poor law had predicted that the introduction of a compulsory measure would lead to a fall-off in charitable donations.[59] This appears to have happened and there are a number of references to charitable bodies facing particular financial difficulties at this time;[60] redefining their activities;[61] or ceasing activity entirely.[62] The houses of industry and foundling hospitals were quasi-public institutions and were clearly intended to be replaced by the workhouses.[63]

However, the voluntary mendicity societies either disappeared entirely or changed the focus of their work with the introduction of the poor law. The Dublin Mendicity Institution discharged 1,000 paupers from the institution shortly after the opening of the Dublin workhouses and the Poor Law Commission reported that 1,500 persons were admitted to the South Dublin workhouse in the first month, 'the great majority of whom had previously been supported in the Dublin Mendicity Institution'.[64] Although the Dublin mendicity society itself remained in operation, its working was 'modified very materially'.[65] Jordan reports that the Belfast house of industry closed in 1841.[66] Similarly, Durnin reports that the first occupiers of the new Londonderry workhouse were 100 adults and children from the city's mendicity institute (established in 1825), which appears also to have closed.[67]

Nonetheless, the census data indicate that the poor law did not lead to a freeze on the establishment of private institutions in the period with a number of new establishments being set up in the period from 1830 to the onset of the Great Famine.

CONCLUSION

This chapter has set out an overview of philanthropy and poor relief before the poor law in the period from about 1800 to the 1830s. Although there was no 'old poor law' in any meaningful sense of the term, there was a pre-existing system of poor relief. We have seen that poor relief – before the poor law – involved a complex mix of systems of relief and that it is difficult to use a distinction such as 'public' and 'private' in the period. Support was provided through a range of institutions, legal, civic and religious, and also through complex and geographically varied patterns of

---

59 See, for example, Sir Francis Workman Macnaughton, *Observations on the state of the indigent poor in Ireland* (London, 1830). Of course, it is possible that donations to poor relief ceased but that donations were redirected to other forms of charitable giving. **60** See, for example, Alison Jordan, *Who cared?: charity in Victorian and Edwardian Belfast*, at pp 23–4; Woods, *Dublin outsiders*, pp 113–19. **61** Woods, *Dublin outsiders*, pp 113–19. **62** Patrick Durnin, 'Aspects of poor law administration and the workhouse in Derry 1838–1948' in Gerard O'Brien (ed.), *Derry and Londonderry: history and society* (Dublin, 1991), pp 537–56. **63** In many cases, the local bourgeoisie favoured a swift transfer to the poor law (presumably because the new taxation arrangements were more favourable to them). **64** Woods, *Dublin outsiders*, p. 116 and *Seventh annual report*, p. 44. **65** See Woods, p. 117 et seq. **66** Jordan, *Who cared?*, pp 21–4. **67** Durnin, 'Aspects of poor law administration and the workhouse in Derry 1838–1948', pp 537–56.

private giving. This initial study suggests that patterns of support were regionally varied with, for example, a lack of (grand jury or Exchequer funded) houses of industry in Ulster and, conversely, most of the country's mendicity institutions being established in that province.[68] There were no houses of industry in Connacht and only two mendicity institutions, in Galway and Sligo, the only two medium-sized towns in the province. The lack of formal relief structures presumably reflects the general poverty and lack of resources in the province and the limited urban base. It is interesting to note that a similar tripartite division between an austere north, an impoverished west and the rest of Ireland continued even after the establishment of a national poor law in 1838.[69]

Unfortunately the extent to which poor relief relied on a 'mixed economy' of supports and the informal nature of many of these supports makes it difficult (if not impossible) to get any clear picture about the extent of relief in pre-Famine Ireland or to compare this in any meaningful way with comparative data such as that collated by Peter Lindert.[70] Nonetheless the type of detailed local study proposed below – including the examples contained in this volume – should begin to develop a much clearer picture of the level of support provided so as to enable such a comparative picture to emerge.

Clearly much more detailed research and, in particular, local study, is required to give a more comprehensive picture, particularly as to private, community and religious relief.[71] This would also allow a more detailed assessment of the actual impact of the introduction of the poor law in 1838 and whether this led to a fall in private giving or simply a redirection with, for example, the establishment by mainly religious bodies of a number of Magdalen asylums and similar institutions in the period. Indeed, there is a long list of issues which deserve further research, several of which are explored in this volume. These include: the perspective of the poor; the role of gender in poor relief; the role of landlords and employers in the provision of relief; and the ideologies of relief. The role of philanthropy has the potential to tell us a lot about Irish society in the nineteenth century and about both how it changed and (in some ways) how it stayed the same.

---

68 Based on a review of official and other publications of the time, mendicity societies (or similar institutions) have been identified in Antrim, Ballymena, Ballyshannon, Bangor, Belfast (though called a house of industry), Carrickfergus, Coleraine, Enniskillen, Larne, Lisburn, Londonderry, Monaghan, Newry, Newtownards (also called a house of industry), Shankill/Lurgan – all in Ulster; Birr, Drogheda, Dublin, Dundalk, Portarlington – all in Lenister; Clonmel, Cork, Limerick, Waterford – in Munster. In Connacht, the only societies were in Sligo and Galway. However, the Dublin body was by far the largest institution. **69** See Mel Cousins, *Poor relief in Ireland, 1851–1914* (Oxford, 2011). **70** Peter Lindert, 'Poor relief before the Welfare State: Britain versus the Continent, 1780–1880', *European Review of Economic History* (1998), pp 101–40. **71** See, for example, the ongoing project in Queen's University, Belfast: 'Welfare and public health in Belfast and its region, c.1800–1973'. Details at http://www.qub.ie/schools/SchoolofHistoryandAnthropology/Research/HistoryResearchProjects/WelfareandpublichealthinBelfast/ProjectDetails/

'The best relief the poor can receive is from themselves': the Society for Promoting the Comforts of the Poor

LAURENCE M. GEARY

The poor man, by sin and wickedness, will make poverty insupportable, for
Lying makes him despised
Drunkenness ruins himself, and his family
Idleness produces Beggary
Discontent is Unhappiness
Swearing is serving the Devil without wages
Stealing leads to the Gallows
And,
What is worse than all, wickedness, which makes him unhappy in this
world, carries him into everlasting misery in the next.
On the other hand, by religion, in low circumstances, he may become as
happy, as this world can make him
For
Honesty gains him a character
Truth makes his word respected
Sobriety preserves his health
Kind behaviour makes his home pleasant
Cleanliness makes it comfortable
Industry drives out want
Contentment is real happiness
Faith in Christ and holy prayers make holy lives
He generally sees his children follow his example
A good conscience gives him peace at last
and
Everlasting happiness crowns all.[1]

---

1 *The twenty-sixth report of the Society for Bettering the Condition and Increasing the Comforts of the Poor* (London, 1806; Dublin: reprinted for W. Watson and son, 1806), p. 110.

ESTABLISHMENT AND ETHOS

In the closing years of the eighteenth century, Ireland was rocked by rebellion and civil war, racked by famine and disease, and rent by political corruption and turbulence. In the previous half century, the Irish population had more than doubled to some 5 million people, and had increased by 1 million, or by 25 per cent, in the 1790s alone. The population continued to expand, albeit at a decelerating rate, in the opening decades of the nineteenth century. Growth on this scale magnified the pressures on the urban and rural poor, whose homes were invariably overcrowded, poorly ventilated and lacking in both comfort and basic sanitation. The diet of the poor had gradually contracted to a few staples, and agricultural labourers, cottiers and small farmers had become dangerously dependent on potatoes for food and survival. Severe food shortages and price inflation in the years 1799–1801, resulting from a combination of unseasonable weather and political and social upheaval, had a negative impact on urban industrial employment, notably in the textile and service industries.[2]

The Irish poor were in a particularly vulnerable and invidious position in that they were almost entirely dependent on private charity and voluntary welfare initiatives if they needed assistance. Historically, facilities for the care of the poor and the sick had been located in abbeys and monasteries but the suppression of these institutions by King Henry VIII in the 1530s resulted in the demise of their relief and other charitable activities. During the reign of Henry's daughter, Elizabeth, a legal and compulsory relief system for the unemployed and unemployable was established in England but the Elizabethan poor law was not extended to Ireland, so that the Irish poor did not have a legal right or entitlement to public assistance, and a parish-based poor law network similar to that in England did not exist in Ireland.[3]

It was against the background of deteriorating economic and social conditions for the poor and the absence of a statutory poor law that the Society for Promoting

2 See, inter alia, Liam Kennedy and Leslie Clarkson, 'Birth, death and exile: Irish population history, 1700–1921' in B.J. Graham and L.J. Proudfoot (eds), *An historical geography of Ireland* (London, 1993), pp 158–64; Roger Wells, 'The Irish famine of 1799–1801: market culture, moral economies and social protest' in Adrian Randall and Andrew Charlesworth (eds), *Markets, market culture and popular protest in eighteenth-century Britain and Ireland* (Liverpool, 1996), pp 163–193, at pp 164–8; Cormac Ó Gráda, *Ireland. A new economic history, 1780–1939* (Oxford, 1994); Dr Barker, 'Extract from an account of the house of recovery for fever patients, lately established at Waterford', *Second number of the reports of the Society for Promoting the Comforts of the Poor* (Dublin: Wm Watson & Son, 1800), pp 89–107 (hereafter *SPCP*); Thomas P. Power, *Land, politics and society in eighteenth-century Tipperary* (Oxford, 1993), pp 58–9; L.A. Clarkson, 'The demography of Carrick-on-Suir, 1799', *Proceedings of the Royal Irish Academy. Section C: Archaeology, Celtic Studies, History, Linguistics, Literature*, 87C (1987), pp 13–36. 3 For the eighteenth-century background to philanthropic associational activity in Ireland, see James Kelly, 'Charitable societies: their genesis and development, 1720–1800' in James Kelly and Martyn J. Powell (eds), *Clubs and societies in eighteenth-century Ireland* (Dublin, 2010), pp 89–108.

the Comforts of the Poor was founded in Ireland in 1799, initially in Cork, Dublin and Carrick-on-Suir, County Tipperary, and in a number of other Irish centres in the following years, including Sligo, Kilkenny and Donamyne (now Donaghmoyne), County Monaghan, in 1800,[4] New Ross, County Wexford, in 1801[5] and Stillorgan, County Dublin, in 1802.[6] These bodies were independent of one another but, collectively, they drew their inspiration, language of discourse and, possibly, their ideals from the English Society for Bettering the Condition and Increasing the Comforts of the Poor, which originated in London in late 1796 and which in turn may have been influenced by earlier initiatives in Munich and, particularly, Hamburg. The general sentiments and much of the content of the literature that emanated from the Irish Society for Promoting the Comforts of the Poor derived from the published reports of the English parent body and role model.[7]

In both countries, the Society for Promoting the Comforts of the Poor was inspired by religious sentiment, philanthropy, and self-interest. It was a predominantly male, middle-class association, with some aristocratic leverage, which operated under the patronage of church and state, and its attitude to the poor was condescending and paternalistic, underpinned by a degree of anxiety about maintaining the social contract. The Society's members feared that disaffection among the lower orders would undermine social structures and they thought that the general weal could best be served by improving the lives, living conditions and morals of the poor. Part of the impetus behind the establishment of the English Society was a sense that enforcing industry by statute and compelling the poor to labour in workhouses had failed, and that a more socially inclusive approach was required. The Society's literature proclaimed 'that the best relief the poor can receive is from themselves', a consummation that could best be achieved by encouraging industry, temperance, prudence, cleanliness and good order among them. The emphasis was on practical, rather than theoretical, philanthropy, on promoting self-help, discouraging dependency on regular assistance, and disabusing the poor of any sense of charitable entitlement.

In both context and concept, the Society defined the poor as the labouring

---

4 *Second number of the reports of the SPCP*, pp 3, 113–16.   **5** *Third number of the reports of the Society for Promoting the Comforts of the Poor* (Dublin: Wm Watson & Son, 1801), pp 47–51. **6** Revd John Reade, 'A report of the Stillorgan Charitable Institution for Bettering the Condition of the Poor', Apr. 1807, *Eighth number of the reports of the Society for Promoting the Comforts of the Poor* (Dublin: Wm Watson & Son, 1807), pp 79–80.   **7** The English SBCICP published thirty reports in five volumes. The thirtieth report appears to have been the last, at least in the original format. In a postscript, the Society stated that it intended 'to vary the mode of publication'. This report, which was dated 22 Dec. 1807, was the culmination of what the Society called 'eleven years of attentive investigation', *The thirtieth report of the Society for Bettering the Condition and Increasing the Comforts of the Poor* (London, 1808; Dublin: reprinted for W. Watson and son, 1808), p. 333. The Irish SPCP continued its publications for another two years, the ninth, and final, number appearing at the end of 1809, *Ninth number of the reports of the Society for Promoting the Comforts of the Poor* (Dublin: Wm Watson & Son, 1809).

classes, the working poor, those independent, self-sustaining members of society who provided for themselves and their families through their own labour. Such individuals were regarded with compassion, as 'deserving' of assistance, in contrast to healthy, unemployed adults, who were perceived as 'undeserving' and looked upon with contempt. Idleness was seen as a manifestation of individual laziness or other character defect, not as a consequence of economic or social circumstances. The term 'poor' was employed in the Society's literature as 'a general and known term', not as an odious or invidious one, and in both England and Ireland the Society was keen to stress that, unlike vice and idleness, 'no disgrace attached either to poverty or wealth'.

It was not the Society's intention to interfere with the conduct of individuals or to embroil itself in contentious and divisive political or social matters. Thus, at a time of intense religious and political dissension in Ireland, the Society's focus was firmly on social welfare, on improving the condition of those who languished at the lower end of the socio-economic scale. The objective was to secure the established social order by promoting the general happiness and welfare of the poor, and this could best be achieved by maintaining the existing gradations of wealth and rank, the current balance between the different social classes, rather than subscribing to any notion of social equality. According to the Society's prospectus, the essential preconditions to effecting any general improvement in the status of the lower classes were 'industry on the part of the poor, personal attention, solicitude and superintendence on the part of the rich'. Any amelioration in the manners, habits and comforts of the poor would promote personal happiness and national prosperity, and improve both the appearance of the country and the security of the middle and upper classes. The writer contended that the eradication of misery and vice from contemporary society was a visionary and unattainable objective but a reduction in its prevalence and a corresponding increase in general virtue and happiness could be achieved.

The Dublin Society for Promoting the Comforts of the Poor appears to have been the co-ordinating body in Ireland and was largely responsible for the various reports and manuals that were produced. The president and patron was the lord lieutenant, Marquis Cornwallis; the vice-presidents were the lord chancellor, the earl of Altamont, Lord Kenmare, the bishop of Ferns, Right Hon. John Foster and Right Hon. David Latouche, and the secretary was William Disney. The committee included representatives of the nobility, the Anglican clergy, Fellows of Trinity College, and medical practitioners, among them Dr Colles, Dr Perceval and Surgeon George Renny.[8]

Five sub-committees were appointed to inquire into different aspects of the lives and circumstances of the labouring classes in Dublin and the provinces. They sought to acquire and disseminate information on subjects as diverse as friendly societies; agricultural improvement societies; gaols; county infirmaries and local dispensaries;

---

8 *The first number of the reports of the Society for Promoting the Comforts of the Poor* (Dublin: Wm Watson & Son, 1800), p. i.

village shops and mills; public kitchens and soup shops; the dwellings of the poor and
the type of fuel the latter used for cooking and heating; the education of the poor;
employment, particularly among the female poor; beggars and begging, and possible
ways of diminishing or eliminating mendicancy altogether. The Society's publications, which were intended to provide practical information on these and other
topics, to promote economy and independence, and to teach the values of industry
and temperance, were deliberately kept short and simple so that they might be
understood by everyone.[9]

In late 1799, the sub-committee inquiring into the state of the labouring classes
in rural Ireland contacted various people, including a number of clergymen, seeking
information on the state of the labouring poor in their neighbourhoods. One of the
more robust responses came from James Hosford of Brookeville, County Cork. He
claimed that any plan for promoting the comforts of the poor would be 'useless and
nugatory, mere patch and botchwork' unless it secured employment for the rapidly
expanding population. Hosford argued that it was the government's duty to provide
work for these people, or, failing that, to assist in their removal to the colonies, or,
more drastically,

> to put a speedy check to the further propagation of the human species in
> Ireland, by operating on the males and females as is done with other animals,
> or at least to adopt Dean Swift's proposal of fatting and eating the multitudes
> of children that swarm about our cities, towns, villages, roads and cabins, and
> that, in the present state of things, are by physical necessity, nothing else but
> thieves, robbers, traitors and rebels in embryo.

According to Hosford, the prevailing features of the cabins of the labouring poor
were 'dirt, darkness and smoke, pigs, turf, potatoes, children and poultry within,
dunghills and lodgements of putrid water without'.[10] These sentiments were echoed
in a report from Kilrush, which categorized the homes of the poor of west Clare as
'miserable beyond description – damp, cold and dirty'; none had windows, few had
chimneys, and every cabin had 'a dunghill at its door'.[11]

The bishop of Dromore, referring to County Down and, perhaps, the north of
Ireland generally, was more discriminatory, claiming that only Catholics lived in such
conditions. 'In this country', he wrote, 'the habitations of Protestants are dry, clean
and comfortable, the papist cabins, filthy and comfortless, though they have each
equal opportunities for decency'. A west Cork clergyman was inclined to blame the
prevailing living and social conditions in his neighbourhood on the improvidence of
the poor and on 'the infatuating pleasure of whiskey'. A clergyman who lived in

9 Ibid., pp i–xxii.   **10** Royal College of Physicians of Ireland Archives (hereafter RCPI), 6
Kildare Street, Dublin 2, TPCK/6/7/2 (1), Society for Promoting the Comforts of the Poor,
James Hosford to the sub-committee inquiring into the state of the labouring classes in the
country, 17 Dec. 1799. I am grateful to Harriet Wheelock and Robert Mills for their
courtesy and assistance.   **11** Ibid., Anon to the sub-committee, 26 Oct. 1799.

Glanmire, just north of Cork city, commented that the high price of coal and the lack of locally produced turf were detrimental to the morals of the poor, prompting them to steal timber and to break up fencing for firewood. He added that a cotton factory in his parish, and a woollen factory in the neighbouring one, provided a considerable amount of employment locally. Factory work offered wages and thereby lessened poverty, which was reflected in the comparative cleanliness of the homes of the ordinary people of the locality. However, he thought that these factories had a very negative impact on the morals of those who were employed in them. 'The order of the day on every Sunday is debauchery', he complained. 'It is hard to stem the torrent against the opposed force of whiskey.'[12]

A member of the sub-committee, possibly the secretary, suggested, in two undated draft reports, that the rural poor were more deserving of assistance than their urban brethren, on the grounds that they were 'more numerous', 'more virtuous', 'more industrious and more stationary'. He added that they were also more amenable to 'habits of industry and virtue' and more likely to inculcate such habits in their families, and, thus, there was a greater chance of securing a permanent improvement in the condition of the rural poor.[13]

These ideas were further refined in a draft document headed 'Proposed as part of preface'. According to the anonymous author, experience had shown that agricultural labourers were less frequently reduced to poverty than industrial or factory workers, a situation that applied more particularly to those who laboured in 'great factories' than to those who worked at home. He claimed that factory workers had a more variable income, changed their dwelling more frequently, and parted from friends who might have assisted them or restrained their 'excesses'. They were less influenced by 'education and association, the guardians of a great proportion of whatever virtue is in the world', and had little fear of gaining a bad reputation because it could so easily be left behind. Their labour earned money, but it did not produce food and the other immediate necessities of life, and money could be 'misused or misapplied'. Industrial or factory workers were often redundant, temporarily unemployed, either from lack of demand for their produce or from their own 'impatience' to raise wages 'by combination', an activity that also taught them to resist or evade the laws of the country. Their circumstances were more likely to lead them into habits of intoxication; they laboured in an unhealthy environment, were much

12 Ibid., Thomas Beatty, bishop of Dromore, Garvaghy, County Down, to the sub-committee, 9 Dec. 1799; Revd John Chetwood, Glanmire, County Cork, to the sub-committee, 10 Feb. 1800; J. Wright, Aghadown Glebe, County Cork, to the sub-committee, 16 Apr. 1800. See also [W.M. Pitt], *A letter from Major Pitt, of the Dorset Regiment, to the Society for Promoting the Comforts of the Poor, established at Carrick-on-Suir, in the county of Tipperary* (Dublin, 1800). Pitt claimed that 'real distress' still prevailed to 'a lamentable extent' in Carrick in the autumn of 1799, and opined that the main causes of poverty were 'sickness, old age, want of employment, children becoming orphans, and very principally idleness and intemperance', p. 4. 13 Ibid., TPCK/6/7/2 (1), Society for Promoting the Comforts of the Poor.

exposed to epidemic diseases, and when sick had 'the dangerous opportunity' to pawn their clothes or their work tools, which meant that they continued in idleness after recovering from illness.[14]

It is not possible to determine whether these were the sentiments of a single individual, the sub-committee inquiring into the state of the labouring classes in rural Ireland, or the Society for Promoting the Comforts of the Poor generally, but they do suggest a more tolerant attitude to small farmers and agricultural labourers, the rural poor, than to factory workers. The former were perceived as more deserving, more amenable to society's dictates, while the urban proletariat were regarded as inherently or potentially dissolute, shiftless and dangerous, prone to drink and combination, a threat to civil society and material wealth.

INDIVIDUAL SOCIETIES AND INITIATIVES

To redress the conditions described by Hosford and by numerous other commentators, be they Irish residents or visitors, improving societies and philanthropic initiatives were launched in various parts of the country around the turn of the nineteenth century. Although there were variations in nomenclature, the inspiration and ethos as well as practical advice and direction derived from the publications of the Society for Promoting the Comforts of the Poor.

In May 1799 a survey by church wardens in Cookstown, County Tyrone, revealed that between 50 and 60 families 'were in great poverty and distress'. Many of the poor had 'no bed but a little straw upon the damp ground, and no covering but the rags they wore by day, and some poor women had not had a shift on for two years'. Many were afflicted with poverty-related illnesses, against which the physician's ministrations were largely ineffective. The inhabitants responded to these findings by inaugurating the Cookstown Charitable Institution which was intended 'to provide relief for the really deserving poor, to exclude the idle and worthless, to relieve sickness, to prevent beggary, and encourage industry'. This initiative was based on a similar scheme in Hamburg, an account of which had appeared in one of the reports published by the English Society for Bettering the Condition and Increasing the Comforts of the Poor.

The regulations governing the Hamburg society were adopted in Cookstown, with slight modifications to suit local circumstances. One of the criteria was that individuals receiving aid were obliged to have been resident in the parish for at least three years. The Cookstown Charitable Institution offered various forms of assistance, including medical relief and medicine, clothing and bedding, and weekly allowances, or other financial support, such as payment of debts, money to purchase fuel, or the provision of flax to those who were capable of spinning. The physician, who gave his services free of charge, attended every Saturday from 12 noon to 3 p.m., and the town's apothecaries furnished medicines at cost price.

14 Ibid., TPCK/6/7/2 (2), Society for Promoting the Comforts of the Poor.

Eighty-six individuals were relieved by the institution between 11 May and 4 November 1799: 53 received medical attendance; 70 received clothing, bedding and a weekly allowance; 25 widows and 7 others who were employed in spinning received financial support according to their needs. In addition, 20 blankets, 165 yards of flannel, 187 yards of linen, 100 yards of drugget and 5 frieze coats were distributed among the needy.[15]

The object of the Donamyne Society for Bettering the Condition of the Poor was 'to relieve the distress of their poorer neighbours and to promote industry and morals amongst them'. Assistance was limited to 'deserving objects'. It was specifically stated at a meeting of the Society on 14 January 1800 that 'the importunate beggar' should not receive relief that was intended 'for retired and modest distress'. Initially, relief took the form of clothing and spinning wheels, but later the Society subsidized food prices for the poor, and, in order to encourage industry, provided flax and spades at half price, the latter because 'many labourers were out of employment through want of spades'. As with many of these societies, some of the principal office-holders were clergymen, including the secretary, who claimed that the consequences of the charity's activities 'in promoting harmony and improving the connection between the different classes of society' were 'beyond calculation'.[16]

The Society for Promoting the Comforts of the Poor of the Town and Neighbourhood of New Ross evolved in January 1801 from a pre-existing poor relief committee in the town. The scarcity and high cost of provisions in the locality, and a lack of employment, had immiserated many who were inclined to be industrious, and had led to a sharp escalation in public begging. The task that the New Ross Society took upon itself was to supervise the distribution of aid to the needy and to improve the district generally. The committee also proposed to revive the dispensary, 'for the purpose of compounding and dispensing medicine, and affording surgical assistance' and, if the funds allowed, to establish a fever hospital in order to curb the spread of infectious disease. The members specifically cited the positive experiences of Manchester and Waterford, where fever hospitals had been established.[17]

In the winter of 1802, Revd John Reade was appointed curate in Stillorgan, County Dublin, where, he discovered, there was a deficiency of bed clothes among the poor and many slept on the earthen floor because they did not have bedsteads. In the winter half of the year, the exorbitant demands of the huxter rendered fuel, 'that great comfort of the poor', so expensive that it was entirely beyond the means of the common labourer, who invariably resorted to 'the hedgerows and improvements of the surrounding gentry'. Under the aegis of the Stillorgan Charitable Institution for Bettering the Condition of the Poor, Reade opened a shop and a coal

15 The Miss Olivers, 'An account of Cookstown Charitable Institution', *The first number of the reports of the SPCP*, pp 44–9.   **16** 'An account of the Donamyne Society for Bettering the Condition of the Poor, communicated by one of its members', *Second number of the reports of the SPCP*, pp 113–16.   **17** *Third number of the reports of the SPCP*, pp 47–51.

store, to supply the poor cheaply with their basic requirements. He maintained a dispensary at his home, where he kept 'a constant supply of plain or simple medicines', and he claimed to have restored the health of many individuals. Reade ministered to their spiritual as well as their physical needs and he detected 'a great improvement' in the 'moral and religious conduct' of his poor Protestant parishioners because of the number of religious books they had received gratis from the charity. He noted that they had become 'more frequent communicants and more strict observers of the Sabbath'.[18]

The Society for Promoting the Comforts of the Poor was particularly keen on establishing friendly societies and in fostering and supporting such institutions where they already existed. Friendly societies provided insurance-style services to their members, specifically financial support in sickness, old age and bereavement, in return for small weekly or monthly subscriptions, and their utility in 'promoting the happiness of individuals' was recognized in a 1796 Act of the Irish parliament, which encouraged these societies and afforded them legal protection.[19] There were at least four such schemes in Dublin:

- the Friendly Brothers, or Staple Union, which began in 1790
- the Amicable Society, which was established in 1796
- the Friendly Brothers of the St Audeon's Society
- the Friends of Industry, Donnybrook.

There were two in Carlow:

- the Carlow Club, which had ninety members and originated in 1769
- the Fraternal Union and Friendly Union Club, which commenced in 1777.

The Athy Farmers' Friendly Union began in 1789 and a friendly society was established at Collon, County Louth, a decade later. Two of the Carlow schemes dissolved in the wake of the 1798 Rebellion, as did two others in County Wexford.[20]

In 1786, two such schemes were formed in the parish of Stradbally (possibly Queen's County, although the county is not specified in the report), one to relieve sick and infirm artisans or tradesmen, such as smiths, carpenters and masons, the other

---

18 Revd John Reade, 'A report of the Stillorgan Charitable Institution for bettering the Condition of the Poor', pp 79–93; idem, 'A report of the Stillorgan Charitable Institution for Bettering the Condition and Promoting the Comforts of the Poor', 31 Aug. 1808, *Ninth number of the reports of the SPCP*, pp 101–31. 19 36 Geo III, c. 58, 'An act for the encouragement and relief of friendly societies', 15 Apr. 1796. See also *The first number of the reports of the SPCP*, appendix 1, pp 1–12. For a general discussion on Irish friendly societies, see A.D. Buckley, '"On the club": friendly societies in Ireland', *Irish Economic and Social History*, 14 (1987), pp 39–58. See, generally, Peter Clark, *British clubs and societies, 1580–1800. The origins of an associational world* (Oxford, 2000), chapter 10, Benefit Clubs, pp 350–87. 20 *The first number of the reports of the SPCP*, appendix 1, pp 31–5.

for the benefit of day labourers. Within a short time, each scheme had about 150 subscribers. Intending members had to be less than forty years of age and of sound mind and body. They were placed on probation for one month, while 'their character and modes of life' were investigated. Once accepted, they paid an admission fee of one English shilling and thereafter the monthly subscription was 10.5 pence for artisans and 11 pence for labourers. Members who did not pay their dues regularly and on time were expelled.

The Stradbally societies offered support in illness and in bereavement. Subscribers who became ill and were unable to work received 6d. a week for six weeks and 3d. thereafter, at a time when, it was reported, the maximum that could be earned locally by a labourer working six days a week was 4s. Two sworn members were obliged to visit the invalids each day 'and report faithfully whether their sickness was real or pretended'. On the death of any subscriber, his widow and family were allowed 30s. for a coffin and expenses. In addition, each member contributed an English shilling towards the family's general support. One example was provided, that of the widow and four boys of a deceased labourer. She received £7 10s. English, which she used to apprentice the two older boys, aged eleven and twelve, and to clothe and school her younger sons.

Death and its trappings were accorded due and proper respect. Within a short time of their foundation, the funds of each of the Stradbally schemes enabled their respective stewards to purchase 'a black velvet pall, twelve linen scarves, fourteen hat bands, two cloaks, caps and poles for conductors'. Non-attendance at the funeral of a deceased member was punishable by a fine of 6d. According to Revd Dr Forster, who reported on the activities of the two friendly societies in Stradbally parish, the poor labourers and artisans who were members 'felt inexpressible satisfaction, knowing they would be buried, not like dogs, without a coffin, but in a kind of state unknown to persons of their rank'.

Stradbally's two friendly societies provided practical support in illness and in death but their rules were also designed to secure the members' morals. According to Forster, expulsion and forfeiture of entitlements was the punishment for any individual who was convicted 'by two or more witnesses, before a council appointed and sworn, of being drunk, or cursing and swearing, of being concerned in any riot, of using indecent or opprobrious language, of stealing and robbing, or of being guilty of any crimes forbidden by the law in force here'. Long experience had convinced Forster that the encouragement of industry, prudence and sobriety constituted the most effectual method of improving the condition and the morals of the poor, although the ameliorative intent appears to have been somewhat diluted by the offer of 'one quart of 3d. ale' to each member as an inducement to attend the monthly meetings at which the business of the friendly societies was transacted.[21]

---

21 'Extract of two letters received from the Revd Dr Forster of Stradbally to Dr Perceval, with observations by the latter', 16 July 1799, in *The first number of the reports of the SPCP*, pp 24–7.

A convivial element was also a feature of the friendly society that was established at Castletown Delvin in the summer of 1800. Two years later, at the annual general meeting on 4 June, 'a small portion of liquor' was distributed to the members to commemorate the king's birthday 'with sober joy and gratitude'. Each member of the society was presented with a specially struck medal which bore the inscription 'Delvin Friendly Society'. The writer presumed that the medal would be regarded

> as a badge of merit, wherever honest industry and frugality are valued, marking in the wearer a well timed exertion of those virtues to prevent his being a burthen to his employer, or a dependent on the charity of his neigh-bours, when sickness, or old age shall have incapacitated him from labour.[22]

Charitable loan societies lent small sums of money, which were generally repaid in weekly instalments, to promote employment and welfare among industrious labourers and others. Benevolent or charitable loan funds existed in Dublin, Limerick, Waterford, Armagh, Raphoe and Carrick-on-Suir.[23] The Waterford initiative was launched in 1768 and over the remaining years of the century more than 10,000 individuals were lent varying amounts of money.[24] A loan fund was established at Castletown Delvin in the spring of 1800, 'in order to facilitate the purchase of various articles necessary to the employment of the cottagers, and to the cropping of their gardens and lots'.[25] A similar initiative commenced in the parish of Killishee and district, Swordlestown, County Kildare, in 1800. According to one of those involved, Robert Graydon, loan funds possessed the great advantage of assisting the industry of the poor 'without encouraging their idleness, or even their indolence'. Graydon added that these initiatives established a link between the upper and lower classes which was 'necessary to the proper support of order and an honest application to labour', both of which were 'the mainsprings of general prosperity in every country'.[26] The Cashel Charitable Society, which was established on 13 December 1806, launched a number of initiatives in its first year, including a charitable loan, under which money was lent to 218 individuals. As a result, according to the Society's spokesman, 'industry has been encouraged, beggary diminished, and many enabled to earn an honest livelihood, who must otherwise have been helpless to themselves and

---

22 Robert Stearne Tighe, 'Extract from an account of a benevolent loan, and a friendly society, established at Castletown Delvin', *Fifth number of the reports of the Society for Promoting the Comforts of the Poor* (Dublin: Wm Watson & Son, 1802), pp 110–21, at p. 114.   23 Robert Graydon, 'Extract from an account of a benevolent or charitable loan, for lending small sums of money (to be repaid by weekly instalments) to industrious labourers and others, in the parish of Killishee and district, Swordlestown, Co. Kildare, *The first number of the reports of the SPCP*, appendix 6, pp 97–104, at p. 104.   24 William Hobbs, 'Extract from an account of the charitable loan established at Waterford', *Second number of the reports of the SPCP*, pp 73–6, at p. 73.   25 Tighe, 'Extract from an account of a benevolent loan, and a friendly society, established at Castletown Delvin', p. 110.   26 Graydon, 'Extract from an account of a benevolent or charitable loan', p. 100.

a burthen to the public'. Spinning wheels and clothing were also provided, the recipients repaying the cost by instalment.[27]

Agricultural societies, for the general improvement of farming practices, were encouraged. One such, which was inspired by the Sussex Agricultural Society in England, was the Castleknock Farmers' Society in County Dublin, which was launched on 27 November 1797 to improve agriculture and to reward 'faithful, industrious and sober servants, labourers and others employed in the business of husbandry'.[28] One such reward was a premium of 25 per cent offered by residents of the parishes of Castleknock, Clonsilla and Mulhuddart on any savings made by the industrious poor during the summer months, when demand for their labour was greatest. The combined sum was paid to the saver at Christmas. Such a scheme was considered desirable 'from want of regular habits of frugality and foresight'.[29]

The Castletown Delvin Farming Society was formed on 30 July 1801, with three objectives: to improve 'agriculture and farming in all its branches', to better 'the condition of the labouring poor', and to enforce the laws of the land, particularly those that were more directly linked to the objectives of this society, including the protection of farmers' crops and property, the preservation of trees, and the removal of dirt, ordure and other offensive matter. In order to better the condition of the labouring poor, the founders wished to encourage 'frugality, industry and sobriety' among them, to promote cleanliness, and to punish 'all drunkenness, vice and immorality'.[30]

The Society for Promoting the Comforts of the Poor published accounts of a number of schools that had been established whose primary function appears to have been the promotion of religious education rather than pedagogy. These included a school at North Strand, Dublin, which opened in 1786 and catered for boys and girls. Some practical subjects were taught, along with the 'principles of religion and morality, and the elements of education'.[31] A Sunday school was established at Derryloran, County Tyrone, in 1789, where the focus was on reading and religious instruction.[32] A scripture school for boys opened at New Ross, County Wexford, on 15 October 1798 and for girls on 27 April 1799, under the aegis of 'The Friends of Education'.[33] Broadly linked to these initiatives were Sabbatharian societies,

27 Robert Patten, 'first annual report of the Cashel Charitable Society, instituted Dec. 13th, 1806', 9 Dec. 1807, *Ninth number of the reports of the SPCP*, pp 164–170. 28 *The first number of the reports of the SPCP*, pp 11–23. 29 Revd Dr O'Connor, 'Extract from an account of a scheme for the encouragement of the prudent and industrious labourers of the united parishes of Castleknock, Clonsilla and Mulhuddart', *Sixth number of the reports of the Society for Promoting the Comforts of the Poor* (Dublin: Wm Watson & Son, 1804), pp 167–70. 30 Revd Henry Wynne, 'Extract from an account of the Castletown Delvin Farming Society', *Sixth number of the reports of the SPCP*, pp 171–2. 31 'An account of the Sunday and daily school on the North Strand, by a lady, communicated by Dr Stokes', *The first number of the reports of the SPCP*, pp 28–39. 32 'An account of the Derryloran Sunday school, communicated by the Miss Olivers', *The first number of the reports of the SPCP*, pp 39–44. 33 William Napper, 'Extract from an account of a society established at New Ross, under the denomination of "The Friends of Education"', *The first number of the reports of the*

including one formed in St Mark's parish, Dublin, for enforcing 'the due execution of the laws for regulating the sale of spirituous liquors by retail, and for the due observation of the Sabbath day'. According to one of the members, the country's statute books contained many 'salutary provisions' which were creditable to the legislature but a disgrace to those whose duty it was to enforce them.[34]

The Society for Promoting the Comforts of the Poor encouraged the establishment of village shops to supply the poor with basic commodities as cheaply as possible. They were designed to meet the prevailing distress and were thus intended to be a temporary rather than a permanent feature. A village shop was established at Delgany, County Wicklow, in October 1799, to supply food, clothing and medicines at cost price to labourers who had resided in the parish for two years. A factory was subsequently established in the village and employed females in the manufacture of some of the items that were sold in the shop.[35] On 27 January 1800, the Castleknock Farmers' Society provided a loan of £10 to establish a shop in the village.[36] A similar shop, which was supported by subscriptions, opened at Donnybrook, Dublin, on 14 February 1800 and continued for more than six months. The shop supplied coal, turf, potatoes, meal and herrings at less than cost price to those recommended by subscribers to the charity, a saving to the poor of at least 25 per cent. As the price of these basic commodities remained high, subscriptions were again raised at the beginning of 1801 and the shop re-opened in early March.[37]

The Society for Promoting the Comforts of the Poor was acutely aware of the close and circular relationship between poverty and illness, between disadvantage and disease outbreaks, and the tendency of contagious diseases, once generated, to ascend from the lower to the higher social classes. The threat that the fevers and fluxes of the poor posed to rank and wealth prompted the Society to encourage and support medical charities, such as a privately funded dispensary at Killaloe, County Clare,[38] the Sick Poor Institution, Meath Street, Dublin,[39] and a dispensary that opened in February 1801 in St George's parish, also in Dublin. The physicians attending the dispensary found that fevers were the most prevalent disorders among the poor,

SPCP, pp 57–65. **34** William McAuley, 'Extracts from an account of a society formed in St Mark's parish, for inforcing (sic) the due execution of the laws for regulating the sale of spirituous liquors by retail, and for the due observation of the Sabbath day', *Second number of the reports of the SPCP*, pp 108–12, at p. 112. **35** William Disney, 'An account of a village shop at Delgany, in the county of Wicklow', *Third number of the reports of the SPCP*, pp 1–4. **36** Revd Dr O'Connor, 'An account of the village shop established at Castleknock, in the county of Dublin', *Third number of the reports of the SPCP*, pp 5–10, at p. 5. **37** Dr Perceval, 'Extract from an account of a village shop established at Donnybrook', *Third number of the reports of the SPCP*, pp 15–20. See also William Disney, 'Extract from an account of a village shop at Cookstown, in the county of Tyrone', *Third number of the reports of the SPCP*, pp 11–13. **38** The bishop of Killaloe, 'An account of Killaloe school and dispensary', *The first number of the reports of the SPCP*, pp 50–7. **39** 'An account of the Sick Poor Institution, Meath Street, communicated by the sub-committee for inquiring into the state of existing charitable institutions in the city of Dublin, and neighbourhood thereof', *Second number of the reports of the SPCP*, pp 82–8.

'proceeding partly from the scarcity and bad quality of food, and partly by the want of cleanliness in their wretched habitations'.[40] More significantly, much of the impetus for the development of fever hospitals in Ireland, again following the English example, came from the Society, notably in Waterford in 1799,[41] Cork in 1802,[42] and two in Dublin, the first a thirty-bed hospital that opened on 1 February 1802 on the Circular Road, near the turnpike-gate, Dorset Street, 'for the reception of the sick poor of the northern district';[43] the second, which was to play a significant role in Dublin's public health in the nineteenth and twentieth centuries, opened at Cork Street on 14 May 1804.[44]

In addition to the features outlined above, the Society for Promoting the Comforts of the Poor reported on and supported a miscellany of initiatives that contributed to the physical and moral well-being of the poor, including the wearing of wooden shoes, which were less than half the price of the common brogues, 'twice as durable, much drier and easier to walk in',[45] the cultivation of vegetables,[46] and the creation of employment for the female poor.[47] The Society for Promoting the Comforts of the Poor gave its approval to the House of Refuge, Upper Baggot Street, Dublin, which was intended for destitute females under the age of twenty. According to a report on the institution dating from early 1802, 'there is perhaps no class of human beings more destitute of resource, or more helplessly exposed to the temptations of vice, and the arts of designing villainy'.[48]

CORK: A CASE STUDY

The most active of the Irish societies, certainly the one for which most information appears to be extant, was the Cork Society for Bettering the Condition and

40 'Extract from an account of what has been done, and is doing, for the relief of the poor in the parish of St George's', *Fifth number of the reports of the SPCP*, pp 128–30.   **41** Barker, 'Extract from an account of the house of recovery for fever patients, lately established at Waterford', pp 89–107.   **42** *Annual report of the house of recovery of the city of Cork, from 8 Nov. 1802 to 8 Nov. 1803* (Dublin, 1804), pp 8–10; John Milner Barry and Charles Daly, 'Second annual report of the Cork house of recovery, for the prevention and cure of fevers, from 8 Nov. 1803 to 8 Nov. 1804', *Seventh number of the reports of the Society for Promoting the Comforts of the Poor* (Dublin: Wm Watson & Son, 1805), pp 68–9.   **43** 'Extract from an account of what has been done, and is doing, for the relief of the poor in the parish of St George's', pp 128–30.   **44** William Disney, 'Extract from an account of the house of recovery, or fever hospital, in Cork Street, Dublin', *Seventh number of the reports of the SPCP*, pp 1–13. For these initiatives and some account of the various institutions referred to, see Laurence M. Geary, *Medicine and charity in Ireland, 1718–1851* (Dublin, 2004), chapters 3 and 4, dispensaries and fever hospitals.   **45** 'Advantage of wooden shoes', *Second number of the reports of the SPCP*, Appendix 8, p. 111.   **46** 'Hints for the cultivation of cabbages', *Second number of the reports of the SPCP*, Appendix 9, pp 112–13.   **47** *The first number of the reports of the SPCP*, pp 65–71.   **48** Revd Dr Guinness, 'Extract from an account of the house of refuge, established in Upper Baggot Street, the 1st of Feb., 1802', *Sixth number of the reports of the SPCP*, pp 161–7, at p. 166.

Increasing the Comforts of the Poor, whose aims, activities and potential impact might serve as a model or template for these associations generally. The Cork Society, the first of its kind in Ireland, originated among the management committee of the Benevolent Society, which had been established by the city's Methodists to relieve illness and poverty and was, presumably, limited to their own communion. The Benevolent Society developed and extended beyond its Methodist base in the mid-1790s and its exposure to the city's socio-economic realities, augmented by the publications of the English Society for Bettering the Condition and Increasing the Comforts of the Poor, suggested that prevention was a better option than attempting to redress the city's widespread poverty and distress. The Cork Society was formally launched and a constitution adopted in the wake of public meetings in the city in the spring of 1799.[49]

The president was the bishop of Cork and Ross. There were 5 vice-presidents, one of whom was the Scottish-born entrepreneur John Anderson of Fermoy, a committee of 28, and a 7-man sub-committee that included the Society's treasurer and secretary. The annual subscription was half a guinea. At the spring assizes in 1799, the grand jury of the city of Cork endorsed the Society's objectives, stating that it was fully conscious of the great benefits that were likely to accrue from the Society's endeavours. The grand jury resolved to give its 'most strenuous aid' and to recommend the Society to public notice and protection.[50]

The driving force behind the Cork Society was its secretary, the Dublin-born, 32-year-old Unitarian minister in Princes Street, Revd Thomas Dix Hincks.[51] In February 1799, Hincks informed the Cork public that 'the very lamentable state' to which thousands of the city's residents were reduced demanded their immediate attention. The poorhouse and the existing public charities were unable to relieve the prevailing distress and the dispensary and Benevolent Society could not cater for the mass of the sick. Hincks added that the streets of Cork were filled with beggars and distress was increasing.[52] In the following year, 1800, the high price of food prompted the Cork Society for Bettering the Condition and Increasing the Comforts of the Poor to establish two soup kitchens in the city for the sale of cheap soup to the poor. During the closing months of that year a daily ration was dispensed free of charge to about 1,500 individuals, 'most of whom had no other resource'. The Society recom-

---

49 The meetings were held on 12, 19 Feb., 22 Mar. 1799. T.D. Hincks, *An address to the inhabitants of the city and neighbourhood of Cork, on a subject of importance* (Cork, 1799), pp 13–19; *Address to the publick, from the committee of the Cork Society for Bettering the Condition and Increasing the Comforts of the Poor* (Cork, 1799), pp 11–13; Revd Joseph Stopford, 'An account of the rise and progress of the Cork Society for Bettering the Condition and Increasing the Comforts of the Poor', *The first number of the reports of the SPCP*, pp 1–10. **50** *Address to the publick*, pp 13–16. **51** For Hincks see Alexander Gordon, 'Hincks, Thomas Dix (1767–1857)', Revd David Huddleston, *Oxford dictionary of national biography* (Oxford University Press, 2004; online edition, Jan. 2008); Enda Leaney, 'Hincks, Thomas Dix' in James McGuire and James Quinn (eds), *Dictionary of Irish biography* (Cambridge, 2009) (http://dib.cambridge org/viewReadPage.do?articleId=a4023). **52** Hincks, *An address to the inhabitants of the city and neighbourhood of Cork, on a subject of importance*, pp 3–4.

mended these soup shops to all classes, claiming that they provided cheap, wholesome and nourishing food to those who could no longer afford to purchase their customary provisions.[53] Hincks described the opening years of the nineteenth century as 'successive seasons of scarcity'. In February 1802, he referred to 'the hard struggle with famine' and the extreme difficulty with which many procured 'the bare support of life', and, he added, all the Society's efforts were directed at establishing and supervising 'soup houses' and the procurement and sale of meal, rice and other foods at reduced prices.[54]

Unlike James Hosford of Brookeville, County Cork, who blamed the prevailing wretchedness on what he called 'the oppression or neglect of former centuries' and on government indifference and inactivity,[55] Hincks detected the hand of providence in the ordering of society. 'The distinction of mankind into rich and poor was the appointment of the all-wise creator', he wrote, and suggested that such a distinction was necessary for their mutual happiness. He added, somewhat disingenuously, that the different social classes were 'a support and a blessing to each other', a sentiment that was unlikely to have found much purchase among the poorer classes. Hincks was keen to stress the moral dimension in any attempts at social amelioration. He insisted that reformers needed to focus on improving 'the moral character' of the people rather than on immediate and short-term palliatives, on promoting what he termed 'the essential and permanent welfare' of the lower orders. He acknowledged that the Irish poor were often dirty, drunken, idle and ungrateful but claimed that they were not always responsible for their condition and circumstances, noting that little effort had been made to reform them or to encourage improvements among them. Hincks observed, in a nod to the Enlightenment, that it was only in recent years that the improvement of the lower classes had been attempted scientifically, which he defined as the science of doing good, of promoting the welfare, morals and happiness of the poor.

In keeping with the general sentiments of the Society for Promoting the Comforts of the Poor, Hincks stressed that the term 'poor' was not one of reproach. He defined the poor as 'all those valuable members of the community who support themselves by their daily labour, and who when burdened with large families, or when sickness renders them incapable of working, may become objects of commiseration'. Hincks divided the poor into the following categories:

- those who were able and willing to work
- those who were prevented from working by illness

53 Archdeacon W. Thompson, 'Report of the proceedings of the committee of the Cork Society for Bettering the Condition and Encreasing (sic) the Comforts of the Poor', *Third number of the reports of the SPCP*, pp 26–8.   54 *Report of the proceedings of the general committee of the Society for Bettering the Condition and Increasing the Comforts of the Poor, in the year 1801* (Cork, 1802), pp 3–28.   55 RCPI Archives, TPCK/6/7/2 (1), Society for Promoting the Comforts of the Poor, James Hosford to the sub-committee inquiring into the state of the labouring classes in the country, 17 Dec. 1799.

- widows and the elderly who were unable to support themselves
- poor children, particularly orphans or those whose parents had deserted them
- beggars.[56]

In an 1802 publication Hincks provided a comprehensive list of the charitable institutions that existed in Cork and linked them to his fivefold classification of the poor.[57] Rather than survey the full complement of Hincks' initiatives and charities, this paper will focus on those for which the Cork Society was responsible, or on those promoted in its publications.

The Cork Society's first objective was the establishment of a friendly society whose members paid a monthly premium which insured them against sickness and provided old-age and death benefits. This initiative, which accorded with the Society's stated principle of encouraging independence among the poor, was launched in 1799. The rules adopted were akin to those employed by a number of similar societies in England. Membership of the Cork Friendly Society was open to any reputable individual, irrespective of gender, station or class, between the age of fifteen and fifty, with the singular exception of mothers-to-be. One of the reasons given for their exclusion was that a movement was afoot to establish a lying-in or maternity hospital in the city, which would assist 'distressed females' at a time when they were 'peculiarly objects of compassion'. The promoters of the Friendly Society were determined to prevent 'the idle, the dissipated, the turbulent and the dishonest' from benefiting at the expense of 'the honest, the quiet, the sober and the industrious'.[58] In the light of this stated intent, there is some irony in the fact that 148 of the 209 individuals who joined the Friendly Society in its first year worked in the Beamish and Crawford brewery.[59]

Individual subscriptions, which were paid on admission and monthly thereafter, were 1s. 1d. for those under 30 years of age, 1s. 4d. for those aged between 30 and 40, and 1s. 9d. for those in the 40–50 age group. The Friendly Society's funds were augmented by voluntary contributions and by fines levied on members who failed to pay their monthly subscriptions (3d. for the first default, 6½d. for the second), or who solicited charity (2s. 8½d.), or who were intoxicated while in receipt of relief from the society (3s. 3d.). When sick, each member was entitled to a weekly allowance, which was determined by the amount already subscribed. Those who were aged sixty or over could opt for an annuity instead of the weekly payments when they were ill or infirm; the amount of the annuity was age-dependent, the older the individual, the greater the entitlement.

The regulations disallowed relief to members 'for any disease, distemper, or infirmity' that had been contracted prior to membership; for 'any distemper contracted

56 Thomas Dix Hincks, *A short account of the different charitable institutions of the city of Cork, with remarks* (Cork, 1802), pp iii–vi.   **57** Ibid., pp 9–43.   **58** *Address to the publick*, pp 3–9. **59** Thompson, 'Report of the proceedings of the committee', *Third number of the reports of the SPCP*, p. 31.

by lewdness'; for 'any lameness, misfortune, or accident occasioned by quarrelling, rioting, drunkenness, or gaming'; and for imprisonment on a charge of treason or felony. Membership could be revoked for feigning illness or infirmity, attempting to defraud the society, defaulting on the payment of three consecutive monthly subscriptions, or, in case of default, failing to pay the prescribed penalties. In addition, 'notorious' drunkards or gamblers or those who were criminally convicted could have their membership cancelled, in which case the individual concerned forfeited any claim or title to the society's funds.[60]

The Cork Society's next initiative was to encourage 'cleanliness, industry and good conduct' by offering small sums of money as rewards to two different categories of the poor: 'well-behaved, faithful and industrious servants, both male and female, who resided within the liberties of the city of Cork', and residents of the liberties who kept their persons and homes 'in the best state of cleanliness' during the six months ending 30 April 1800. Applicants for the latter reward had to be subscribers to the Cork Friendly Society if they were under fifty years of age; they were obliged to whitewash the interior and exterior of their homes at least once during the review period; they were forbidden to make or keep a dunghill 'in the public street or road'; the pavement outside the residence was to be kept clean and well swept; any porcine occupants were to be removed, and the absence of a dog was regarded 'as an additional recommendation'.[61] Not surprisingly, perhaps, there was not a single applicant, although the initiative was better supported subsequently; on the third occasion on which a reward was offered, in the spring of 1802, more than 100 individuals applied.[62]

The lying-in or maternity hospital that was mentioned in relation to the Friendly Society was duly established in Hanover Street in March 1800. According to the Cork Society for Bettering the Condition and Increasing the Comforts of the Poor, this was an institution that was badly 'wanted in this populous city'. The lying-in hospital consisted of eight beds and was overseen by a ladies' committee. Fourteen doctors agreed to attend in rotation when their services were required, and a midwife resided constantly at the hospital. In a characteristically supercilious and patronizing observation, the male-only members of the Society hoped that 'the ladies of Cork will remember that their duty to the poor is a personal service enjoined by the highest authority ... and that by their exertions and punctuality of attendance they will make this institution which is now dependent on them a credit to themselves and to this city'. A number of ladies donated baby clothing to the hospital, clothes that were clearly old and unwanted or surplus to their owners' requirements. However, according to the Cork Society, they served their intended purpose

---

60 Lord Teignmouth, 'Extract from an account of a friendly society, at Cork', *The eleventh and twelfth reports of the Society for Bettering the Condition and Increasing the Comforts of the Poor* (London, 1800; Dublin: reprinted for W. Watson and son, 1800), pp 171–5. **61** *Address to the publick*, pp 7–10. **62** Hincks, *A short account of the different charitable institutions of the city of Cork,* pp 11–12.

perfectly well, a response that neatly captured the social cleavage between the dispensers and recipients of charity.[63]

Other initiatives that the Cork Society launched or espoused included the Cork Charitable Loan, which was established either in 1780 or July 1781, depending on which of Hincks's publications is consulted. Between 29 August 1783 and 12 June 1799, 5,105 individuals were lent sums of up to three guineas. The latter sum was repaid at the rate of two British shillings a week for forty-two weeks, at the end of which a guinea was returned to the borrower and an application for a new loan could be submitted.[64]

The Cork Charitable Repository, the initiative of seven young governesses, opened in George's Street on 18 August 1800, to supply 'strong and comfortable clothing' to the poor at affordable prices and, secondly, to encourage industry among them by providing an outlet for the sale, without commission, of their handiwork.[65]

Separate schools of industry for male and female children, each capable of accommodating fifty pupils, were established in 1801 in an attempt to check the alarming levels of beggary, idleness and theft that prevailed among the offspring of the poor. The children were housed, fed and trained in the expectation that they would eventually secure employment and thus provide lawfully for their own future. The Cork Society donated £200 to the project, and this sum was augmented by voluntary subscriptions and the proceeds of a charity concert. According to the Society's second annual report, the beneficial effects of the schools were 'legible in the altered countenances and in the improved manners, habits and dispositions of children, whose former haggard and emaciated figures were the emblems of famine, and whose uninstructed idleness and vitiated habits of life' projected them as the future outcasts of society. In immediate and practical terms, there were fewer 'juvenile pilferers' on the city's streets.[66]

The Cork Society's most significant achievement was the establishment of a fever hospital, or house of recovery as these institutions were euphemistically designated at the time. Fever was widespread in many parts of the country during and after the 1798 Rebellion, and became unusually virulent in Cork in 1801, exacerbated by food shortages and the high price of provisions. The Cork Society for Bettering the Condition and Increasing the Comforts of the Poor requested the prominent local physician Dr John Milner Barry to investigate the extent of the epidemic in the city and to propose remedies. His inquiries revealed that there had been an average of

63 Thompson, 'Report of the proceedings of the committee', *Third number of the reports of the SPCP*, pp 25–6, 34.   64 T.D. Hincks, 'Account of the Cork charitable loan, with observations', *Second number of the reports of the SPCP*, pp 76–82, at p. 81; idem, *A short account of the different charitable institutions of the city of Cork*, pp 13–15.   65 T.D. Hincks, 'Extract from an account of the Cork charitable repository', *Third number of the reports of the SPCP*, pp 13–15; appendix, p. 45.   66 *Report of the proceedings of the general committee of the Society for Bettering the Condition and Increasing the Comforts of the Poor, in the year 1801* (Dublin: William Watson and son, 1802), pp 4–6; Hincks, *A short account of the different charitable institutions of the city of Cork*, pp 39–41.

2,600 fever cases annually in Cork during the previous decade, and he recommended the establishment of a fever hospital, similar to those in London, Manchester and Waterford, to combat the high incidence of infection.

The undertaking was entrusted to the city's Benevolent Society and a committee was appointed under the chairmanship of the bishop of Cork. In a public appeal for funds, the committee commented on 'the alarming prevalence of fever amongst the poor', stating that more than 4,000 fever-stricken individuals had applied to the city dispensary for relief in 1801. The committee observed that the dispensary was 'a most useful resource' but was limited to relieving the infected; the fever hospital on the other hand was intended to prevent the disease and thus extinguish it altogether. The Cork fever hospital opened in November 1802, and in its first year 254 patients were admitted. The essential principle was to isolate the infected in hospital as quickly as possible. On removal, the patient's home was whitewashed, ventilated and fumigated, the bed clothes were soaked and washed and the furniture was cleaned and disinfected, all at the hospital's expense.[67]

Hincks reflected the prevailing medical belief when he stated that the separation of the sick from the healthy and the disinfection of patients' homes and belongings were essential to check 'the progress of infection'. According to Hincks, the possibility of relapse, the contagious nature of the disease and its communication from the poor to the middle and upper classes suggested that a subscription to the fever hospital was 'not merely the dictate of charity but of self interest', sentiments that were shared by the hospital's administrators and physicians.[68] Hincks' observations captured the combination of philanthropy and utilitarianism that constituted the philosophical foundations on which fever hospitals were established and supported in the eighteenth and early nineteenth centuries, as well as the mixed motives that prompted much charitable and philanthropic endeavour at this time, not least involvement in associations such as the Society for Promoting the Comforts of the Poor.

CONCLUSION

This chapter's epigraph captures the essence of the Society, with its focus on personal responsibility, moral rectitude and religious sentiment. The Society emphasized the virtues of independence, respectability, sobriety and thrift, it encouraged mutuality, social improvement and practical philanthropy, and disavowed idleness, indolence, mendicancy and vice. The various branches of the Irish Society for Promoting the

67 Ibid., pp 7–8. For the establishment and early development of the Cork fever hospital, see Laurence M. Geary, 'John Milner Barry and public health in early nineteenth-century Cork', *Journal of the Cork Historical and Archaeological Society*, 106(2001), pp 131–42.
68 Hincks, *A short account of the different charitable institutions of the city of Cork*, pp 29–31; *Annual report of the house of recovery of the city of Cork, from 8 Nov. 1802 to 8 Nov. 1803* (Dublin, 1804), pp 17–18.

Comforts of the Poor were not original in their aspirations or activities; they were modelled on similar associations in England and Hamburg particularly, and were open to external ideas and influences.

In the case of Cork at least the Society for Promoting the Comforts of the Poor was a subscription-based, secular and male-dominated association, although some specifically female initiatives were encouraged, such as the lying-in hospital and the charitable repository. A number of medical practitioners were actively involved in the Society's branches, and were key to the establishment of fever hospitals, notably John Milner Barry in Cork and Dr William Barker in Waterford, while Dr Colles, Dr Perceval and Surgeon George Renny were on the committee of the Dublin Society. The Society had a distinctly Protestant flavour and few, if any, Catholics appear to have been actively or managerially involved. Protestant clergy, both Anglican and Dissenting, constituted the largest professional element in the Society, one of the more energetic being the Revd Thomas Dix Hincks in Cork. Hincks and many of his fellow activists were members of a network of educational, religious, improving and philanthropic associations in Ireland at the time; Revd Dr O'Connor of Castleknock, for example, was a prominent member of the Society for Promoting the Comforts of the Poor and earlier, in 1792, had been one of three founders of the Association for Discountenancing Vice and Promoting Christian Religion.[69]

It is difficult to measure the reach and success of an association such as the Society for Promoting the Comforts of the Poor. The Society provided practical assistance in times of crisis, most clearly seen in the case of Cork in the extremely difficult years at the turn of the nineteenth century. Like many voluntary associations the Society for Promoting the Comforts of the Poor was relatively short lived. As an active initiating and coordinating body it appears to have existed for no more than a decade, although some of the Society's initiatives survived its demise, most significantly the fever hospitals in Waterford, Cork and Dublin, and the lying-in hospital in Cork. As poverty, sickness and disease were closely linked, the provision of health care made a positive contribution to reducing poverty and social distress. Missing from the equation – and the extant literature offers little assistance – is the way in which the recipients of the Society's attention, the deserving or respectable poor, viewed the intervention – some might say intrusion – of such a paternalistic, patronizing and agenda-driven association in their humble, workaday lives.

---

69 J. Warburton, J. Whitelaw and Robert Walsh, *History of the city of Dublin, from the earliest accounts to the present time; containing its annals, antiquities, ecclesiastical history, and charters; its present extent, public buildings, schools, institutions etc.; to which are added, biographical notices of eminent men and copious appendices of its population, revenue, commerce, and literature* (London, 1818, 2 vols), 2, pp 885–93.

Charitable loan fund societies
in Ireland, *c.*1820–1914

EOIN McLAUGHLIN

INTRODUCTION

The charitable loan fund society (LFS) was prevalent in nineteenth-century Ireland. At their peak, in 1845, LFSs made loans of £2.99 million (equivalent to €283 million in modern monetary value) to the 'industrious poor' of Ireland.[1] This was equivalent to 37 per cent of the savings held by Joint Stock Banks and 102 per cent of the savings held in Trustee Savings Banks (TSB).[2] Yet despite this former significance they have been understudied by historians of Ireland to date. This essay aims to address this lacuna by providing the reader with an overview of the history of charitable LFSs in Ireland in the period 1820 to 1914.[3]

LFSs were quasi-mutual financial societies that issued loans to the 'industrious poor'. Membership of these societies was made up of debenture (bond) holders and trustees and they issued small loans to non-members, with a maximum amount of £10 (€890) set by legislation.[4] There were three distinct types of LFSs in operation

---

1 This figure refers to £1.85 million in loans made by 263 loan fund societies registered with the LFB and an estimated £1.14 million in loans made by *c.*161 Reproductive Loan Funds. The latter was estimated by assuming Reproductive Loan Funds issued the same as the average LFS registered with the Loan Fund Board (£7,089) in 1845. 2 The use of the abbreviation TSB is anachronistic as savings banks were only referred to as TSBs in the 1863 Savings Bank Act. The figure for LFSs registered with the LFB is 64% of TSB deposits: Annual reports of the Loan Fund Board and *Thom's Directory*. 3 See Aidan Hollis and Arthur Sweetman, 'Microcredit: can we learn from the past?', *World Development*, 26:10 (1998), pp 1875–91; 'Microcredit in prefamine Ireland', *Explorations in Economic History*, 35 (1998), pp 347–80; 'The life-cycle of a microfinance institution: the Irish Loan Fund Societies', *Journal of Economic Behaviour and Organization*, 46 (2001), pp 291–311; 'Microfinance and famine: the Irish loan fund societies during the Great Famine', *World Development*, 32:9 (2004), pp 1509–23. See chapters 1, 2, 5, 6 in Eoin McLaughlin for an alternative and broader interpretation of LFS history, 'Microfinance institutions in nineteenth-century Ireland, vols 1 & 2' (PhD Thesis, Department of History, NUI Maynooth, Oct. 2009). See chapters 1, 2, for an alternative and broader interpretation of LFS history in Eoin McLaughlin, 'Microfinance institutions in nineteenth-century Ireland' and Eoin McLaughloin, '"Profligacy in the encouragement of thrift": savings banks in Ireland, 1817–1914, *Business History*, 56 (2014), pp 569–91. 4 The exception being those registered as Friendly Societies as these were bona fide mutuals where membership was a prerequisite for both borrowing and saving. Eoin McLaughlin, 'A note on mutual savings and loans societies in nineteenth-century Ireland', *Irish Economic and Social History*, 40 (2013), pp 48–98.

in the period 1820–1914. Reproductive Loan Funds, associated with the London Relief Committee (1823–48), were set up in response to a famine in the west of Ireland. There were separate LFSs registered with the Loan Fund Board (LFB). There were distinct LFSs that were registered under Friendly Society legislation, societies where membership was a requirement to avail of services. The information we possess mainly relates to the activities of LFSs associated with the LFB. There are some indicators as to the location and activities of the other two strands of LFSs; however, only Reproductive Loan Funds and LFSs registered with the LFB were established under charitable auspices, hence this paper will focus on their intertwined history.

Charitable LFSs had been in existence since the early 1700s, but there was a proliferation of such societies in the early nineteenth century. They were in vogue from the 1820s to the mid-1840s, and in that period there was an increase in the number of LFSs, a greater geographic distribution, and a significant change in their *modus operandi*. This paper will outline the salient factors that led to an increase in the number of LFSs in the 1820s, 30s and 40s, and the prominent events that led to their decline thereafter. It will outline some of the reasons why they were established and illustrate where they were located. The paper will also analyse the legal structure and constraints under which LFSs operated. There was a flurry of LFS legislation between 1820 and 1843; however, the 1843 Loan Fund Act regulated the LFS system until the last LFSs were wound up in the 1970s.[5]

ORIGINS AND EXPANSION OF THE LOAN FUND
SOCIETY SYSTEM IN IRELAND, c.1820–1842

The tradition of LFSs can be traced to a loan fund established by Dean Swift for unemployed weavers in Dublin in the early eighteenth century. He provided interest-free loans to enable them to purchase yarn; he personally supervised these loans and the fund appears to have ceased after his death.[6] The spirit of this endeavour was followed by the Dublin Musical Society (DMS), although distinct from Swift's initiative, it raised money from concerts and used this capital to issue interest-free loans. At its peak, the DMS operated a small branch network, but this went into decline in the late eighteenth century.[7] These eighteenth-century LFSs

---

5 'An act to consolidate and amend the laws for the regulation of charitable loan societies in Ireland', 6&7 Vict., c.91. The last reference to the loan fund societies is in the *Annual report of the Minister for Agriculture and Fisheries 1975*, A.1/55, prl 5514, p.126. But the latter reports from the Department of Agriculture are not as rich as those published by the Loan Fund Board and no details are given of actual loan fund business activity.   6 R.R. Madden, 'Origin of the Loan Fund system in Ireland, vol. 1', c.1857, NLI, MS 4466, p. 36; Thomas Sheridan's biography of Dean Swift states that 'the fund remained undiminished until the last'; Thomas Sheridan, *The life of the Revd Dr Jonathan Swift, Dean of St Patrick's* (Dublin, 2nd ed.; [London, 1787]), p. 234.   7 *First annual report of the Commissioners of Loan Fund Board of*

shared similarities with their nineteenth-century counterparts such as regular weekly repayment of loans and the use of personal security in the form of sureties. The early LFSs issued interest-free loans and they did not pay interest on deposits. This, however, changed dramatically in the 1820s with the creation of the London Relief Committee.

The London Relief Committee was formed in response to a famine in the west of Ireland in the early 1820s.[8] Money was raised in Britain, and further afield, for the relief of famine in Connacht and Munster, and despite initial fears of a poor response, the London Relief Committee was in fact oversubscribed. After famine conditions abated, the board decided on a number of ways to distribute the surplus funds in an attempt to promote sustainable development in affected areas of Connacht and Munster (see table 1). The surplus funds amounted to the extraordinary sum of £60,000 (€5.2 million). Out of this surplus, £40,000 (€3.5 million) was 'appropriated under trustees to the encouragement and assistance of the poor of the distressed Provinces of Ireland, in the manufacture of flax and wool, by means of small loans repayable with interest'.[9] It must be stressed that the Reproductive Loan Funds were established contemporaneously to the industrialization of linen and wool manufacturing in the UK. The introduction of Reproductive Loan Funds followed a decline in the hand woven linen and woollen industries in Ireland. Linen production was beginning to concentrate in east Ulster.[10] Thus, it is questionable whether the provision of small loans could have been effective against the onset of industrialization.

The surplus funds earmarked for lending by the London Relief Committee were allocated to local trustees responsible for the distribution of loans to the industrious poor in the designated areas. The local LFSs created with capital from the London Relief Committee were designated as Reproductive Loan Funds, which were distinct from societies that derived capital from sources in Ireland. Table 1 illustrates the distribution of the capital of Reproductive Loan Funds. As can be seen they were primarily active in counties in Connacht and Munster, with the notable exception of Waterford. The activities of the London Relief Committee led to the passing of an act of parliament in 1823 specifically for the encouragement of LFSs in Ireland. As a result other LFSs, unaffiliated with the London Relief Committee, emerged in Ireland, including areas in Munster and Connacht.

LFSs that were unaffiliated with the London Relief Committee operated on a unit-independent basis in the sense that their capital was not controlled by a central agency such as the London Relief Committee. These unaffiliated LFSs raised their

Ireland, HC 1839 (578), 29, 619, Appendix, p. 1. **8** *Report of the committee for the relief of the distressed districts in Ireland, appointed at a general meeting held at the City of London tavern, on 7th of May, 1822; with an appendix* (London, 1823). **9** Ibid., p. 24. **10** Frank Geary, 'The evolution of the linen trade before industrialization: why did firms not replace the market?' in Brenda Collins, Philip Ollerenshaw and Treveor Parkhill (eds), *Industry, trade and people in Ireland, 1650–1950: essays in hour of W.H. Crawford* (Belfast, 2005); and Philip Ollerenshaw, 'Industry, 1820–1914' in Liam Kennedy and Philip Ollerenshaw (eds), *An economic history of Ulster, 1820–1939* (Manchester, 1985), pp 62–108.

Table 1 Distribution of the capital of the Reproductive Loan Funds, 1824–45

County	Population 1821 (%)	Grant 1824 (£)	1843 (£)	1844 (£)	1845 (£)
Clare	7.20	3,000	5,697	5,909	5,919
Cork	25.28	5,500	8,028	8,844	10,155
Galway	11.68	6,000	7,060	8,551	8,592
Kerry	7.48	4,000	5,777	5,908	5,999
Leitrim	4.32	2,000	1,200	1,805	1,859
Limerick	9.60	5,300	6,370	7,381	7,465
Mayo	10.14	4,500	9,377	11,038	11,083
Roscommon	7.22	4,000	4,500	7,313	7,392
Sligo	5.06	3,200	3,870	5,106	5,215
Tipperary	12.01	2,500	2,500	3,078	3,105
Total	2,889,320	40,000	54,379	64,934	66,784

Note: Population 1821 refers to the distribution of population in the 10 counties in 1821. The total refers to the population of the 10 counties.
Sources: Census of Ireland, 1821; *First report of the Irish Reproductive LFS Institution*. HC 1844 (173), 42, 531; *Report of the Irish Reproductive Loan Fund Institution*. HC 1845, (591), 36, 265; *Second annual report of the Corporation of the Irish Reproductive Loan Fund Institution*. HC 1846, (539), 22, 405; *Third annual report of the Corporation of the Irish Reproductive Loan Fund Institution*. HC 1847, (714), 17, 331; *Fourth annual report of the Corporation of the Irish Reproductive Loan Fund Institution*. HC 1847–48, (730), 29, 425.

capital through charitable bequests and deposits. The growth in the number of LFSs led to the creation of a government supervisory body, LFB, in 1836. The LFB published annual reports of LFSs registered with it from 1838 and from these reports we can get a clearer understanding of the spatial distribution of LFSs in Ireland. However, these reports only published information relating to LFSs registered with the LFB. Owing to political wrangling by the London Relief Committee, the LFB did not bear any responsibility for Reproductive Loan Funds as they were exempt from LFB jurisdiction. Map 1 displays the spatial distribution pertaining to Reproductive Loan Funds, LFSs registered with the LFB and Trustee Savings Banks (TSBs), *c.*1842. The spatial pattern is interesting as it shows that there were very few unit-independent LFSs operating in Connacht and Munster. Most of the LFSs active in these areas of the country were related to the London Relief Committee. TSBs were the inverse of a LFS in terms of institutional purpose as they focused on savings rather than lending, but paralleled the organizational structure of LFSs in terms of trusteeships, and were primarily located in the east of the island. Curiously, many TSBs were located in the same building as LFSs. This indicates that there was a closer connection between the two strands of microfinance designed to help the working poor than previously known.[11]

Reproductive Loan Funds aside, growth in the number of LFSs appears to have

11 *Return from each savings bank in United Kingdom, of the house or building in which business is transacted; names of each trustee and manager; number of days on which bank was open, Nov. 1850–51*, HC 1852 (521), 28, 757.

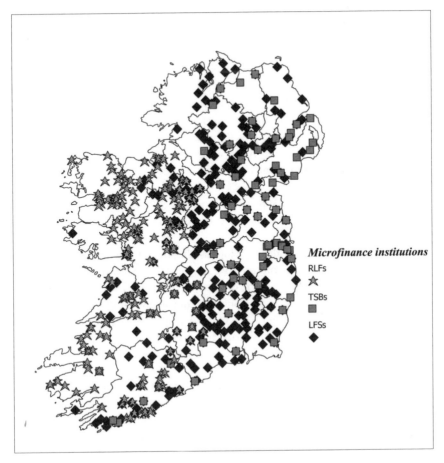

Map 1 Reproductive Loan Funds, Loan Fund Societies and Trustee Savings Banks, *c*.1842
Sources: Fourth annual report of the Commissioners of the Loan Fund Society Board of Ireland,
HC 1842, 24, 247; John Tidd Pratt, *Progress of savings banks, an account of the number of
depositors and of the sums deposited in savings banks, in Great Britain and Ireland, divided
into classes, on the 20th November in each of the years 1829 to 1844, both inclusive and the
increase or decrease in each year* (London, 1845).

taken place principally in the 1820s, 30s and 40s. It is difficult to explain exactly why
growth took place in this period, but there is a number of demand and supply side
indicators as to what may have influenced the growth in LFSs. The initial growth of
LFSs is contemporaneous to banking crises in the post-Napoleonic wars' period
when many private banks failed.[12] The LFSs may have been adopted as they filled a
void vacated by private banks. Furthermore, the Bank of Ireland, chartered by the
Irish parliament in 1783, was given a monopoly on joint stock banking in Ireland and

12 Cormac Ó Gráda, *Ireland: a new economic history, 1780–1939* (Oxford, 1994), p. 55.

given a geographic monopoly on note issuing within a 65-mile radius of its head-quarters in Dublin.[13] This monopoly status also influenced the bank's *modus operandi* as it did not attempt any branch expansion.[14] Following banking reforms in the 1820s, joint stock banks were permitted to form but the Bank of Ireland retained its geographical monopoly until 1845.[15] LFSs appear to be related to this shortage of banking facilities. For example, the Abbeyleix LFS issued loans amounting to £27,567 in 1843, much greater than the average LFS issue of £5,540 for the same year. The LFB inspector report suggested that 'the fact of Abbeyleix being within the circle of the Bank of Ireland, and Banks of discount being consequently precluded from setting up, may in a measure account for the large number of borrowers from that town'.[16]

LFSs also received official support and encouragement. The *Third report of the commissioners for inquiring into the condition of the poorer classes in Ireland* stated that:

> It appears from the evidence before us, that the poor who have occasion to borrow small sums of money have in general to raise them at exorbitant interest, and that when they are obliged to purchase any necessaries they stand in need of on credit, they are compelled to pay double, or nearly double, the market price; we therefore recommend that there shall be a Loan Fund Society established in each district, and that it be administered according to such regulations as the Commissioners shall approve.[17]

LFSs received legislative encouragement in the 1836 and 1838 LFS acts.[18] They were given legal privileges, such as tax exemptions and speedy recovery of loans through local courts; however, they were required to operate under the proviso that their profits be used for charitable purposes.

An important contemporary development that may explain the growth in the number of LFSs was the introduction of a contemporary public poor relief system that was intended to be funded by local taxation, with the tax payable by 'every occu-pier of rateable hereditaments'.[19] A noteworthy clause in the legislation was the exemption given to tenants of properties valued at less than £5. This placed the burden of taxation on landlords and larger farmers, thus giving them incentives for tax avoidance schemes.

Further evidence of the importance of the poor law comes from contemporary

13 'An act for establishing a bank, by the name of the governors and company of the Bank of Ireland, 1781–82', 21 & 22 Geo. 3, c. 16 [I], section 14.   **14** F.G. Hall, *The Bank of Ireland, 1783–1946* (Dublin, 1948), p. 172.   **15** 'Bankers (Ireland) Act, 1845', 8 & 9 Vict., c. 37, sections 1, 12, 13.   **16** *Fifth annual report of the Commissioners of the Loan Fund Board of Ireland*, HC 1843, [470], xxviii, 29.   **17** *Third report of the commissioners for inquiring into the condition of the poorer classes in Ireland*, HC 1836, xxx, 1, section xxv, 27.   **18** 'An act to amend the laws relating to loan societies in Ireland', 6 & 7 Will. 4, c. 55; 'An act for the amendment of the laws relating to loan societies in Ireland', 1 & 2 Vict., c. 78.   **19** 'Poor Relief (Ireland) Act, 1838', 1 & 2 Vict., c. 56, section lxi.

pamphleteers who were opposed to the introduction of compulsory poor laws. The pamphleteers argued that an LFS system could be a private alternative to the public poor law by offering loans at concessional interest rates to the 'industrious poor' and using profits from lending activities to fund a poor law system. In this alternative system 'rates' would be paid as interest bearing debentures rather than as a tax. The advocated model of poor relief was based on a superficial understanding of Continental poor relief institutions, primarily Mont-de-Piété, which were public pawnbroking institutions found throughout Europe.[20] Continental Monts-de-Piété were modelled on a medieval form of pawnbroking that aimed to curb usury by charging borrowers rates of interest lower than the market rate. Importantly, they were given monopoly powers and operated branch networks. In addition, they implemented loan floors and did not place upper bound restrictions on lending. Profits earned from lending were fed into charitable ventures; most notably the Parisian Mont-de-Piété funded the *Hôpital General* and other public works.[21]

Confusingly, the pamphleteers interchanged references to Monts-de-Piété and LFSs, but the overwhelming majority of institutions formed were LFSs and not Monts-de-Piété. Circumstantial evidence suggests that the poor law was a significant explanatory factor in the growth of LFSs in the period 1823 to 1843 as the greatest number of LFSs registered with the LFB was in that period. In effect, it appears that LFSs were promoted as a means of tax avoidance. This, coupled with governmental support, suggests that supply side factors were important determinants in the growth of LFSs in this period. In his study of the implementation of the poor law system in the 1830s, Peter Gray argued that the proposals from the 1836 report were initiated independently of the 1838 Poor Law and that these were designed to complement the poor law system.[22] The charitable LFS system appears to conform to this view.

However, there was a lack of understanding by the propagators and practitioners as to how public relief in the form of a Mont-de-Piété worked on the Continent and the methodologies implemented in nineteenth-century Ireland had a number of limitations. Monts-de-Piété operated in a monopoly as private pawnbroking was rendered illegal. The Parisian Mont-de-Piété, which inspired efforts in Ireland, also operated a large branch network which meant it realized economies of scale. In Ireland, LFSs operated under a loan ceiling of £10, which is discussed below. In nineteenth-century France, the municipal Mont-de-Piété of Paris did not issue loans for less than 3 francs (£0.12).[23] This effectively meant that the French Monts-de-Piété were able to raise more income, to cross-subsidise small loans and raise more profits for expenditure on public relief works. This, however, was not possible in the competitive Irish LFS system.

20 Pawnbroking in the British Isles has primarily been a private enterprise, by contrast on the Continent pawnbroking was a public monopoly. See Eoin McLaughlin 'An experiment in banking the poor: the Irish Mont-de-Piété, c.1830–1850' *Financial History Review*, 20 (2013), pp 49–72. **21** Cheryl L. Danieri, *Credit where credit is due: the Mont-de-Piété of Paris, 1777–1851* (New York, 1991), p. 2. **22** Peter Gray, *The making of the Irish poor law, 1815–43* (Manchester, 2009), p. 173. **23** Danieri, *Credit where credit is due*, p. 189.

INSTITUTIONAL STRUCTURE OF LFSs
IN NINETEENTH-CENTURY IRELAND

LFSs, both Reproductive Loan Funds and those registered with the LFB, were regulated by legislation. Substantial acts of parliament were passed in 1823, 1836, 1838, and
1843 that regulated the activities of LFSs for the duration of their existence.[24] Minor
amendments to this legislation came in 1844, 1872, 1900 and 1906; however, there
was no drastic overhaul of the LFS system between 1844 and the time the last
remaining LFS was wound up in the south of Ireland in the 1970s.[25]

In order to fully understand the operations of LFSs, and appreciate the controversies that developed within the system, it is important to analyse key features of the
legislation. First and foremost, LFSs registered under the LFS legislation cited above
were *not* mutual societies. According to the 1823 act, any number of persons could
form a society in any part of Ireland 'for the purpose of establishing a Society for a
Charitable Loan, or for providing implements of labour by way of Loan, for the
industrious classes of Ireland, or for providing implements of labour, and receiving
back payment for the same by instalments, with the legal interest due thereon'.[26] The
New Ross (No. 3) Loan Fund Society, for example, stated that its managers were
'shareholders whose chief object is to confer benefit on the poorer classes of society,
without reference to their political opinions'.[27] The important point to note is that
membership was not a requirement for lending or saving in LFSs. Therefore, the
incentive structure differed from other financial mutuals, such as savings and loans in
the United States or later cooperative banking institutions.[28] Also, the LFSs were
established for lending to the industrious poor within a specified area. In terms of
the outline in section 2, it seems that this was due to their advocation of being an
alternative to the poor law system. Ostensibly, this feature also enabled them to have
better local information regarding the credit worthiness of borrowers.

Maximum interest rates on LFS activity were determined by legislation. Initially
the interest on savings was 6 per cent per annum under the 1836 act, but this was
reduced to 5 per cent per annum under the 1843 act. This was a relatively high

---

24 'An act for the amendment of the laws respecting charitable loan societies in Ireland', 4
Geo. 4, c. 32; 'An act to amend the laws relating to loan societies in Ireland', 6 & 7 Will. 4,
c. 55; 'An act for the amendment of the laws relating to loan societies in Ireland', 1 & 2 Vict.,
c. 78; 'An act to consolidate and amend the laws for the regulation of charitable loan
societies in Ireland', 6 & 7 Vict., c. 91.   **25** 'An act to amend an act of the last session, to
consolidate and amend the laws for the regulation of charitable loan societies in Ireland', 7
& 8 Vict., c. 38; 'Loan Societies (Ireland) Act, 1843, Amendment Act, 1872', 35 & 36 Vict.,
c. 17; 'Charitable Loan Societies (Ireland) Act, 1900', 63 & 64 Vict., c. 25; 'Charitable Loan
Societies (Ireland) Act, 1906', 6 Edw. 7, c. 23.   **26** 'An act for the amendment of the laws
respecting charitable loan societies in Ireland', 4 Geo. 4, c. 32, preamble.   **27** *Fourth annual
report of the commissioners of the Central Loan Fund Board,* 1842 [392], xxiv, 87.
28 Christopher L. Colvin and Eoin McLaughlin, 'Raiffeisenism abroad: why did German
microfinance fail in Ireland but prosper in the Netherlands?', *Economic History Review,* 67
(2014), pp 492–516.

interest rate as contemporary savings banks offered a rate of 3.42 per cent from 1828 to 1843 and 3.04 per cent from 1844 to 1862.[29] The yield on UK government debt, Consols, fluctuated between 4 and 3 per cent between 1820 and 1860.[30] Loans were issued at a discount whereby interest was subtracted from the initial loan amounts. The low rate of discount was due to the fact that LFSs were intentionally designed to curb usurious/exorbitant rates of interest. Initially the discount rate was set at 6 pence in the pound (2.5 per cent), but this was reduced to 4 pence under the 1843 act (1.67 per cent), which equated to APRs of 6.52 per cent and 4.35 per cent respectively. For example, if £10 was borrowed from a LFS, the borrower would receive £9.83 and would repay the full £10 in weekly instalments.

The issue of interest was not without controversy. There was a contemporary view that the discount rate of 6 pence in the pounds equalled 12 per cent per annum and when the discount rate was reduced in 1843 the corresponding annual interest rate was calculated as 8 per cent per annum. The 1896 inquiry into LFS activity calculated the discount charged for the use of an instalment over the combined number of days (e.g., 7+14+21...+140 = 1470) in the loan term and calculated annual interest rates of 12 and 8 per cent.[31] Whereas the Moate LFS argued that the interest rate, which was 6 pence in the pound, was 2.5 per cent over the twenty week loan term and thus equalled 6.5 per cent per annum (52 weeks).[32] A more extreme view was taken by the Revd C.K. Irwin, a former member of a Loan Fund Society (1838–9) and a Church of Ireland clergyman in Portadown, County Armagh, who argued that the rate was as high as 130 per cent if costs were included in the calculation.[33] It is unclear why exactly rates were reduced in 1843. Hollis and Sweetman have argued that it may have been due to lobbying at the behest of the joint stock banks.[34] Another significant piece of evidence suggests that they were restricted to protect the stability of the banking system. This is noticeable from the actions of Thomas Mooney, founder of the ill-fated Agricultural and Commercial Bank of Ireland, who attempted to establish a bank under the guise of a LFS.[35]

The reduction in the interest rate on savings from 6 to 5 per cent and the

29 Charles Eason, 'The trustee savings banks of Great Britain and Ireland, from 1817 to 1928', a paper read before the Statistical and Social Inquiry Society of Ireland (Friday 15 Nov. 1929), p. 5. **30** Sidney Homer and Richard Sylla, *A history of interest rates*, 4th ed. (New Jersey, 2005). **31** See 'Appendix 1.2. Methodology used to calculate annual interest rates in the 1897 LFS report' in Eoin McLaughlin, 'Microfinance institutions in nineteenth-century Ireland', vol. 2. **32** For example, if 6*d*. in the pound for 20 weeks was 2.5%, then 1 week would equal 0.125% (2.5/20) and 52 weeks would equal 6.5 (0.125 ★ 52.14): *Fourth annual report of the commissioners of the Central Loan Fund Board*, pp 83–4. **33** *Select committee on loan fund societies, 1854–55*, HC 1854–55 (259) vii, 321. **34** Hollis and Sweetman, 'Microcredit in prefamine Ireland', p. 377. A private bank is financed by the capital of its partners, and shares in the bank are not traded publicly. By contrast, a joint stock bank is financed through the sale of shares, and these shares are publicly traded. **35** Aidan Hollis & Arthur Sweetman, 'Complementarity, competition and institutional development: the Irish loan funds through three centuries', 1997, mimeo; *Select committee on joint stock banks report, minutes of evidence, appendix, index*, HC 1837–38 (626), vii, 1, question 611, p. 42.

reduction of discount on loans from 2.5 to 1.67 per cent meant a lower interest rate spread in LFSs. However, LFSs had recourse to fines as a source of income. 'Reasonable' fines were permitted in legislation with no limit placed on them; hence, they were widely used. Another aspect of the LFS legislation was that loan renewals were illegal in the sense that a LFS was not supposed to issue a loan to an existing borrower until the extant loan was repaid. Available evidence leads us to believe that many LFSs did not adhere to this law.

The scale of activity of LFSs was restricted by law with maximum loan sizes fixed at £10 (€920) over the course of the history of LFSs. This cap on LFS activity coincides with a similar loan ceiling imposed on private pawnbroking.[36] Private pawnbrokers also operated under interest rate restrictions and loan ceilings throughout the nineteenth century until pawnbroking laws were reformed in 1964. However, these loan ceilings were not binding as pawnbrokers could offer private loans over this amount. In addition, it was stipulated that the loans were to be short term with a set maximum of 20 weeks. Loans were to be repaid in instalments, either weekly – most common until the 1843 act – or monthly. The average loan sizes in LFSs were in the region of £3 to £4 in the 1830s and 40s; these were significant amounts given contemporary average weekly wages, in the region of four shillings and six pence (£0.23) in the 1840s and less for the 'poor', around 2s.[37] There was considerable regional variation in LFS loan use. According to Porter's account of the activity of 80 LFSs in 1840, 59 per cent of loans were for agricultural purposes, roughly half of which were used for the purchase of livestock. The remaining loans were distributed as follows: 18 per cent were for industrial uses, such as flax, yarn, loans, iron, coal etc, 13 per cent were used for 'dealing' and 9 per cent were used to clear debts and pay rent.[38]

LFSs issued collateral-free loans; however, they used collateral substitutes in the form of a surety system whereby borrower loans were guaranteed by two sureties. As sureties were liable for loans if the borrower defaulted, this helped overcome problems such as *ex ante* and *ex post* moral hazard.[39] LFSs also screened borrowers by making them fill out application cards, at the borrowers' expense, stating the purpose

---

36 'An Act to establish the business of a pawnbroker, and to authorize such persons as shall be duly qualified to carry on the same, to lend money on pawns or pledges, and to receive interest at a higher rate than heretofore was recoverable by law', 26 Geo. II, c. 43. [Ire]. **37** A.L. Bowley, 'The statistics of wages in the United Kingdom during the last hundred years. (Part iv): agricultural wages', *Journal of the Royal Statistical Society*, 52:3 (Sept. 1899), pp 555–70.   **38** Henry John Porter, 'A statistical account of loan funds in Ireland, for the year 1840', *Journal of the Statistical Society of London*, 4:3 (Oct., 1841), pp 209–24.   **39** Ex ante moral hazard refers to changes in behaviour before an event and ex post refers to behaviour after an event. In this context, ex ante moral hazard is the problem that borrowers may be untruthful about the purpose for which a loan is to be used. For example, a loan is issued for a relatively risk free purpose but the borrower then engages in a risky venture. Ex post moral hazard refers to problems after a loan has been issued. The borrower may be untruthful regarding the success of the loan and may default on loan repayments.

of the loan. At a meeting of the society applications were discussed and loans allo-cated on the basis of committee approval. In this sense they were able to overcome adverse selection problems by using decentralized information.

LFSs were intended to be non-profit banking institutions and profits, after all expenses were accounted for, were allocated to charitable pursuits. This was unlike contemporary Friendly Society loan funds, which distributed profits amongst members. Theoretically, this gave LFSs a dual-charitable function; first they issued loans at concessional rates of interest, and second they used profits from LFS activity to fund charitable ventures. However, the stipulation that profits be allocated to charity gave some LFSs an incentive to increase their expenses in order to minimize their profits.

Another interesting feature of LFS legislation was the fact that the liability of management and staff of LFSs was limited.[40] This was similar to contemporary devel-opments within the TSBs that also limited the liability of trustees.[41] The ostensible aim of such legislation was to encourage the formation of such LFSs, but it had the adverse effect of reducing the incentive for management to monitor staff activity as they were not liable for losses accruing to staff defalcation (fraud or misappropriation of funds). This resulted in a form of moral hazard. Many depositors in LFSs and TSBs saved in these institutions based on the reputation of their trustees, but these trustees were not liable for the actions of their staff and thus did not fulfil their obli-gations. This resulted in a number of high-profile frauds in the case of the savings banks,[42] institutions which were primarily focused on savings, and lesser known frauds in the case of the LFSs,[43] which were greater in number though smaller in scale in terms of monetary value.

The most notable aspect of the LFS legislation was the creation of a government body responsible for the supervision and regulation of LFSs: the Loan Fund Board (1836–1914). The LFB was created under the 1836 LFS act and its office was located in Dublin Castle.[44] The main function of the LFB was to act as a supervisory body. It registered and licenced LFSs, and made annual off-site and on-site inspections; annual audits of accounts and inspection of societies. Interestingly, it was also given the power to make loans to individual societies, essentially lender of last resort powers commonly associated with Central Banking today. The LFB was given power to wind up societies and place societies in receivership. It could also remove certifica-tion from a society and this meant that they would lose legal privileges; however, LFB sanctions were subject to appeal.

The LFB was given the responsibility of regulating and supervising the LFS system; yet, it was given limited resources, monetary and non-monetary, to achieve

40 'An act for the amendment of the laws relating to loan societies in Ireland',1 & 2 Vict., c. 78, section xv. **41** 'Savings Bank Act, 1844', 7 & 8 Vict., c. 83, section vi. **42** Cormac Ó Gráda, 'Savings banks as an institutional import: the case of nineteenth-century Ireland', *Financial History Review*, 10 (2003), pp 31–55. **43** *Select committee on loan fund societies*, HC 1854–55 (259), vii, 321, paragraph 297–303, pp 15–16. **44** R. Barry O'Brien, *Dublin Castle and the Irish people* (London, 1912).

these goals. There was no statement of the source of funding of the LFB in the 1836
act nor the 1838 act. It was given a budget of £600 per annum in the 1838 act,[45] but
there does not appear to be a source of funding included in the 1836 or 1838 acts.[46]
Instead, money was lodged on an *ad hoc* basis in the Bank of Ireland in the name of
the LFB. This was potentially an insecure source of funding if there were major political changes. The LFB, in a draft bill written and published by it in 1842, argued that
it should be funded by a levy on profits of LFSs.[47] However, as an alternative to this
a funding proposal was introduced in the 1843 LFS act that instead gave the LFB a
monopoly on the sale of stationery to LFSs under its jurisdiction. The 1843 act stipulated the LFB charge societies 1*d*. for promissory notes and 1*s*. for debenture
forms.[48] The charge for promissory notes was increased to 2*d*. in 1872, but the cost
of debenture notes remained constant. The LFB used the income from the sale of
promissory notes in the early 1840s to purchase government stock and the dividend
payments from its investment portfolio were also an annual source of income. In the
period 1844–1879 dividends payments made up an average of 13 per cent of LFB
income.[49]

The LFB issued debenture forms to LFSs. In these societies, management were
not liable for the amount of debentures, neither was the LFB as it did not directly
issue the debenture form. In some cases this led to debenture holders taking greater
interest in the society; but in most cases it gave debenture holders a false sense of
security as they believed that government stamped debenture forms were equivalent
to government guaranteed debt. In essence, this created another form of moral
hazard. The outline of LFB stationery was included in a schedule in the 1843 LFS
act,[50] but very few of these notes appear to have survived. Plate 1 is a copy of a LFB
promissory note issued by the Culdaff LFS in County Donegal, showing the LFB
stamp (with the imprimatur of the crown), which would have also been present on
debenture forms.

THE FAMINE YEARS, 1845–51

The first serious test of the LFS system came during the Famine of the 1840s. This
exogenous and systemic shock highlighted a number of faults within the structure of

---

45 'An act for the amendment of the laws relating to Loan Societies in Ireland', 1 & 2 Vict.,
c. 78, section 10.   **46** 'An act to amend the laws relating to Loan Societies in Ireland', 6 &
7 Will. 4, c . 55, section 2; 'An act for the amendment of the laws relating to Loan Societies
in Ireland', 1 & 2 Vict., c. 78, section 7.   **47** *Fourth annual report of the commissioners of the
central loan fund board*, p. 24.   **48** Promissory notes were forms wherein a borrower
acknowledged the debt and outlined the terms of the loan. Debenture forms stated that a
person was owed a certain amount, with interest, by the LFS; essentially a bond.
49 Annual reports of the Loan Fund Board, 1838 to 1880.   **50** 'An act to consolidate and
amend the laws for the regulation of Charitable Loan Societies in Ireland', 6 & 7 Vict., c.
91, schedule A.

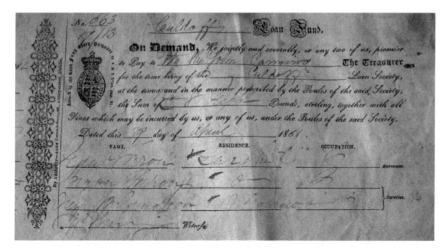

Plate 1 Promissory note from the Culdaff loan society, 1860
Source: 'Culdaff loan society account book,' 1860, NLI, MS 23063
(reproduced with permission of the NLI).

LFSs. Firstly, the Famine witnessed the closure of all Reproductive Loan Funds operating in Munster and Connacht. The Reproductive Loan Funds had operated virtually unsupervised since they were formed. They were intended to be placed under the supervision of the LFB by the 1836 LFS bill,[51] but lobbying by the London Relief Committee exempted them from the supervision of the LFB.[52] However, following this exception the London Relief Committee did not replace LFB supervision with an equivalent substitute and the actions of Reproductive Loan Funds were unmonitored. This culminated in widespread fraud. The Reproductive Loan Funds were wound up in 1848 and their capital vested with the British Treasury to be used for charitable ventures in their original counties in Connacht and Munster.[53] As the Reproductive Loan Funds were wound up, the history of charitable LFSs in the post-famine period is primarily concerned with LFSs registered with the LFB.

As noted above, LFS propagators argued that these voluntary institutions could be an alternative to the compulsory poor law. However, the famine conditions indicate shortcomings in such arguments. First, there was a withdrawal of LFS debentures. This suggests that charity was income sensitive and it is highly doubtful,

---

51 A bill to amend the laws relating to loan societies in Ireland, HC 1836 (251), iv, 385 and Loan societies (Ireland.) A bill [as amended by the committee] to amend the laws relating to loan societies in Ireland, HC 1836 (309), iv, 395; A bill for the amendment of the laws relating to loan societies in Ireland, HC 1837 (486), iii, 337; A bill for the amendment of the laws relating to loan societies in Ireland, HC 1837–8 (293), iv, 523; A bill [as amended by the committee] for the amendment of the laws relating to loan societies in Ireland, HC 1837–8 (482), iv, 539. **52** 'Loan Societies (Ireland) Act, 1836', 6 & 7 Will. 4, c. 55. **53** The Treasury acted as a trustee for the fund; 'Irish Reproductive LFS Act, 1848', 11 & 12 Vict. c. 115.

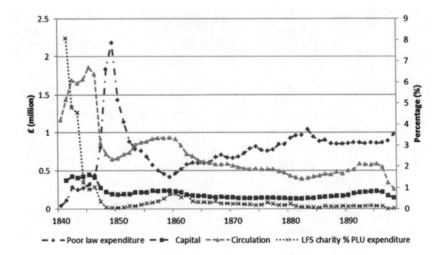

Figure 1 Poor law expenditure, Loan Fund Society capital, Loan Fund Society circulation and Loan Fund Society charitable expenditure as a percentage of poor law expenditure. *Source*: Annual reports of the LFS Board and *Thom's Directory*.

given the extremely difficult conditions, whether such a voluntary organization would have been able to cope, relatively speaking, as well as the much maligned and criticized poor law. Second, propagators of the LFS system had argued that the LFSs could expend profits on charitable relief. In the initial years of the poor law system the charitable expenditure of the LFSs associated with the LFB was relatively high compared to poor law expenditure, for example it was 8 per cent of poor law expenditure in 1841. However, LFS charitable expenditure during the Famine was dwarfed by that expended by the poor law system: the amount of LFS charitable expenditure fell to 0.11 per cent of poor law expenditure between 1847 and 1851. This is understandable as the profitability of the LFSs was pro-cyclical – they were profitable in economic upswings, but made losses during downturns. The cyclical nature of the LFS system in essence explains the failure of the LFSs as agents of poor relief. Figure 1 highlights this fact by comparing the absolute values of poor law expenditure with LFS circulation and LFS capital and also by comparing the percentage of ratio of LFS charitable expenditure to poor law expenditure.

At the onset of the Famine, the LFB issued the following circular to LFSs in 1846:

> The Loan Fund Board wish to direct the especial attention of your Committee to the necessity which exists at the present time for great caution being exercised in the issue of loans. The Board apprehend that in certain districts a pressure may be felt during the ensuing season which may render it difficult for borrowers to meet engagements previously made with the managers of Loan Fund Societies. The board also consider it desirable to direct the attention of the Managers to the importance of retaining at all times

a sufficient Reserve Fund, which will place beyond all risk the security of the funds entrusted to their care by the depositors, and which will enable them, whenever such a course may be considered desirable, to dissolve their society, without loss being sustained by any parties who may have been connected with it.[54]

Available evidence suggests that LFSs followed the LFB advice.[55] The LFSs had evolved into hybrid charitable banking institutions and developed conflicting responsibilities; one to depositors and another to desperate borrowers.

Map 2 illustrates the effect of the Famine period on LFSs registered with the LFB. As can clearly be seen there were many LFS failures in the period from 1842, the peak year in number of LFSs registered with the LFB, to 1851. Due to famine conditions and the fact that LFSs made loans to low income borrowers we would expect a large number of failures in the period. However, events did not turn out as expected. As noted above, many LFSs began to retract credit services, thus limiting their exposure to famine conditions, but failures occurred nonetheless. In evidence to the 1855 LFS committee of inquiry, R.R. Madden, secretary of the LFB from 1850 to 1880, indicated that failure was due to widespread fraud.

POST-FAMINE, 1860–1914

Following the Famine, LFS activity declined significantly, as shown in table 2. This was the result of structural economic changes, competition from joint stock banks and the Post Office Savings Bank, and an ossified institutional structure unreformed since the 1843 act. But despite these changes the LFS system was able to persist and actually grew in the period 1880 to 1896. What made the LFS system sustainable?

The answer lies in events in the late 1890s which led to a government inquiry into the LFS system. The immediate issue that brought attention to the LFS system were two court cases that created panic and precipitated a loss of confidence.[56] The court decisions adjudicated that the loans, for which cases were brought, were issued in violation of the 1843 loan fund act,[57] and that the borrower was exonerated from the repayment of the debt under the loan fund legislation.[58] The initial verdicts were challenged, but the appeals were dismissed. In the judgment of the case of 'the treasurer of the Enniskillen loan fund society [County Fermanagh] v Green' it was found that as the borrower did not reside within the area which the Enniskillen LFS had given as its area of operations, the loan could not be pursued in the petty session

---

54 *Eight annual report of the commissioners of the Loan Fund Board of Ireland* (218) HC 1846, xxii, 385. **55** 'Report and account of the Cashel Loan Fund Society 1848', NLI, MS 41,872. **56** *The treasurer of the Enniskillen loan fund society v. Green* [1898] 2 Ir. R. 103 (QB); *Skey v. Shield* [1899] 2 IR 119 (QB). **57** Renewals were illegal under loan fund legislation, and interest was reduced under the 1843 act. **58** A headline from a newspaper in 1897 was 'decision in favour of borrowers', *Anglo-Celt,* 7 Aug. 1897.

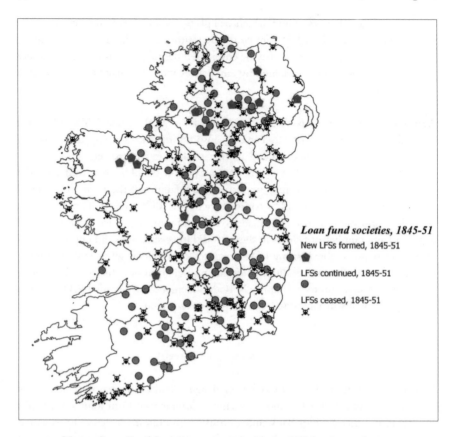

Map 2 Loan Fund Societies registered with the LFB in 1842 and 1851.

courts system. The main issues that arose from the case were: that the sum of money being sought was in fact a renewal of a loan issued seventeen years previously, that the borrower was residing outside the loan fund's stated jurisdiction, that the loan fund had violated its own rules, and that there had been a change of treasurer since the original loan was made and the new treasurer could not sue for the debt in the name of the old.[59]

The point regarding the society violating its own rules referred to the fact that the borrower and sureties were already in debt to the society. In the case the borrower was previously indebted to the society, as he was the surety for his sureties. Also his sureties were already in debt to the society, as they themselves had outstanding loans. It was stated that:

> No money, however, had been advanced to any of the defendants on the 30th January, 1896, nor for many years previous, this note being the last of a series

59 *The treasurer of the Enniskillen loan fund society v. Green* [1898] 2 Ir. R. 103 (QB).

Table 2 Inter-decadal percentage change in population and LFS variables, 1841–1911

Decennial period	Population (Rural)	Population	Number of LFSs	Capital	Circulation	Number of loans
1841–51	−19.85	−24.24	−54.10	−49.73	−50.55	−53.55
1851–61	−11.49	−12.29	−14.63	15.23	16.10	−4.68
1861–71	−6.67	−9.82	−22.85	−35.11	−34.40	−36.78
1871–81	−4.37	−6.90	−2.46	−5.18	−24.53	−32.14
1881–91	−9.08	−12.13	26.58	49.95	25.71	9.99
1891–1901	−5.22	−11.40	−36	−47.21	−57.94	−51.48
1901–11	−1.54	−5.16	−20.31	−14.52	−9.86	−18.76

Sources: LFS Board reports, *Thom's Directory*, and Census of Ireland

of renewals of an original note given more than seventeen years ago. It had been the custom of this society to allow borrowers to renew their loans every three months, the borrowers first paying all fines incurred under the previous note, and the interest which would accrue due on the new note, in the present case in all amounting to the sum of 9s 4d. The defendant had already paid £44 to the society, by way of renewal fines and interest on the original note.[60]

The borrower was also residing five miles outside of the district stated to be the area where the Enniskillen LFS operated. What the courts deemed to be at odds with the act was the fact that the loan fund act deemed that LFSs were to be for the benefit of the industrious poor within a stated area. Provided they operated within the area stated there would be no legal doubt surrounding the recovery of debt, but if the LFS operated outside its stated area, then the LFS ceased to abide by the loan fund laws. It is interesting that some of the elements in this case were so instrumental in derailing the LFB system as the reverberations seem to suggest that the faults highlighted in this case were universal amongst LFSs in Ireland. Shortly after Enniskillen LFSs v Green, an appeal from the Castlederg LFS in County Tyrone was dismissed. The resulting case determined that loan renewals were in fact 'contrary to the provisions of the loan fund act, 1843'.[61]

These decisions created panic amongst LFS members. There had been an increase in the number of LFSs in the period 1880 to 1896, and the verdicts, which were upheld, endangered any capital invested in loan funds. It meant that loans made via the LFSs could only be recovered if they were made in adherence to the 1843 act and to the rules that the societies had lodged with the LFB, and the subsequent parliamentary report published in 1897 showed that the majority of LFSs had not adhered to the law. The problem was compounded by the fact that LFSs, as they had

60 Ibid., pp 104–5. **61** *Skey v. Shield* [1899] 2 IR 119 (QB).

registered under the 1843 loan fund act, were thereby disqualified from suing for promissory notes (i.e., debts)[62] under the alternative petty session acts.[63]

Loan funds, by registering under the loan fund acts, had taken advantage of the tax exemption which did not require the stamping of promissory notes, but by doing so they were prevented from suing for debts outside of the loan fund act – suing for debt required a stamp on the promissory note. In the opinion of one of the judges in the Enniskillen case there was nothing stopping a LFS from trying to recover a debt in court as the judgement did not necessarily invalidate the debt; only the judgement meant that the LFS could not recover debts under the petty sessions act.[64] As the 1843 loan fund act specially made reference to loan recovery in the petty session courts, this meant that LFSs could not adequately and economically enforce debts. Although recourse to higher courts could have been possible, this would have increased the transaction costs associated with debt recovery. Given the low value of LFS loans it is quite possible that the increased transaction costs would have been greater than the size of the loan. This resulted in a liquidity crisis in the LFS system, as loans could not be recovered and depositors could not redeem their deposits. Both factors, increase in transaction costs and liquidity crisis, instigated a collapse of the Irish LFS system.

How did LFSs survive under interest rate restrictions imposed by the 1843 act? Evidence from the parliamentary enquiry in 1896 found that LFSs had charged rates of discount and paid rates of interest on savings higher than the legal maximum. Given that the LFS system was supposed to be monitored by the LFB, in 1895 and 1896 every society was the beneficiary of an on-site inspection, it must be asked how such a state came into being. In fact, it was done through misinformed advice from the LFB. It arose due to confusion regarding a clause in the 1843 LFS act that permitted LFSs to issue a limited portion of loans as 1½*d*. 'interest' monthly loans (0.625 per month and 7.5 per cent APR).[65] However, the LFB misinterpreted the act and advised LFSs that they could charge a higher discount rate on monthly loans, a rate of 3.125 per cent (8.15 per cent APR) instead of the rate of 1.67 per cent (4.35 per cent APR) stated in the act. The inquiry into the LFS system in 1896 found that the majority of LFSs were charging discount rates over the legal maximum. Unsurprisingly, when the law was properly enforced the majority of the LFSs went out of operation.

The regulatory failure of the LFB can be explained by its institutional structure. The legislative powers of the LFB were inadequate; it could wind up LFSs but not enforce its recommendations. The LFB issued a number of communiqués but these

---

62 Essentially IOUs, except the loan funds were required to use special promissory notes with an LFB stamp. **63** The key feature of the loan fund legislation was an exemption from stamp duty. This also included an exemption of stamps on promissory notes. But such an exemption effectively excluded loan funds suing for debts issued that contravened the 1843 loan fund act: (BPP, LFB 1898, p. 7) **64** The treasurer of the Enniskillen loan fund society v Green, [1898] 2 Ir. R. 103, pp 116–17. **65** 'An Act to consolidate and amend the laws for the regulation of charitable loan societies in Ireland', 6 & 7 Vict., c. 91, section 28.

were ignored by LFSs. Most notably, it advised LFSs against issuing renewals and recommended that LFSs reduce the interest on debentures. The annual on-site inspection by the LFB was ineffective. In the period 1847 to 1896 the LFB ordered the dissolution of 47 LFSs, 64 per cent of which came in the period 1847–60.[66] However, in the same period 250 LFSs ceased. Many cases were due to 'defalcations by officials'.[67] Despite these on-site and off-site annual inspections, numerous cases of fraud went undetected by the LFB. Perhaps a greater indictment of this failure was the fact that in the year prior to the collapse of the LFS system each LFS received an annual on-site inspection and submitted its annual accounts to the LFB but there was nothing deemed untoward from either on-site or off-site inspections. A noticeable facet of the institutional history of the LFB was the fact that during the period 1850 to 1880 the powers of the LFB were vested in a long-standing autocratic secretary, R.R. Madden. The LFB began to encourage the formation of societies and after Madden's retirement several were in fact formed.

LFSs were intended to be charitable institutions and titles of legislation relating to LFSs reflect this – they were deemed charitable LFSs. However, in the period 1860 to 1914 it is unclear how 'charitable' LFSs were. Instances similar to the borrower who had not repaid a loan of £10 after 15 years despite paying £44 in various charges were recounted in local newspapers. The treasurer of the Newtownstewart LFS stated that there were 'permanent borrowers' on the society's books.[68] The spirit of the LFB was to regulate the LFS system and prevent such scenarios from developing but it failed. In essence, this is a case of regulatory capture, whereby the industry (LFSs) captured the regulator (LFB) that was intended to supervise them. But the case of the LFSs displays an element of double capture whereby the charitable LFSs were captured by unscrupulous managers who disregarded the welfare of borrowers as was the intention of the LFS system. One such example was a LFS that was established in Gortin, County Tyrone, three years prior to the LFS enquiry. According to evidence, borrowers felt so aggrieved by their treatment that they had attempted to establish a new society in the area.[69]

This double capture scenario arose from how the LFB was funded as it received its income from the sale of stationery. These arrangements were implemented in the 1840s but were unreformed in the post-Famine period despite changes to the scale of the LFS system. As a result the LFB was underfunded. As noted above, there was minor reform in that there was an increase in the amount of income the LFB received for promissory notes, but this did not eliminate the LFBs' dependence on the industry it was supposed to regulate for its income. Under these arrangements, the LFB was incentivized to encourage LFSs to issue more loans. Also the LFB could recognize and register new LFSs. The following public notices were published in

---

66 Calculated from an appendix in the 1896 LFS report and *Report of the committee appointed to inquire into the proceedings of charitable loan societies in Ireland, established under the Act 6 & 7, Vic. Cap 91.* HC 1897, [C8381], 23, 383. **67** Ibid., paragraph 169, p. 25. **68** *Tyrone Constitution*, 2 Oct. 1896. **69** Ibid., 25 Sept. 1896.

Thom's Directory in the late nineteenth century: 'The LFS Board will gladly co-operate with local gentlemen who desire to have the benefits of the public LFS system extended to their districts.'[70] Many of the LFSs formed between 1880 and 1896 were in the north-west of the island. Revd Fr Grimes, PP, complained in evidence to the 1896 LFS inquiry 'that there were too many loan fund societies in the district [Sixmilecross, County Tyrone], and it was a temptation to the poor to borrow from more than one of those societies at the same time. There were three loan funds within a radius of six miles.'[71] In relation to another society in Beragh, County Tyrone, Grimes stated that 'there are too many of these banks in the neighbourhood [and he could] fix an instance of a man having to sell his farm owing to have to pay off loans in so many loan funds'. It must be noted that there was a religious angle to Grimes' evidence; he claimed that 'two thirds of the borrowers are small Roman Catholic farmers whereas the officials are all Protestants, they have not given anything of the profits to Roman Charities'.[72]

The result of this double capture was that it adversely affected borrowers and depositors. Borrowers were subjected to excessive fines and experienced cyclical debt. It also altered depositor incentives as there was a belief that LFSs registered with the LFB had a government guarantee. There was a belief that the LFB was a government regulator. The LFB stamp, which featured the crown, gave a misleading signal to depositors and this led to moral hazard as depositors did not monitor the running of the LFSs as they believed their deposits were guaranteed by the government. However, this was not the case and the LFS acts specifically stated that the LFB was not liable for LFS debentures. In fact, the government refused to acknowledge responsibility for the LFB and denied that it was a government department. This was despite the fact that it was created by legislation and had an office in Dublin Castle. When the LFB was dissolved, its role and staff were transferred to the Department of Agriculture and Technical Instruction. A plausible explanation for the government's actions can be seen in the contemporary financial context. There was a contemporary fraud in other financial institutions that had strong government involvement – TSBs in England.[73] TSBs were the inverse of LFSs; essentially LFSs were trustee credit banks. If the contemporary UK government admitted liability for financial institutions where such liability was not enshrined in legislation but instead based on the existence of government auditing then TSBs could also call for compensation. As the scale of TSB activity was much greater than Irish LFSs, the government would have been wary of setting a dangerous precedent.

If we look at the amount of LFS capital, shown in figure 2, in the period 1860–1914 we can see that there was a significant increase in LFS capital in the period 1880–96 before falling dramatically.

A plausible explanation for this increase in LFS capital can be found in the rate of interest paid by LFS debentures. These were set at a maximum of 5 per cent by

70 *Thom's Directory*, 1889.   71 *Tyrone Constitution*, 25 Sept. 1896.   72 *Tyrone Constitution*, 2 Oct. 1896.   73 Oliver H. Horne, *A history of savings banks* (London, 1947).

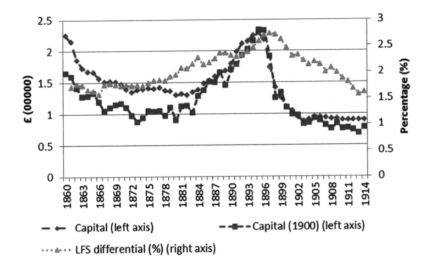

Figure 2 Loan Fund Society capital, nominal and real (1900 prices), and differential between LFS debentures and UK Consols, 1860–1918

Sources: Annual reports of the Loan Fund Board, *Thom's Directory*, and Liam Kennedy, 'The cost of living in Ireland, 1698–1998' in David Dickson and Cormac Ó Gráda (eds), *Refiguring Ireland: essays in honour of L.M. Cullen* (Dublin, 2003), pp 249–76. Estimated Consol yield from Jan Tore Klovland, 'Pitfalls in the estimation of the yield on British Consols, 1850–1914', in *Journal of Economic History*, 54 (1994), pp 164–87. *Note*: LFS differential = 5 % LFS debentures – UK Consol yield

legislation. If we compare this rate to prevailing interest rates we can see that it was higher than the yields of government bonds. There was a trend of declining bond yields in the late nineteenth century, the result of these falling yields would have been to increase the nominal risk premium of LFS debentures. Figure 2 includes a differential between LFS debentures and UK Consols. As can be seen there was an increase in this differential as bond yields continued to increase, from 1880 to 1896 there was also an increase in LFS capita. However, the increase in the nominal risk premium did not mean a decrease in the real risk associated with investment in LFSs. Many of the newly formed LFSs may have believed that loan renewals and higher rates of discount were normal income generating procedures of LFSs. When the law was enforced many of these societies found it difficult to repay depositors and many LFSs were a very risky venture.

CONCLUSION

This contribution has briefly explored the history of charitable LFSs in nineteenth-century Ireland. It discussed the importance of the London Relief Committee in establishing LFSs in Connacht and Munster. When the London Relief Committee wound up the Reproductive Loan Funds there was a much smaller LFS presence in these provinces. From 1848 to 1914, LFSs registered with the LFB were the dominant form of charitable LFSs on the island. However, these diverged from their original *raison d'être* and began to exploit borrowers.

When the Congest Districts Board conducted its baseline reports one of the questions asked was whether or not the districts had access to joint stock banks or LFSs. Of the 84 districts only 12 had access to LFSs, and of these 12 some had to travel considerable distances; for example the report for Grange, County Sligo noted that the residents had access to LFSs in Drumcliff, County Sligo and Bundoran, County Donegal.[74] By contrast, 75 per cent of the districts had access to joint stock banks.[75] This suggests that LFSs were absent from the poorest communities, by contemporary definition, on the island. In his report on the Rosses, County Donegal, one inspector harshly criticized the LFS system, stating that 'the district is fortunate in not having any LFSs within or near its limits'.[76] In a report on Ballyshannon, County Donegal, a different inspector observed that the 'the general opinion seems to be that the effect morally of the Loan Fund is not good'.[77] The report on Grange, County Sligo, stated that 'the borrowing is a very costly process, for not only has the borrower to pay the interest on the loan, but he must also bring in and pay two securities, and if his loan is not paid to date he is fined. The interest charged is very high and it is difficult to see where the profits, which must be very great, go to.'[78] Given reports of a similar ilk, perhaps the absence of LFSs was a blessing. However it must be stressed that LFSs did provide benefits to borrowers. The chairman of the 1896 inquiry stated:

> they had inquired into about thirty societies and found none of them working properly except one in Donegal where the clerk was working for a very small salary, and the maximum fine imposed was 1d. There seemed to be some virtue in the societies until they came to Tyrone where they found the state of affairs in a horrible position and the unfortunate borrowers drawed out.[79]

Writing in 1841, in the conclusion to a LFB inspection report, the secretary remarked:

> I have gathered sufficient evidence to convince myself, had I previously been disposed to doubt the fact, that the Loan Fund System will speedily become a most mighty engine of either good or evil, and will exercise a vast influence on the moral and social condition of the people of this country. Where

---

74 Baseline report no. 25, Grange, Mr Gahan, 12 Dec. 1895, p. 8.　**75** CDB baseline, TCD, OL Microfilms, 395.　**76** Baseline report no. 12, The Rosses, Mr Micks, 27 May 1892, p. 7. **77** Baseline report no. 20, Ballyshannon, Mr Gahan, 6 Oct. 1894, p. 5.　**78** Baseline report no. 25, Grange, Mr Gahan, 12 Dec. 1895, p. 8.　**79** *Tyrone Constitution,* 25 Sept. 1896.

conducted with sound discretion, the condition and character of the surrounding population cannot fail of being essentially improved; but where conducted in a spirit of reckless extravagance, by parties who have only their own selfish ends in view, no system could be more calculated to retard the march of peace, order, and civilization.[80]

The history of charitable LFSs in Ireland highlights the danger of the latter. The main fault of the LFS system was that from 1843 it went unreformed. Despite the initial benefits to borrowers, the LFSs were incapable of adapting to changing economic circumstances, and were vulnerable to corruption. The history of the charitable LFS system in Ireland has valuable lessons for the developing world today where similar microfinance institutions have been established in an attempt to improve the lives of borrowers. A recent enquiry into such initiatives in India has revealed patterns of multiple indebtedness and circular debt that precisely echos the circumstances described in the 1896 LFS report.[81] Ireland's experience is an important lesson for modern microfinance institutions and warns of the dangers of complacency in long-standing charitable institutions.

---

80 *Fourth annual report of the commissioners of the central loan fund board*, p. 30.   **81** Report of the sub-committee of the central board of directors of Reserve Bank of India to study issues and concerns in the MFI sector, Jan. 2011. http://www.rbi.org.in/Scripts/Publication ReportDetails.aspx?UrlPage=&ID=608 [Accessed 28 May 2012].

'The monster misery of Ireland': landlord paternalism and the 1822 famine in the West

CONOR McNAMARA

This chapter examines the impact of the 1822 famine on the rural poor in the west of Ireland and the response of landowners as a social group to the crisis. It focuses in particular on the organization of relief in County Galway and the consequences of the calamity for tenants on a single landed estate in north Galway and south Roscommon. It also examines the importance of social stratification in the period, which, although less acute than later in the century, was an important factor in determining the distribution of charitable relief. The numbers of landless cottiers had risen steadily from the late eighteenth century, creating a cohort that was especially vulnerable to fluctuations in food supplies, and heavily dependent upon philanthropy for survival in times of need. Famine was caused by the partial failure of the potato harvest in August 1821 due to an unseasonably wet late summer, resulting in a drastically reduced potato crop, which began to run out in many areas in late April 1822. Throughout the crisis landowners, along with the clergy, acted as the facilitators of both government and private relief, which was premised on the basis that centralized aid supplemented local efforts at tackling distress.[1] Thus, the willingness of landowners to organize, fund and administer relief was the defining factor in the alleviation of both hunger and fever. In isolated districts, where landlord absenteeism was a major factor, extreme distress and actual deaths from starvation occurred on a significant scale. But this philanthropic impulse was not entirely selfless: some landlords and farmers seized the chance suddenly available to them to secure improvements to their holdings at no expense to themselves. The story of the 1822 Famine is one of both crisis and opportunity, and in which philanthropy served often contradictory purposes.

---

1 Timothy P. O'Neill, 'Minor famines and famine relief in County Galway, 1815–25' in Gerard P. Moran (ed.), *Galway: history and society: interdisciplinary essays on the history of an Irish county* (Dublin, 1996), pp 445–85.

'THE ANGEL OF DESTRUCTION': THE 1822 FAMINE

The first reports of extreme distress emerged in mid-April as the annual supply of potatoes ran out in nine counties across the west.[2] The annual 'hungry months' of summer were often times of intense hardship for the landless who produced their own supply of potatoes in garden plots rented from farmers in return for labour. These were harvested in late August and were expected to provide sustenance for an entire family for a full year. This cottier class were largely outside the cash economy, exchanging their labour for right of residence on small plots of land, and were unable to purchase food when crops failed. Thus, even the partial failure of the crop was enough to plunge millions into extreme food shortage. The government was later informed by a parliamentary committee that had been appointed to investigate the state of the poor that:

> the nature of the late distress in Ireland was peculiar ... the potato crop which furnishes the general food of the peasantry had failed: but there was no want of food of another description for the want of support of human life. On the contrary the crops of grain had been far from deficient and the prices of corn and oatmeal very moderate.[3]

It was a lack of money, rather than the absolute lack of food, that created devastation. This factor was identified as an additional source of distress by the *Connaught Journal*, which pondered whether 'the abundance of provisions in neighbouring counties is but tantalizing them' [the starving poor].[4]

It was to the relatively privileged that responsibility for relief fell. Meetings of landowners and clergy commenced in the last week of April, with a typical meeting of gentlemen at Ennis organized 'for the purpose of taking into consideration the distressed and, indeed, actually starving state of the peasantry of that county'.[5] At the same meeting it was reported that the rural poor in outlying districts had been living on one meal per day for the previous month and that 'three fourths of the inhabitants are in absolute want of food and have neither means to purchase nor repay anything given to them by way of loan'.[6] During the same week similar meetings were held at Limerick, Galway and Castlebar with the price of potatoes reported to have risen to 8*d.* per stone in Galway, the equivalent of a full day's wage for an agricultural labourer in the west,[7] and potatoes which normally fetched less than 2*d.* per stone in Ennis were available for no less than 6*d.*[8]

On the west coast conditions were, as always, much more severe than elsewhere

---

2 Donegal was the sole western county where the potato crop was unaffected. There was a smaller than normal harvest reported in parts of Tipperary. 3 *Condition of the labouring poor in Ireland and application of funds for their employment: report from the select committee on the employment of the poor in Ireland, minutes of evidence and appendix*, p. 4. HC, 1823 (561), vol. 6, p. 331. 4 *Connaught Journal*, 24 Mar. 1823. 5 *Freeman's Journal*, 2 May 1822. 6 Ibid. 7 Ibid. 8 Ibid., 3 May 1822.

and the *Connaught Journal* reported that on the Aran Islands people were being 'forced to sustain nature on limpets and such other shellfish as may be collected along the shore. If this is not poverty, if this is not the extreme of want, language has no meaning.'[9] In Galway town and west Galway, the *Galway Advertiser* reported:

> The pawnbrokers are so full of the articles which the operative classes are in the habit of pledging and no purchasers to be found at the auctions for unre-deemed goods, that no more money can be advanced on this description of property. We know many poor persons thus situated who, having no alterna-tive, have absolutely sold their shirts and shifts and other cotton wearables as rags to the paper-stuff buyers for the purposes of stopping the ravages of hunger. Fever is very prevalent and many have died and some are buried without coffins. Numbers are dying from the worst of food, eating wild salt leafs, seaweed and shellfish. Several have drowned in endeavouring to obtain these fish and weeds.[10]

The *Mayo Constitution* regretted the 'awful and most melancholy duty of announcing the frequent visitation of death to the habitations of our unhappy fellow creatures, who have by the use of nettles and other weeds, for a while averted the blow until, in fact, their stomachs refused to receive this unnatural food'.[11]

COUNTY CENTRAL COMMITTEES

From the onset of the crisis there was a general belief that the famine was precipi-tated by the dire lack of full-time employment for the rural poor, and aggravated by absentee landownership. This factor left a very significant portion of the rural popu-lation dependent upon casual work, which was paid in kind rather than wages, leaving hundreds of thousands unable to purchase food.[12] A government committee was told in 1823 that 'they [the rural poor] are unaccustomed to have recourse to markets and indeed they seem rarely to have the means of purchasing'.[13] The Mayo Committee for the Relief of the Distressed Districts decried 'the drain of absent landed proprietors who draw from this impoverished county every year, a sum exceeding one hundred thousand pounds ... there appears to be an abundance of oatmeal and oats in this county, some hoarded up by speculators ... the people are starving in the midst of abundance'.[14] According to the *Connaught Journal*, the price of potatoes in the markets suggested that it was a shortage of employment and a lack of money in circulation rather than a general deficiency in the potato supply that

9 *Connaught Journal*, quoted in the *Freeman's Journal*, 4 June 1822.   10 Ibid., 6 June 1822.
11 *Mayo Constitution*, quoted in the *Freeman's Journal*, 6 June 1822.   12 For editorials on the topic, see *Connaught Journal*, 24 Mar. 1823; *Roscommon and Leitrim Gazette*, 11 May 1822.
13 *Condition of the labouring poor*, p. 331.   14 Report of the Committee for the Relief of the Distressed Districts in Mayo, published in the *Freeman's Journal*, 25 May 1822.

were responsible for the pronounced distress in Galway.[15] The marquis of Lansdowne told parliament that in County Kerry 'the misery and starvation which the poor now suffer was endured in the face of plenty, but that plenty was beyond their means'.[16] Sir Edward O'Brien of Clare was the most prominent public representative to forcibly highlight the extent of the crisis, telling the House of Commons in early May that

> a small portion of oatmeal, mingled with nettles or watercress was the daily allowance of food for many thousands of people in the south ... with thousands of able men about the country without the means of life, or the possibility of gaining a day's labour at the lowest possible price. They had no means of getting either money or money's worth to support them ... the destroying angel was already out.[17]

The *Mayo Constitution* claimed that while the entire population of the parish of Island-Eady were starving and without food and four people had already perished, 'hundreds of dying victims, are this instant awaiting their cruel fate with awful resignation ... the only persons of any consideration belonging to this parish are at present out of this country'.[18] While landlord absenteeism was highlighted as a major contributory factor to the crisis, some farmers also took advantage of the situation. The Committee for the Relief of the Distressed Districts in Cork noted that there were 4,500 people in a state of starvation in Skibbereen alone but farmers were no longer hiring casual labourers. The result was that many landless people were

> gladly working for food without hire, or any provisions to take home to their wives and children, the consequence is that men, women and children are almost all naked and wander the country begging and almost starving, carrying and circulating contagion in all quarters.[19]

While a lack of money in circulation among the poor and want of employment aggravated by landlord absenteeism were consistently highlighted by commentators, landowners were centrally involved in the relief effort. The state's response to the crisis was centrally co-ordinated by a five-man Government Relief Board that operated alongside two main voluntary charitable organizations, the London Tavern Committee and the Dublin-based Mansion House Committee.[20] Throughout the crisis these three central bodies donated money and foodstuffs, which were, in turn, distributed by individual county central committees that co-ordinated aid distribution to baronial committees and parochial committees. The Government Relief

15 *Connaught Journal*, quoted in the *Freeman's Journal*, 7 May 1822. 16 *Freeman's Journal*, 13 May 1822. 17 Ibid., 3 May 1822. 18 *Mayo Constitution*, quoted in the *Freeman's Journal*, 27 May 1822. 19 Report of the committee for the relief of the distressed districts in Cork, in *Freeman's Journal*, 30 May 1822. 20 The five members of the Government Relief Board were William Gregory, William Disney, Peter La Touche, Thomas Luscombe and George

Board held its first meeting on 13 May but their efforts were pre-empted by English philanthropy, which saw the London Tavern Committee, composed of London merchants, MPs and landowners, establish their own relief committee on 7 May, followed by a similar enterprise in Dublin organized at a public meeting called by the lord mayor in the Mansion House on 16 May.[21]

The immediate failure of Irish landowners to respond adequately to the crisis, in contrast to the speed and perceived generosity of the landowners and merchants who constituted the London Tavern Committee, was highlighted in newspaper editorials and speeches by prominent individuals. After the first meeting of the London Committee on 7 May, the *Globe* newspaper noted with alarm that 'there is no appearance of any intention to meet or subscribe in Dublin'.[22] English philanthropy was not confined to the London Committee and regional committees and fundraising events were organized across Britain throughout the month of May. Upwards of £500 was raised by a Manchester committee and £1,700 by a Liverpool committee in mid-May during the same week in which a 'grand dress ball' was held in the Great Room at the King's Theatre in London and a special comedy performance took place at Drury Lane Theatre. Similar fundraising events were reported across Britain by the *Worcester Journal*, the *Cambridge Chronicle*, the *Exeter Flying Post* and the *Edinburgh Star*, among others.[23] In relation to fundraising endeavours in England, Daniel O'Connell told the inaugural meeting of the Mansion House Committee that it was

> in no small degree mortifying to national vanity, that they should have heard of subscriptions for the relief of the distressed peasantry in Ireland in London, Liverpool, Chester and other places, not only before meetings were convened, but before they were told an official account had reached Dublin of the extent of the crisis.[24]

At a meeting of gentlemen in Cork city on May 11, a speaker decried the:

> utter abandonment of which the gentry of this country have been guilty, of all those obligations which their situation in life imposes on them ... It is with pain we add that this unfeeling apathy exists in this quarter to as great a degree as elsewhere ... the distresses of the poor are no more spoken of, except among the poor themselves, than if they were in the midst of plenty, and had the means of purchasing.[25]

Large private donations from prominent English institutions and individuals helped sustain the Irish relief effort with the Bank of England, the East India Company, the

Renny. **21** The London committee was officially titled the London Committee for the Relief of the Distressed Irish but was generally referred to as the London Tavern Committee. **22** *The Globe*, quoted in the *Freeman's Journal,* 9 May 1822. **23** *Freeman's Journal*, 20, 22 May 1822. **24** Ibid., 17 May 1822. **25** Ibid., 14 May 1822.

duke of Devonshire and the officers of the 57th Regiment (then stationed in Galway) contributing a total of £2,400 for relief.[26] Large donations from the London Committee were channelled to leading church figures in the west with the Archbishop of Tuam, Charles Le Poer Trench, Revd Archdeacon Grace of Westport and Revd Smith of Castlebar dispersing £1,900 to local committees in the second week of May.[27] By the second week of June, only a number of weeks after the London Committee's establishment, a total of £40,265 of English aid was distributed throughout eleven counties.[28] In the first week of June, cargoes of seed potatoes sailed from Bristol and Liverpool, arriving at sixteen western ports. The London Committee donated a total of 2,961 tons of seed potatoes throughout the crisis.[29]

Throughout early May, county central committees were organized across the west and began co-ordinating relief to a series of baronial and parish committees in their respective counties. Relief in Galway was organized by two central committees: the Galway Committee for the Relief of the Poor, chaired by landowner William Martin Burke of Marblehill, and the Tuam Committee for the Relief of the Poor, chaired by Charles Le Poer Trench, archbishop of Tuam. The Central Relief Committee in Dublin stipulated that all money raised for relief was to aid local contributions and that gratuitous relief was to be avoided, with aid distributed through employment in public works. The government later concluded that

> purely gratuitous relief can seldom in any case be given without considerable risk and inconvenience: but in Ireland where it is more particular, it is important to discourage habits of pauperism and indolence ... it is obvious that gratuitous relief can never be given without leading to the most mischievous consequences.[30]

Fifty-one landowners in County Galway were selected by a provisional sub-committee organized by the Central Relief Committee in Dublin representing the most prominent landed families in the county, including members of the Daly, Lambert, Trench, D'Arcy, Blake, Martin and Persse families.[31] The Galway Committee met daily in Loughrea and co-ordinated the activities of a number of baronial committees, which in turn organized the relief effort of parochial committees. Both Protestant and Catholic clergy were involved at a local level on parochial committees, with money used to provide provisions and seed potatoes at a reduced cost, with the proviso that they did not interfere with local markets. Small works were preferred to large schemes as it was hoped that this would encourage

---

26 Printed Report of the London Committee for the Distressed Irish, printed in the *Freeman's Journal*, 13, 16, 24 May 1822. **27** Ibid., 12 June 1822. **28** Report of the London Tavern Committee, p. 347, quoted in T.P. O'Neill, 'The famine of 1822' (MA, UCD, 1965), appendix, unpaginated. **29** Vessels landed potatoes at Sligo, Westport, Galway, Kilrush, Tarbert, Limerick, Castlemaine, Skibbereen, Tralee, Bearhaven, Crookhaven, Bantry, Kinsale and Cork. **30** *Condition of the labouring poor*, p. 331. **31** Printed resolution of the Galway Central Relief Committee, 16 June 1822, NLI, Bellew Papers, MS 27,273(5).

landowners to contribute, and in this respect the Mansion House Committee preferred parish committees to county committees, as smaller schemes avoided the scenario of large numbers of desperate people gathering at single schemes.[32]

The Tuam committee organized relief over a very large swathe of the county, consisting of ten baronies in both east and west Galway and from June onwards met four times a week – twice weekly in Tuam and twice weekly in Galway town.[33] A quorum of five members was deemed necessary to conduct committee business and applications for relief from baronial committees could only be made at central committee meetings with applicants expected to produce returns noting the numbers of persons relieved by their endeavours, expenses incurred, the quantity and quality of provisions provided and the amount and value of subscriptions received.[34] Baronial committees were requested to approach local Catholic priests, 'along with one other respectable parishioner', and visit the homes of the distressed in order to compile accurate statistics of the number of those in dire need.[35] They were subsequently allocated resources to alleviate the crisis in their own districts on the original stipulation that the central committee allocate one half of the money with members of the baronial committee allocating the remainder. For labourers on relief schemes, the Galway Committee fixed the quantity of daily sustenance at one quart of meal to each head of family and one pint of meal to each subsequent family member, with those in need of relief but unable to secure a place on a relief scheme receiving one pint per family member.[36] In view of the extreme nature of the crisis, the Galway Central Committee wrote to all baronial committees to advise them not to refuse relief to labourers solely on that basis that they possessed a single cow or horse, which ordinarily could be sold to provide sustenance and to be particularly mindful of the needs of the under-tenants of non-resident landlords.[37]

As well as aid sent directly to county central committees, the government appointed three senior engineers, Alexander Nimmo, Richard Griffith and John Killally, to supervise the setting up of public schemes to provide employment and food to the starving. Griffith supervised public works in Limerick, Cork and Kerry and spent a total of £17,043; Nimmo supervised works in Galway, Mayo, Leitrim, Sligo and Roscommon, spending £26,893; and Killally supervised road works totalling £14,725 in County Clare and south Galway.[38] In Galway, as elsewhere, priests and ministers were prominent on local committees, with schemes generally overseen by leading members of the county's most prominent gentry families who supervised the spending of £12,953 on thirty government-sponsored projects.[39] Various members of the extended Blake, D'Arcy and Daly families, traditionally

32 O'Neill, 'The 1822 famine', p. 32. **33** Printed resolutions of the Tuam Relief Committee 1822, NLI, MS 27/274. **34** Ibid. **35** Ibid., 16 June 1822 (MS 27,273/5). **36** Ibid., 15 July 1822 (MS 27,273/6). **37** Ibid., 2 July 1822 (MS 27,273/5). **38** *Employment of the poor in Ireland: copies of the reports made to the Irish government by the civil engineers employed during the late scarcity in superintending the public works, account of appropriation of sums expended to provide employment for Irish poor.* HC 1822 (249), 10, p. 437. **39** Ibid., pp 44–6.

among the county's most prominent landed families, acted as principal overseers on eight schemes, with Archbishop Charles Le Poer Trench personally overseeing eight schemes and Lord Clonbrock overseeing three.[40]

Along with direct government grants county central committees co-ordinated the distribution of large amounts of direct grants of money and provisions donated by the government and the London and Dublin committees. A total of £87,953 was dispersed for relief during the crisis in Galway with the government granting £48,663, the London Tavern Committee donating £31,357 and the Mansion House Committee £3,230.[41] Despite the London Committee's proviso that they would only distribute funds to individual counties on the basis of matching charitable contributions raised locally for relief, only £4,703 was disbursed from private sources in County Galway. In addition to money, the London Committee also landed cargoes of 715 tons of potatoes, 226 tons of meal, 29 tons of rice and 55 tons of biscuits in County Galway alone.

PAROCHIAL RELIEF SCHEMES AND ESTATE MANAGEMENT

It is instructive to examine the impact of the 1822 crisis on the inhabitants of a single landed estate and the degree to which the crisis affected the various groups of employees and tenants who constituted a single community. The property of absentee landlord Ross Mahon consisted of two main portions, with several thousand acres situated in north-east Galway, in the parish of Ahascragh and surrounding districts, and a smaller portion comprising less than a thousand acres situated in south Roscommon, in the parish of Tarmonbarry.[42] As previously discussed, absenteeism was repeatedly singled out as an exacerbating factor during the crisis and the managerial arrangements on the estate were typical of most estates of a similar size with a highly stratified chain of command responsible for day-to-day management. The employment of a hierarchical managerial system involving stewards, agents and head agents acting under the direction of a head landlord, facilitated both the physical and psychological detachment of Ross Mahon from the life of his tenants and employees. On the Tarmonbarry portion of the estate, steward Christopher Quinn reported to land agent Alexander Wallace, who in turn carried out the wishes of head agent Thomas Bermingham, who corresponded weekly with Ross Mahon in Dublin. Similarly, on the Galway portions of the estate, steward Timothy Glynn acted under instruction from agent Henry Comyns, who was directed by Ross Mahon's brother James, who also relied on head agent Thomas Bermingham for the overall supervision of the estate.[43] In such circumstances, the implementation of crucial decisions regarding evictions and rent were heavily influenced by the opinions of stewards and sub-agents, who often disagreed with, or were antagonistic toward one another. The

40 Ibid., p. 44. 41 Quoted in O'Neill, 'The 1822 famine', appendix, unpaginated. 42 See Conor McNamara, *The Mahon Papers: Manuscript Collection List 149*, NLI. 43 Bermingham was also head agent on the neighbouring Clonbrock estate.

detrimental role of absentee landlordism was specifically highlighted at a meeting of the 'principal parishioners' of Tarmonbarry at the height of the crisis in a resolution condemning local landlords. The meeting noted that 'due to the general failure of the potato crop, an alarming scarcity has taken place, so much so, as to threaten an immediate famine and its usual concomitant disease, but also to extend those calamities to the ensuing year from the inability of the poor to crop their land'.[44] The gathering pointed out that there were nearly 400 families in the parish suffering under 'the severe pressure of actual death' and 'that from the non-residence of any landlord or person of property in the parish, we have to regret our inability to raise any sum at all adequate to meet the necessity of the poor on the present occasion'.[45]

By the early months of 1822, even before the annual potato supply began to run out, the tenants on the estate presented a frightening appearance. A number of tenants were without clothing or food, prompting land agent Henry Comyns to write to Ross Mahon:

> I gave some old blankets and rugs to the widow Nicholas Flannery … it was as great an object of compassion as could be seen, it was clearly clothing the naked, she is in a wretched way for want of clothing and want of food, these days herself and her children will starve for want of clothing, [the rugs] will be sufficient, to take her out to beg with them.[46]

In May Christopher Quinn, steward on the Tarmonbarry estate, risked his livelihood by writing to Mahon and asking him to provide assistance to his tenants, claiming:

> the voice of humanity calls on me to represent to you the wretched state of this part of the country, few so badly off as those on your estate, eleven or twelve families only excepting, not only from the general calamity but also from the loss of their potatoes by floods.[47]

In June the London Tavern Committee donated £169 for the poor of the parish of Ahascragh to be administered by Ross, James and George Mahon, along with £50 to the people of the parish of Tarmonbarry, with the money remitted to Mahon's agent, Alexander Wallace.[48] By the end of July, a total of £348 had been donated for the relief of the poor of the parish of Ahascragh, with the London Tavern Committee's contribution of £169, supplemented with £30 from the archbishop of Tuam, £30 from the Dublin Mansion House Committee and £119 donated by local subscribers.[49] There were significant differences of opinion between the agents, stewards and members of the Mahon family over how the money should be distributed

44 Resolution of the principal parishioners and clergy of the parish of Tarmonbarry, 3 June 1822, NLI, Mahon Papers, MS 47,844/1.   **45** Ibid.   **46** Henry Comyns to Ross Mahon, 3 Nov. 1822, NLI, MS 47,843/3–5.   **47** Christopher Quinn to Ross Mahon, 21 May 1822, NLI, MS 47,843/8.   **48** Correspondence of the Committee for the Relief of the Distressed Irish, NLI, MS 47,843/7.   **49** Ibid.

despite the London Committee's official recommendation that all remittances go towards the purchase of provisions and seed potatoes. Such differences of opinion, combined with a multiplicity of agents and stewards and the absence of the head landlord, slowed the process of organizing relief and was detrimental to a co-ordinated response on the estate. George Mahon, who was involved in running the Galway portion of the estate on behalf of his brother Ross, was in favour of using the relief money to promote a new manufacturing enterprise by investing in and distributing wool in its un-manufactured state so that the wives and daughters of tenants might spin woollen yarn, which in turn could be woven into flannel. He argued that such a scheme would keep their tenants' dependents busy all year round, and independent of the seasonal nature of farm work. He argued that under his scheme 600 families in the parish could eventually become self-sufficient.[50] Alexander Wallace, however, proposed that the money be distributed through relief schemes only, which would have recipients working on road repairs on the estate.[51] He subsequently rebuked his employer, telling him: 'in the past, too much indulgence may heretofore have rather injured rather than served your tenantry – a little is now absolutely necessary'.[52] Christopher Quinn, on the other hand, advised Mahon against such a scheme, as 'it would not in the smallest degree alleviate the wants of your tenantry'. Complaining of the actions of head agent Thomas Bermingham, Quinn drew his employer's attention to the dire want of potato seed in the locality and advocated the purchase of same for distribution.[53]

The Mahon estate eventually received funds from the Tuam Central Committee to set up a relief scheme on the estate and £257 was finally spent on the employment of starving tenants in drainage work on the Ahascragh portion of the estate; 255 destitute families were eventually employed on these works, with land agent Henry Comyns noting that 42 tenant families were without any means of sustenance whatsoever.[54] At the beginning of June there were a total of 390 men, women and children in immediate want of food in the small Tarmonbarry district with this number increasing to 540 by the end of the month.[55] The crisis was compounded by the dire lack of seed potatoes as the poor were forced to eat their entire crop and could not afford to purchase more for sowing. On the insistence of the parish priest, the Tarmonbarry Relief Committee distributed oatmeal to starving families engaged in digging drains on the Roscommon portion of the estate, with tenants given two quarts of meal per day, per head of family. Of the 72 heads of families who came forward from the Mahon estate in Tarmonbarry, only 17 were accepted on the working party. Noting that the tenants were without fuel, Christopher Quinn proposed the employment of tenants draining bogs on the estate and, as the tenants

50 George Mahon to Ross Mahon, 19 Aug. 1822, NLI, MS 47,843/6. **51** Alexander Wallace to Ross Mahon, Aug. 1822, NLI, MS 47,843/9. **52** Ibid., 28 Nov. 1821, NLI, MS 47,843/2. **53** Christopher Quinn to Ross Mahon, 31 May 1822, NLI, MS 47,843/8. **54** Note on relief on the Ahascragh portion of the Mahon estate, NLI, MS 47,844/3. **55** Returns of destitute families on the Mahon estate, 1822, NLI, MS 47,845/11.

did not have turbary rights, he suggested to Ross Mahon that a donation of £5 would enable them to purchase turf and potatoes.[56]

With the end of the European Wars in 1815 grain prices in Ireland dropped dramatically and with large profits no longer available from tillage farming, landowners increasingly turned to pastoral farming to maintain the high profit margins that had driven up the price of rents over the previous two decades.[57] The increasing determination of Irish landowners to maintain the high incomes generated by the boom in agricultural prices generated during the Napoleonic Wars steeled many landlords against the pleas of the rural poor to refrain from the wholesale clearance of large numbers of their landless tenants during the first half of the nineteenth century.[58] However, the modernization of the agricultural economy demanded a fundamental structural transformation of rural society as a whole, entailing a steady decline in the demand and role of the landless labouring class, an increasing diminution of the role of middlemen and a mounting preference on the part of landowners for clearances, farm amalgamation and field consolidation.[59] As Samuel Clark has observed, landowners during the period were especially anxious to dislodge squatters who occupied land without official permission and frequently without paying rent.[60] Pastoral farming was also increasingly attractive to landowners, as it required a far smaller investment in casual and full-time labour and generated reliable annual profits from a vast export market.[61] With eviction clearly in mind on the north Galway portion of his estate, Mahon's land agent compiled a return of 71 destitute tenants, renting holdings that were in arrears to the extent of £515 in June 1823. Of this group of tenants, George Mahon noted that 2 heads of families were dead, 10 families were beggars, 19 were insolvent, 21 were 'to be discharged' and 11 families were labelled 'gone away'.[62] The rental returns highlight the fluidity between the landless cottiers on the estate who rented tiny plots of land in return for their labour and very small tenants who paid cash for their plots, supplemented by casual days worked for the landlord and deducted from their rent. Thus, too precise a distinction between the landless and those tenants occupying tiny plots of land in return for cash and labour is misleading. Destitution was concentrated within the lowest class of tenants, with 29 insolvent tenants paying less than £1 in rent per half year, 13 paid less than £2, 16 paid less than £3 and 5 less than £5. Destitute tenants

56 Christopher Quinn to Ross Mahon, 26 June 1822, NLI, MS 47,843/8. **57** For an overview of the commercialization of the rural economy during this period, see Raymond D. Crotty, *Irish agricultural production, its volume and structure* (Cork, 1966), pp 35–46; James S. Donnelly, Jr, *The land and the people of nineteenth century Cork* (London and Boston, 1975), pp 9–73; Cormac Ó Gráda, *Ireland before and after the Famine: explorations in economic history, 1800–1925* (Manchester, 1988), pp 1–35; L.M. Cullen, *An economic history of Ireland since 1660* (London, 1987), pp 100–33. **58** Cullen, *An economic history*, p. 100. **59** See Donnelly, *Land and people*, pp 9–14. **60** Samuel Clark, *Social origins of the Irish Land War* (New Jersey, 1979), p. 31. **61** See Crotty, *Irish agricultural production*, pp 35–46. **62** In addition to these numbers, two tenants were listed as blind and four more as unable or too old to pay. Returns of tenants listed as insolvent, dead and gone away, 1819–22 at Ahascragh (NLI, MS 47,845/5).

were overwhelmingly between two to three years behind in their rents, reflecting the previous two years' bad harvests, and highlighting the amount of debt which their landlord was willing to indulge. Larger debts by small tenants on the estate present a misleading overall picture of this group's inability to pay rent as they were accrued by two distinct groups of people. First, relatively large debts were accrued on tiny plots where the holder had died, fled or was too old or unable to work. Thus, John Donnelan, who was listed as dead, previously paid a half yearly rent of only £1 17s. but had debts totalling £11 12s. listed against his name. Likewise, Malachy Flannery was listed as 'gone way' and paid only 16s. per half year, but had debts of £12 3s. listed against him. The townland of Lunaghton had one single arrears of £56 owed by a group of tenants for conacre, presumably representing the combined debts of a significant group of landless cottiers and small tenants for garden plots. Thus, the vast majority of debt on the estate represented very small sums owed by a significant number of very poor tenants. A very small but financially significant number of large and middling farmers, however, were also unable to pay their rents. James Hughes represented a much more comfortable class of strong farmer but owed £111 12s. from a half yearly rent of £41 4s. Of the 67 other tenants listed as destitute, however, (the status of 3 tenants is unclear) only 5 paid more than £5 half yearly rent.

It was clear to George Mahon that these debts could not be met by his tenants and he recommended to his brother that he discharge the unpaid rents entirely from his rental account and transfer them to an account of bad debts, as 'it is as well to enter them in this way as to keep them on the books, giving a fictitious debt which probably can never be realized or reconciled.'[63] A similar pattern of debt emerged on the Roscommon portion of the estate, where the land agent had previously categorized 22 tenants as 'good tenants', 5 as 'middling' and 10 as 'indifferent', with only 9 tenants listed as 'bad' in May 1819 (9 tenants had no comment).[64] However, despite only 10 tenants being listed as 'bad', Mahon served eviction notices on all 55 Roscommon tenants, along with 14 sub-tenants in October 1825.[65] In anticipation of also being evicted, tenants on the Clooncannon portion of the Galway estate petitioned their landlord in an undated memorial:

> Pray pity your poor people who always did and always will pay their rents well, better drown us then turn us off, for there is no place for us anywhere. We were a quiet easy poor people who did never complain ... but what is that to us if we be turned off, if we will pay you more than anybody and more work than anybody and why would you destroy us, that all the Fathers that came before you took care of us and for all their sakes God Bless you and keep your poor people about who would die for you and leave us where you found us and God prosper you.[66]

63 Galway rental, dated Nov. 1822, NLI, MS 47,845/9.   64 Arrears of rent for the period Nov. 1818 to May 1819 on the Mahon Estate, NLI, MS 47,845/2.   65 List of the tenants served with eviction notices at Tarmonbarry, 29–31 Oct. 1825, NLI, MS 47,846/4. 66 Petition from the tenants of Clooncannon to Ross Mahon, NLI, MS 47,846/3.

The arrival of a bumper harvest in August 1822 did not signal an end to distress in
the west, however, and food shortage remained a serious and recurring phenomenon.
Nakedness among the poorest rural classes remained a problem of particular concern,
with the *Connaught Journal* claiming in February 1823 that it was 'tormented with
letters, long and short, on the subject'.[67] 1824 was to be a year of intense hardship
once again, with the same newspaper scolding Galway landowners for their failure to
provide employment for the landless: 'Shame on some of our resident Gentry who
have their tenantry in a state of starvation, without making some exertion to have
them usefully employed.'[68] The paper noted ruefully, 'we have received a letter from
a respectable Catholic clergyman, dated Ballynahinch, Cunnemara, [sic] June 6th,
which contains the following dreadful announcement: "One-fourth of the inhabitants of this parish are starving. I pledge myself to you, that they are worse than in
1822."'[69] As the Mahon estate demonstrates, in a rural economy where the difference
between eviction and staying on the land was often a debt of £3 or less, casual labour
saved many families from complete destitution and on the small Cornamucklagh
portion of the Mahon estate, 18 tenants and their families were engaged in some
form of casual work for their landlord during 1825.[70] Men were paid a standard rate
of 8*d*. per day (the average in the west at this time): this was also the price of one
stone of potatoes during the crisis of 1822, with children being paid 4*d*., and the hire
of a tenant's horse earning an additional 2*d*. per day. Thus, the value of one day's
work, from sun up until sun down, by one head of family, could be exhausted in one
day's food. Between 17 January and 23 October 1825, 18 tenants and their families
earned a total of £55 18*s*. through their combined labour in the townland, undoubtedly saving many of these families from complete destitution and eviction,
highlighting the pitiful monetary rewards the poor were willing to accept to stave off
catastrophe. Such work was prized and much sought after despite being so badly
rewarded and 13 heads of households among this group of 18 families worked for
their landlord for an average of 75 days per year, with one tenant working 209 days,
three working between 100 and 150 days, with the remainder confined to seasonal
work of between 23 and 95 days.

CONCLUSION

The culpability of landowners in the unremitting decimation of the lowest social
group in rural Ireland, the landless labourers of the west, throughout the nineteenth
century has contributed to the enduring disdain with which landlords have been
held in the Irish popular psyche. While the role of the small and middling classes of
farmers in the economic exploitation of the landless tends to be overlooked in both

67 *Connaught Journal*, 3 Feb. 1823.   **68** Ibid., 16 June 1824.   **69** Ibid., 10 June 1824.
70 Return of labourers complied by Charles Filgate at Cornamucklagh, Oct. 1825, NLI,
MS 47,824.

popular folklore and nationalist rhetoric, the memory of famine clearances by landlords retains the power to evoke genuine emotion in the modern Irish imagination.[71]
Contemporary observers of pre-Famine rural Ireland, however, consistently highlighted the necessity for reforming the rural economy and the failure of the Irish
landowning elite to modernize their estates was a source of constant criticism from
both agricultural improvers and political economists alike. Contemplating the nature
of estate management in the west on the eve of the Great Famine in 1844, English
agricultural improver John Wiggins noted in his study of the Irish land tenure system,
The monster misery of Ireland:

> One cannot at first behold the wretched and filthy habitations, the inadequate
> outbuildings, the ragged habiliments, the poor food, the miserable fences, the
> total neglect of draining, the crops smothered with weeds, and the thousand
> other indications of poverty, without a feeling of conviction that there is
> something wrong, indeed that much, very much, is very wrong between land-
> lord and tenant.[72]

English, rather than Irish, philanthropy, combined with government aid, was primarily responsible for saving many thousands of lives during the famine of 1822 and the
London Tavern Committee, as well as being the first to formulate a coherent
response to the crisis, was by far the most important private donor of aid. Out of a
total of £606,973 expended by various agencies on relief during the crisis, the
London Committee contributed £280,140, compared to £221,437 expended by the
government, with private relief amounting to £85,355 and the Mansion House
Committee's efforts raising £20,044.[73] In addition to money, the committee donated
2,961 tons of potatoes, 1,762 tons of meal, 471 tons of rice and 273 tons of biscuits.[74]
As the spectre of famine receded, the Revd Dr Oliver Kelly, archbishop of Tuam
wrote to the committee: 'it is not in the power of language to convey an overstated
idea of the mass of misery under which these wretched beings laboured when the
bounty and munificence of your committee first enabled me to visit them with your
relief.'[75] Walter Joyce, chairman of the Grand Jury of the town of Galway, wrote that
as a result of the committee's efforts 'prejudices have been softened, new ties of union
and concord have been cemented, and Ireland, disclaiming all foreign relations, has
learned to look to her natural protectors in the hour of our adversity'.[76]

Ostensibly, the organization of relief in the west was relatively sophisticated and

---

71 For a report on a commemoration of the Ballinlass evictions of 1846 at Newbridge,
County Galway in May 2011, see *Tuam Herald*, 26 May 2011.   **72** John Wiggins, *The monster
misery of Ireland: a practical treatise on the relation of landlord and tenant with suggestions for
legislative measures and the management of landed property, the result of over thirty years experience
and study of the subject* (London, 1844), p. 23.   **73** Quoted in O'Neill, 'The 1822 famine',
appendix, unpaginated.   **74** Ibid.   **75** *Report of the committee for the relief of the distressed
districts in Ireland, appointed at a general meeting held at the city of London tavern, on the 7th May,
1822*, p. 168.   **76** Ibid., p. 175.

was ultimately effective, in terms of keeping tens of thousands of people alive and distributing a vast amount of food daily. However, while the achievements of the central relief committees were not insignificant, a number of issues must be considered when assessing the role of landlords who dominated county, baronial and parish committees. These committees acted primarily as facilitators of government and charitable relief, rather than generators of relief, and the vast majority of aid disbursed among the poor originated from direct grants of cash and provisions, provided by the government and the London Tavern Committee, and, to a much lesser extent, the Mansion House Committee. Throughout the crisis, in districts where landlord absenteeism was a major factor, reports of deaths, while shocking, remained haphazard and occasional, consisting predominantly of accounts from individual travellers, newspaper reporters and clergy, as relief efforts were hampered by the absence of formal relief structures. Mass evictions were not a prominent feature of the crisis, however, as events over the preceding years on the Mahon estate demonstrated. During subsequent partial harvest failures (which failed to arouse significant British or national interest) the limits to landlord philanthropy were more evident and despite the prevalence of external relief, debts accrued during the 1822 crisis were not purged, and could spell disaster for poor families.

Relief schemes enabled landowners to have private improvements carried out across their estates, typically in drainage and road maintenance, at no added expense to themselves other than the task of supervising schemes that increased the value of their property. Thus, rather than paying their labourers 8*d.* per day, many landowners could simply let their labourers go and administer food and provisions to the value of 6*d.* to 8*d.* per day, provided to a significant degree by English landowners. There was also serious criticism of the government's public works schemes from one of the government's own engineering experts. Alexander Nimmo supervised road works across all five counties in Connacht and expressed concern to the government that the practice of setting labourers' wages on schemes directly against their landlords' rent de-incentivized labourers and led to corruption by overseers, who were generally landowners themselves, and who were subsequently disinterested in the quality of work carried out.[77] Small schemes such as road repairs and the cleaning out of drains accounted for most of the work done. However, engineers were frequently dissatisfied with the quality of labour carried out by relief claimants, noting in one report: 'the custom of jobbing is so invertbred, [sic] that we could seldom get the work properly done by day labourers for the sum granted by presentment. The peasantry are not trained in those habits of industry, which are always the result of regular industry.'[78]

---

77 *Employment of the poor in Ireland*, p. 437.   **78** Ibid., p. 31.

Charity, paternalism and power on the Clonbrock Estates, County Galway, 1834–44

KEVIN Mc KENNA

Who supports the poor in Ireland today? It is the poor. The rich man looks at the poor over the top of the walls of his beautiful park, or if he meets him on the road, he responds to his entreaties: I make it a duty not to give anything to those who do not work. And he does not provide them with work. He has big fat dogs and his fellow creatures die at his door. Who feeds the poor? The poor.[1]

The two decades prior to Alexis de Tocqueville's visit to Ireland in 1835, following the conclusion of the Napoleonic wars, were unsettled as economic activity contracted and poverty and destitution began to rise. Begging, vagrancy and emigration became commonplace, and in the 1830s the government established the Poor Inquiry to investigate the condition of the Irish poor. The inquiry found that 2,385,000 people, or almost one-third of the population, were living in poverty. A further revelation was that much of the poverty was a result of unemployment among the able-bodied poor who were in need of assistance for over six months in every year.[2] De Tocqueville's travelling companion Gustave de Beaumont visited again in 1837 and in his analysis of Irish society, published in 1839, he concluded that the Irish landed class were responsible for the degenerate state of the country.[3] This was echoed by Third Baron Thomas Drummond who in 1838 declared that property had 'its duties as well as its rights' and that 'the diseased state of society' was attributable to 'the neglect of those duties in times past'.[4] However, this was not a universal phenomenon, as there were estates, such as Clonbrock in County Galway, where landlords were not negligent in the performance of their duty.

Robert Dillon (1807–93), Third Baron Clonbrock, inherited his family's estates of c.27,000 acres in counties Galway, Limerick and Roscommon as a minor at the age of eighteen, in 1826. Clonbrock's family seat in the townland of Clonbrock, adjacent to the village of Ahascragh, was the hub from which the estates were

---

1 Alexis de Tocqueville [Emmet J. Larkin (ed. and trans.)], *Alexis de Tocqueville's journey in Ireland, July–August 1835* (Dublin, 1990), pp 78–9.   2 Laurence M. Geary, 'The poor and the sick in pre–Famine Ireland: charity and the state' available at http://www.stm.unipi.it/ Clioh/tabs/libri/4/13-Geary_187–200.pdf.   3 Gustave de Beaumont [W.C. Taylor (ed. and trans.)] *Ireland: social, political, and religious* (Cambridge, MA, 2006), p. 316, first published as *L'Irlande:sociale, politique et religieuse* (Paris, 1839).   4 Thomas Drummond's reply to the Tipperary magistrates published in the *Freeman's Journal and Nenagh Guardian*, 29 Sept. 1838.

administered and he began his stewardship of the estates at a time when, according
to David Roberts, a flourishing of paternalistic ideas was about to begin that would
last for a further twenty years.[5] Detailed charity accounts kept by Thomas
Bermingham, Clonbrock's principal land agent, for the 1830s and early 1840s provide
evidence that the style of management on the Clonbrock estates was distinctly paternalist and somewhat at variance with the experiences of Gustave de Beaumont.
According to Roberts, 'there were three principal sets of duties (among many) that
the conscientious paternalist of superior rank felt he must perform: ruling, guiding
and helping'.[6] The aim of this essay is to explore the charitable dimension of
Clonbrock's paternalism on the estates managed by Thomas Bermingham, chiefly
located in County Galway, in the vicinity of Clonbrock demesne, Ballydonelan, and
Dalystown between 1834 and 1844 and examine the role that philanthropy played in
cementing the bond between landlord and tenant.

Thomas Bermingham, a well-known land agent in the 1830s and early 1840s, was
fine-tuned to the paternalistic *zeitgeist* described by Roberts and between 1829 and
1848 he authored a number of pamphlets that expressed a paternalistic social outlook.
He persistently campaigned for infrastructural investment in railways and harbours,
and as an experienced land agent much of his pamphleteering was on the topics of
estate improvement and the duties of Irish landlords towards their tenantry.[7] The
distribution of charity on the Clonbrock estates in the years 1834–5 demonstrates, I
believe, that a form of estate-based 'social welfare' existed before the introduction of
the poor law and that this locally distributed charity played an important role in the
legitimation of landed power. I will then proceed to an analysis of the poor law
debates that emerged in the 1830s and the opposition of paternalists such as
Clonbrock and Bermingham to it. I will argue that the introduction of the poor law
in 1838 had no immediate impact on the estate-based distribution of charity but that
as time progressed it went into decline, which had implications for locally based landlord control. The chart below provides a breakdown of the £290 paid out in
charities for the year ending 31 March 1835.[8]

The level of engagement with the tenantry is observable through the charity
accounts, which can leave little doubt that a paternalistic style of management was
pursued on the Clonbrock estates. Fig. 1 shows a breakdown of the charity accounts

5 David Roberts, *Paternalism in early Victorian England* (New Jersey, 1979), p. 28. 6 Ibid.,
pp 4–5. 7 Thomas Bermingham, *Facts and illustrations for the Labourer's Friend Society ... in
a short narrative of the home colonies of Iskerbane and Castle Sampson ...* (London, 1833); idem,
The social state of Great Britain and Ireland considered, with regard to the labouring population ...
(London, 1835); idem, *Letter addressed to the Right Honourable Lord John Russell containing facts
illustrative of the good effects from the just and considerate discharge of the duties of a resident landlord*
(London, 1846), henceforth cited as *Duties*. 8 The 'annual charities' account for this year
also included the sum of £25 paid to the schoolmaster at Kilglass (Clonbrock) school but as
the school was given a specific account in later years it was decided to separate this figure
in order that the data should be consistent. The extra £11, bringing the total expended on
the school to £36, was for improvements to the school. MS 19,696.

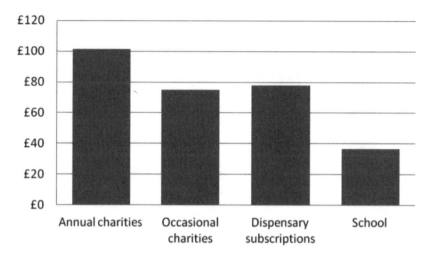

1 Summary of £290 in charities on Clonbrock estates, March 1834–5.
Source: NLI, Clonbrock papers, MSS 19,595–6

for the year ending March 1835. These recorded the name of each individual, and in some cases their address, as well as the sum received. The names entered in the 'annual charity' accounts changed little from year to year and the breakdown in Fig. 2 shows that those in receipt of assistance, such as widows, orphans, and blind girls, were very much in keeping with contemporary notions of the 'deserving poor'. 'Larkin's orphans', one of the five sets of orphans shown, received a sum of £1 10s. that year and they continued to receive between £1 and £2 for the following six years.[9] At the Poor Inquiry Thomas Bermingham stated that widows were in receipt of pensions of £2 and the Clonbrock accounts (see Fig. 2) confirm that seventeen widows were beneficiaries of charity on the estates.[10] However, the average sum of money expended on widows during the year ending March 1835 was £2.7 as some women, such as 'Widow Gordan' from Killosolan, were allocated up to £4, possibly because she had to raise a young family. While these sums of money may have provided some assistance it certainly would have been difficult to live on if compared with the wages of labourers. Bermingham further stated that he paid labourers 8d. per day in the summer and 6d. per day in the winter, which corresponds to an annual income of £9 2s. for a six-day week. However, labourers were rarely able to secure work throughout the year so an annual wage of £5 to £6 would be a more reasonable estimate. It must also be considered that a labourer may have had to support a wife and family on such wages, which makes the £2 pension looks significantly more substantial especially if the widow had already raised a family. As late as 1846 Bermingham considered a £2 pension paid to the 'aged and infirm of the tenants'

9 Clonbrock rental and accounts, 1834–5 (NLI Clonbrock papers, MS 19,595). 10 *Poor Inquiry (Ireland): Appendix F*, H.L. 1836, xxxiii, 83.

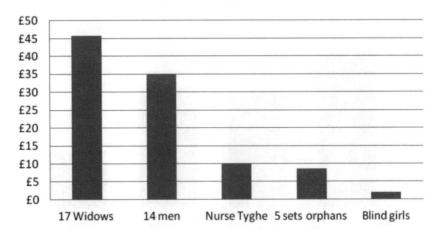

2 Breakdown of £101 in annual charities for the Clonbrock estates, 1834–5
Source: NLI, Clonbrock papers, MSS 19,595–6

enough to make 'them of a consequence, instead of being a burden on their families'.[11] This indicates that there was some concern that vulnerable people should have
a degree of autonomy and that their years of residence on the estate were appreciated to the extent that Clonbrock was prepared to provide them with some form of
financial security. While we know that widows, orphans and blind girls received
charity there is no indication as to why the fourteen men were assisted but it is most
likely that they were aged or infirm as Bermingham believed that they were
deserving of charity.

The provision of medical care to tenants was not unusual and the year ending
March 1835 was no exception as £10 was paid to Nurse Tyghe for attending sick
tenants (see Fig. 2 above). A further £50 10*s.* was subscribed to dispensaries at various
locations across the estates and Ahascragh dispensary, the one closest to the demesne,
received a considerably higher donation of £30 compared to the others, £5 being
the usual donation (see Fig. 1). As Laurence Geary has pointed out, 'the fact that
voluntary subscriptions had to be raised before a presentment could be obtained
from the grand jury meant that philanthropy rather than necessity dictated the
number and location of dispensaries in pre-Famine Ireland'.[12] Before Clonbrock
purchased a number of townlands at Dalystown in 1832, Bermingham informed him
that 'the people about here are rejoiced at the idea of having you as a landlord'.[13]
Clonbrock, it seems, did not disappoint his new tenants and erected a dispensary
there in 1834 at a cost of £27 10*s.* and henceforward subscribed a sum of £5 to it
annually.[14] Furthermore, it appears that Clonbrock's reputation as a benevolent land-

11 Bermingham, *Duties*, p. 7.   **12** Laurence M. Geary, *Medicine and charity in Ireland, 1718–
1851* (Dublin, 2004), p. 63.   **13** Bermingham to Clonbrock, n.d. (NLI, Clonbrock papers,
MS 35,727 (9)).   **14** Clonbrock rental and accounts, 1835–43 (ibid., 19,595–614).

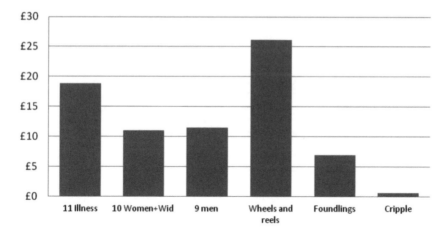

3 Breakdown of £75 of Occasional charities on Clonbrock estates for 1834–5
Source: NLI, Clonbrock papers, MSS 19,595–6

lord worked in his favour. When negotiating the purchase of a number of townlands on this estate Bermingham informed him that the vendor was prepared to sell 'at £18,000, he [the vendor] values them to £19,000 to anyone else but as you take such care of the poor tenants he wishes to give you a preference'.[15] Other vulnerable sections of the community such as orphans and blind children were provided with financial assistance as illustrated in Fig. 2.

'Occasional charity' was somewhat different from 'annual charity' as this account recorded sums of money paid out to individuals who encountered difficulty over the course of a year and most of the names that appear in this account changed from year to year. This account provides insights into the experiences of the labourers and tenants who lived and worked on the estates and the harsh reality of life for some in the 1830s. The chart below shows a breakdown of the £75 in occasional charity distributed for the year ending March 1835.

A total of £19 was allocated for eleven people with illness, seven – all men – were named and the other four, two men and two women, were simply described as 'poor men' or 'poor women', which may indicate that they were not tenants but, perhaps, mendicant beggars. Ten were described as sick or sickly while one had fever[16] and it is notable that there was a significant gender imbalance of nine men to two women in this section. It is hardly likely that men were more prone to illness than women but it must be understood that married women whose husbands were alive did not receive direct payments but by proxy through their husbands and some of the

15 Bermingham to Clonbrock, 12 Apr. 1833 (ibid., MS 35,727). **16** Fever was not a big problem in 1834–5 but this was not the case in the two years that followed when £4. 1*s*. 6*d*. was expended to provide lime for fever sheds, £10 to eleven individuals, as well, as £15 'to poor people in fever about Clonbrock'. Clonbrock rental and acoounts (NLI Clonbrock papers, MSS 19,699, 19,601).

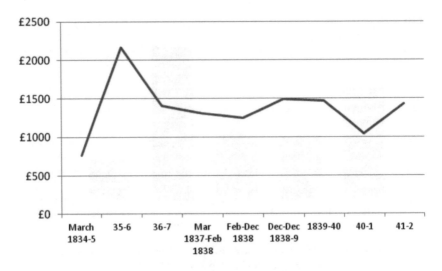

4 Expenditure on improvement projects on Clonbrock estates, 1834–5
Source: NLI, Clonbrock papers, MSS 19,595–6

payments made to men that year may have been for this reason. Of the ten women in receipt of occasional charity seven were named widows and three unnamed 'poor women' who may also have been mendicants. £26 was paid for wheels and reels which indicates that Clonbrock assisted tenants in the development of domestic industries such as spinning. £7 was allocated to foundlings, some of whom were discovered at Lanelough which proves interesting as this townland bordered Clonbrock demesne. This location may have been specifically chosen because there was an awareness that Clonbrock would make some provision for them.

Two contrasting payments stand out in the 'sundry small payments' account, £3 5s. was allowed to L. Finaghty for the trespass of pheasants and 7s. was paid to the doctor for attending Widow Fox's child who had broken her leg.[17] While the considerable sum of £290 was spent on charity it represented just 3.6 per cent of the projected rental of £8,000 on the estates in question.[18] Even landlords who were regarded as possessing a sense of *noblesse oblige* did not believe in 'promiscuous' charity and were critical of many charitable organizations. They advocated assistance for the sick, widowed, orphaned, blind and insane but were loathe to dole out money to the able bodied who were capable of work. A conscientious paternalist advocated work for the able-bodied poor rather than handouts, and Clonbrock spent considerable amounts of money employing labour on various improvement schemes. These projects included the construction of a large mill, reclaiming and draining of land,

---

17 Sundry small payments account 1834–5 (ibid., MS 19,596) **18** Clonbrock rental and accounts (ibid., MSS 19,595–6).

building walls, and making new roads, all of which would have been a boon to the tenantry and their families in providing employment.

Thomas Bermingham was an avid campaigner for state-sponsored public works, which he believed would improve the country's infrastructure as well as provide much needed employment for the poor during the 'hungry months' of late summer and early autumn. He was a founder member, along with Lord Clonbrock, of the Western Railroad and Navigation Company in 1831 and much of his campaigning zeal was focused on the promotion of drainage schemes and railway projects as is evidenced in his pamphleteering.[19] Peter Gray has argued that the development of railways was rarely viewed as connected with the poor law question. 'However, a closer examination of its chronology and the political considerations surrounding its establishment and operations suggests that it can legitimately be regarded as forming part of a common strategy with the poor law bill for the economic development of Ireland and the redressing of the structural problems of poverty in that country.'[20]

By the 1830s Ireland was the only country within the United Kingdom not to have a poor law despite the fact that many of its inhabitants lived in poverty. The Scottish poor law was based on the voluntarism of private benefactors while in England and Wales the workhouse system, introduced in 1834, was funded through local taxation known as the poor rate. The widely held view was that Irish landlords had failed in their duty to the Irish poor so the Poor Inquiry was established in order to determine the best way of combating poverty in the country.[21] It was chaired by Richard Whately, the Church of Ireland archbishop of Dublin, and between 1833 and 1835 evidence was presented to various local hearings across the country from diverse social classes.[22] Thomas Bermingham was optimistic that the information gathered during the inquiry would be put to good use in easing the plight of the poor in Ireland and stated as much in his 1835 pamphlet, *The social state of Great Britain and Ireland considered*.[23] It appeared as the Poor Inquiry was deliberating its findings and there can hardly be any doubt that he was attempting to influence the outcome of the inquiry as he included feasibility studies for his pet projects of river drainage, railway construction and the reclamation of waste land to accommodate the poor.

19 Thomas Bermingham, *First report of the committee on the Western Rail-Road and Navigation Company* (Dublin, 1831); idem, *The social state of Great Britain and Ireland considered, with regard to the labouring population* ... (London, 1835); idem, *A letter to the Rt. Hon. Lord Viscount Morpeth: from Thomas Bermingham, Esq., of Carnamana, Kilconnell County Galway, chairman of the General Irish Railroad Committee: upon the advantages certain to accrue to Ireland by the introduction of railway communication to the river Shannon and to other parts of the kingdom* (London, 1839); idem, *Statistical evidence in favour of state railways in Ireland* (Dublin, 1841). **20** Peter Gray, *The making of the Irish poor law, 1815–43* (Manchester, 2009), p. 173. **21** Kinealy, *This great calamity*, p. 18. **22** For discussion see, Niall Ó Ciosáin, 'The Poor Inquiry and Irish society: a consensus theory of truth', *Transactions of the Royal Historical Society*, 20 (2010), pp 127–39; Gerard O'Brien, 'The establishment of the poor law unions in Ireland', *Irish Historical Studies*, 23 (1982), pp 97–120; idem, 'The new poor law in pre-Famine Ireland: a case history', *Irish Economic and Social History*, 12 (1985), pp 33–49. **23** Bermingham, *The social state of Great Britain and Ireland considered*, p. xx.

However, the report 'adopted a distinctly sceptical tone towards the role of active state intervention in mitigating Irish distress through works of agricultural improvement better undertaken by the proprietors themselves'.[24]

Despite the report's lack of enthusiasm for his favoured means of alleviating poverty, Bermingham continued campaigning for extensive infrastructural investment in railways and drainage. He did not voice any significant opposition to the findings of the Poor Inquiry, but when it became apparent that the workhouse-based English poor law system was being considered, he opposed it. George Nicholls, an English poor law commissioner, was engaged to conduct a further survey of Irish poverty in 1836 and he denied that Irish needs differed from those in England and recommended the creation of large poor law unions and the establishment of workhouses on the English model.[25] Many landlords feared that if the able-bodied poor were given a right to relief in workhouses, as they were in England, then they, as the principal payers of the poor rate, would be bankrupted. They feared that workhouses would immediately become crowded and that the 'virtuous' payers of the poor rate would be forced to support idleness within workhouse walls.

David Roberts has argued that Tory reviewers were suspicious of some forms of philanthropy. 'A philanthropy that meant a personal benevolence in a small community they did not dislike, but a philanthropy that was extended, diffuse, and general won from them only the most pejorative adjectives. They wrote of "platform philanthropy", "claptrap philanthropy", "the pernicious cant of universal philanthropy", "pseudo humanity and philanthropy".'[26] While the expense of funding a workhouse was the landlords' prime motivation in condemning the poor law they also feared that this model would undermine the control that they and their agents exercised at local level. They decided who were the deserving and the undeserving poor, and dispensed charity according to their own dictates so they feared a loss of control to commissioners answerable to a central authority. It could reasonably be argued that Clonbrock performed his paternal duty to his tenantry through estate charities and the provision of employment. However, the general feeling among those in favour of the workhouse-centred model, 'from liberal whigs to humanist tories, was the belief that Irish landlords were failing in their responsibilities to their tenants and to society in general'.[27]

While the poor law bill was being debated in parliament in early 1838, Thomas Bermingham made his position on the matter clear in his *Remarks on the proposed poor law bill for Ireland, addressed to George Poulett Scrope, Esq., Member for Stroud.* Poulett Scrope, an English radical and long-time campaigner for an Irish poor law, was complimented by Bermingham for his persistent advocacy of this cause. However, he believed it necessary to inform Poulett Scrope of alternative methods of poor relief that he thought might be of use at this very important time. From experience

---

24 Ibid., p. 116. **25** George Nichols, *A history of the Irish poor law in connection with the people* (London, 1856), pp 157–62. **26** Roberts, *Paternalism*, p. 74. **27** Crossman, *Local government*, p. 45.

gained travelling around Prussia, Belgium, Switzerland, Savoy and parts of France in the latter part of 1837, Bermingham felt 'satisfied that the English are far behind foreigners in the science of managing the poor, and that we should seek abroad for further information, in order to make the Irish poor law as perfect as all the friends of humanity wish it to become'.[28] He expressed the view that the workhouse system was unsustainable in Ireland, and estimated that the cost of constructing a workhouse and maintaining widows, orphans, the aged and infirm within them would break landed proprietors. He argued there were many excellent institutions, including the deaconries in Ballinasloe and Cloughjordan, where the poor were visited and relieved by private charities, and that the introduction of 'one uniform and expensive plan' would lead to their demise. Other institutions that he held in high regard were dispensaries, and he suggested Ahascragh dispensary, adjacent to Clonbrock demesne, as a model of efficiency since 2,373 persons had been treated for a sum of £180 or 1s. 6d. per individual.[29] Finding common ground with Poulett Scrope he criticized the poor law bill for the absence of any mention of public works, and reiterated his call for railway and river drainage projects. While Bermingham admitted the necessity of poor laws and of institutions such as hospitals, fever hospitals, asylums for 'lunatics', the 'deaf and dumb' and the blind, he expressed no confidence in the workhouse system because of the cost, and the humiliation that he believed the poor would suffer if forced to enter them. Echoing Whately's recommendations he argued for private initiative in the dispensation of charity. Essentially, he was in favour of outdoor relief that treated the sick in dispensaries and provided paid work for the able-bodied poor through public works.

The poor law bill continued its progress through parliament and one month after Bermingham had penned his pamphlet, Frederick Shaw, the Tory MP for Dublin University, proposed to limit workhouse relief to the impotent and elderly poor and to exclude the able-bodied. It was defeated by 134 votes to 75 and represented a significant defeat to those who were trying to frustrate the bill's passage.[30] In the end it proved an insurmountable task and the bill passed on 30 April, but only 25 of 63 Irish MPs voted in its favour, and at least eight other Irish MPs abstained. Such was the significance of the defeat of Shaw's proposal that a petition to the House of Lords was drafted in Galway while the bill was still in the Commons. Many of the grand juries that met around the country for the spring assizes drew up similar petitions demanding the restriction of state relief to the 'impotent poor', along with some form of remunerative employment for the labouring poor. In March, the grand juries of Meath, Cavan, Wexford, Fermanagh, Kings County, Down, and Mayo all submitted similar resolutions. During the 1837–8 session, 116 petitions from various bodies, with 39,922 signatures, were presented against the bill; this swamped the paltry four (with 593 names) in its favour.[31]

The meeting to draw up the Galway petition, attended by Bermingham, was held

28 Bermingham, *Remarks*, pp 3–4.   **29** Ibid., pp 9–10.   **30** Gray, *Irish poor law*, pp 201–3.
31 Ibid., p. 362.

at Tuam courthouse on 29 March and chaired by Sir John Burke, who had been a Whig MP for Galway between 1830 and 1832. Landed paternalists were dedicated to locality and suspicious of any external authority that might undermine their position and this was very much in evidence in the petition agreed. It strongly objected to the 'arbitrary and unlimited powers awarded to the commissioners. Being non-resident, they cannot from experience either sympathize with the necessities, comprehend the resources, or direct judicious relief, of the Irish people.' It further described the bill as oppressive and inquisitorial, 'being calculated to wither the purest sentiments of benevolence. To snap asunder the ties of gratitude and affection'. The petition concluded with a call for the introduction of the Scottish poor law model as well as arguments for the draining and cultivation of wasteland and an appeal to 'assist the efforts of agriculturalists, by affording permanent employment to [a] willing and intelligent peasantry'. It was resolved that Lord Clancarthy, supported by Lords Clonbrock, Gort and Fitzgerald, would present the petition to parliament. It further resolved that Thomas Bermingham and others form a committee to sit in London while the bill was progressing through the House of Lords.[32] It is evident that Bermingham assisted in drafting this petition because of the similarities between it and his *Remarks* pamphlet published a month previously. Both the pamphlet and the petition expressed the views of landed paternalists regarding the duties and responsibilities of property and their fear of interference in local matters. Like many landlords in England who were dedicated to locality, they feared and criticized the centralized Benthamite commissioners, using 'the classic argument of paternalism that only in small, circumscribed spheres, where all were intimately and personally known, could benevolence and property be rightly administered'.[33]

There appears to have been an anxiety that the 'the ties of gratitude and affection' would be broken, and the paternalist relationship would be undermined. It is hardly surprising, therefore, that those who conscientiously managed their estates sought to retain control of local charity. They firmly believed that it could be better administered by the rule of property but they also knew that the dispensation of charity was an essential component of the social glue that was at the heart of paternalism and that the surrender of its control to centralized authorities would undermine their ability to successfully manage the deferential dialectic. Howard Newby has argued that in order for the exercise of traditional authority to succeed, a careful balance needs to be struck between the elements of identification and differentiation which constitute deferential interaction. Encapsulated within the gift, he continues, the identificatory and differentiatory elements of deference find perfect expression and that charity distributed locally at a personal level 'celebrated, symbolized and reaffirmed the deferential dialectic'.[34] There can hardly be any doubt that

---

32 *Tuam Herald*, 31 Mar. 1838.   **33** Roberts, *Paternalism*, p. 257.   **34** Howard Newby, 'The deferential dialectic', *Comparative Studies in Society and History*, 17 (1975), p. 161. Newby uses italics for the words *differentiation* and *identification* to emphasize that they are the two components of the deferential dialectic and they have been similarly italicized in the text.

the charity which the poor received from Clonbrock fostered some level of identification but it also underscored the differentiation that existed between giver and
receiver. As Newby has argued:

> Clearly one does not wish to deny the conscious validity of the philanthropic
> and Christian motivations to charity, but charity has long been, in effect, an
> integral part of the legitimation of social subordination, not only through its
> status-enhancing properties but because it has been used discriminatingly in
> favour of the 'deserving' (i.e., deferential) poor.[35]

The power of the gift was intimately understood by those who opposed the introduction of the poor law and the Galway petition, along with several others, was
presented to the House of Lords by the marquis of Clanricarde on 18 May 1838. He
'came closest to articulating a class interest in expressing the fear that the centralizing
powers of the bill, in common with many other innovations under the present
administration, would continue the process of "gradually and by degrees superseding
the resident gentry"'.[36]

Despite a barrage of petitions and the opposition of Lord Clonbrock and other
Irish landlords the *Act for the effectual relief of the destitute poor in Ireland* was passed by
the Lords on 9 July 1838 by 93 votes to 31.[37] One of the principal arguments against
the introduction of the poor law, and its accompanying poor rate, was that it would
bring a halt to the benevolence of landlords and others who had acted in a charitable
manner. For the first few years following its introduction this does not appear to have
been the case on the Clonbrock estates and the distribution of charity continued
under Bermingham's direction as the graph below illustrates.

In fact, expenditure on charities peaked in the years immediately after the introduction of the poor law. Christine Kinealy has argued that in 1839 there was
localized, yet severe, distress in some parts of the country and the estate accounts
reveal that this was the case among some of Clonbrock's tenants.[38] It is particularly
evident in the £140 expended on 'occasional charities' in 1839 as this figure had not
risen above £80 since 1834.

The bulk of the figure consists of charity dispensed on the Clonbrock and
Ballydonelan estates which amounted to £54 and £58 respectively.

I now want to provide some examples from these estates to illustrate the challenges that the tenantry faced in these trying times, and the response of Clonbrock
and Bermingham to them. Figure 7 shows the breakdown of £54 paid out in occasional charity on the Clonbrock estate in 1838–9. It includes a sum of £7 10s.
recorded as 'weekly charities' paid out to twenty-four 'people in want of food on the
estate' during late July and August, corresponding with the 'hungry months' when

---

35 Ibid., pp 161–2. **36** Gray, *Irish poor law*, p. 211. **37** *Hansard*, III, 44, 30 (9 July 1838).
38 Christine Kinealy, 'The role of the poor law during the Famine' in Cathal Póirtéir (ed.),
The Great Irish Famine (Cork, 1995), p. 107.

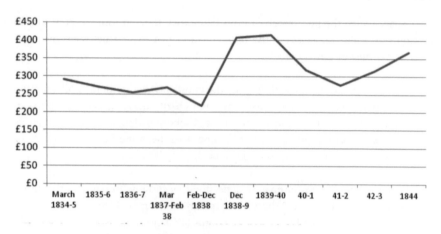

5 Charities distributed on the Clonbrock estates, 1834–44
Source: NLI, Clonbrock papers, MSS 19,595–19,616

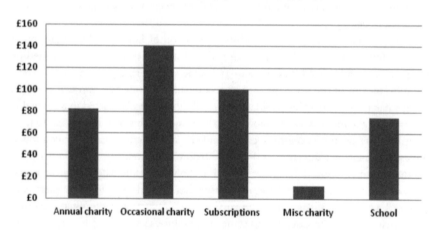

6 Summary of £408 in charities for Clonbrock estates, December 1838–9
Source: NLI, Clonbrock papers, MS 19,605

the people awaited the ripening of the potato crop. 'Weekly charities', distributing small sums of money during the hungry months, were not paid out in previous years, and this reflects Kinealy's 'localized, yet severe, distress in some parts of Ireland'[39] during 1839, and its impact on the poorest of Clonbrock's tenantry. Fever also hit the poorer sections of the tenantry that year and £2 was spent whitewashing fever sheds at Killosolan where the sick were quarantined. Several people suffering from fever received various sums from Clonbrock that year: eight named individuals received sums ranging from 10s. to £2 and a sum of £1 8s. was allocated to give 'oatmeal to poor people in fever, on the estate'. Patt Rogan, Kilglass, suffered from fever for a

39 Ibid.

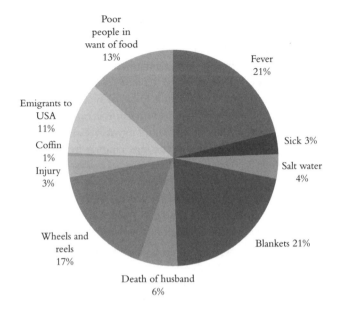

7 Division of £54 in occasional charities on Clonbrock estate, 1838–9
Source: NLI, Clonbrock papers, MS 19,605

number of months and received £1 in March and 4s. in July/August. However, it appears that he did not recover from the fever as the occasional charity account records a sum of 5s. to provide a coffin for him in October. Less than a month later Widow Rogan, probably Patt's wife, also from Kilglass, received £1 because she too was suffering from fever.[40] The account also records two others suffering from unspecified illnesses for which they received sums of money. Three tenants and one tenant's son were given 10s. each to go to 'salt water', indicating that they were being sent to the sea for health reasons; others received compensation for injury while working on the estate or for the death of a spouse. E. Nicholson who was 'hurt by wagons in [the] bog' was given £1. 10s. 'to help bind him to a trade'. James Clarke, whose 'house was blown down by the hurricane' (the night of the 'big wind' on 6 January 1839),[41] received £1 for repairs as well as 5s. on 24 June because of illness. He had not recovered from this illness, it appears, by 23 August as he was a recipient of 10s. to go to 'salt water'. The picture was similar on the Ballydonelan estate where tenants received financial assistance or were sent to 'salt water'; £4 was spent employing nurses to tend to those who had been stricken with fever; and during the 'hungry months' forty-four people were recorded as receiving 'weekly charity'.[42]

In the 1830s and early 1840s, emigration on a voluntary basis was an option for

40 Clonbrock rental and accounts, 1838–9 (NLI, Clonbrock papers, MS 19,605).   **41** For discussion see Peter Carr, *The night of the big wind* (Belfast, 1993).   **42** Clonbrock rental and

those resident on the estate. In 1836–7 eight tenants received £10, while two received £5 to assist with emigration. These payments were not considered charity as the rent on the vacated holdings was increased by five per cent. A rise in rent did not always follow the vacation of holdings by emigrants to America as in the same year four widows and one man were given between £2 and £5 and 'there was no rise of rent expected'.[43] Tenants, it appears, were given financial incentives to encourage their siblings and children to emigrate. These seldom came as cash payments but rather in the form of reduced rents or the cancellation of rental arrears. In 1837–8 five tenants, including two widows, were granted reductions ranging from £4 to £5 each for sending sons or brothers to America.[44] While sums of money were paid to emigrants and their parents in the 1830s and early 1840s emigration was not extensive and in no way systematic or forced. More extensive was the practice of paying 'paupers for going away' and between 1834 and 1844 at least £497 was expended for this purpose. The amounts that people received varied but between £5 and £10 was the usual sum paid. For the year ending March 1835, £100 was paid to fourteen pauper under-tenants of a middleman who was evicted from the estate. Twelve of these received £5 each, Widow Derham 'who had ten in family' received £20, while John Colohan 'who had been a useful man in trying occasions' received £10.[45] There is no mention of these paupers going to America that year and those that were paid money in subsequent years were not referred to as emigrants either. What became of them is unclear; they may have been accommodated on other portions of the estate as, in the late 1820s, Bermingham had relocated tenants from a townland on an overcrowded portion of the Roscommon estate to a new settlement in the vicinity.[46] However, it is just as likely that those who had been paid to 'go away' had to find another place to live; this would not have been easy given the intense competition for land so they may have had little option but to emigrate. Despite the obvious difficulty which some tenants were facing on the estate in 1839 only two women were provided with assistance to emigrate and unusually these sums were recorded in the charity accounts: Bridget Downey, of Kilglass, and Honor Toohy, were given £2.10s, and £2 respectively to emigrate to America.[47]

The introduction of the poor law in 1838 does not seem to have interfered with the distribution of charity on the Clonbrock estates; neither does it appear to have diminished Clonbrock's ardour for improvements. There was continuous expenditure on the latter which provided work for the labouring population on the drainage of Crith bog, adjacent to Clonbrock demesne, and individual tenants were also encouraged to drain their land for which they received compensation (see Fig. 4). From 1838 to the end of 1841, following the introduction of the poor law, the amount

accounts, 1838–9 (NLI, Clonbrock papers, MS 19,605). **43** Ibid., 1836–7, MS 19,600. **44** Ibid., 1837–8, MS 19,602. **45** Ibid., 1834–5, MS 19,596. **46** Thomas Bermingham, *Facts and illustrations for the Labourers' Friend Society … in a short narrative of the home colonies of Iskerbane and Castle-Sampson …* first published in 1833, addendum to *The social state of Great Britain and Ireland considered* (London, 1835). **47** Clonbrock rental and accounts, 1838–9 (NLI, Clonbrock Papers, MS 19,605).

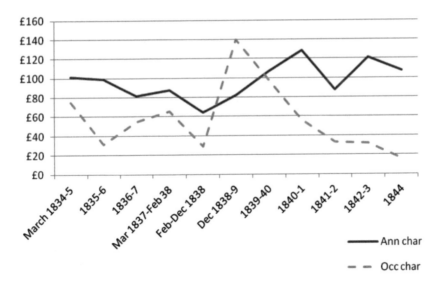

8 Annual and occasional charities for Clonbrock estates, 1834–44
Source: NLI, Clonbrock papers, MSS 19,595–617

expended on 'occasional charities' rose significantly but this figure fell to £33 in 1842, indicating that the poor law was beginning to have an impact on estate based charities. This was Bermingham's last full year as agent and despite the decline in the amounts spent on charity he granted rent reductions of £54 to a number of tenants for reasons that could be deemed charitable. Lawrence Shanaghan received £3 for 'great loss of cattle on mountain', John Kennedy received £3 for failure of his wheat crop, and £6 was given to John Kissane 'a long time sick by which he got insane'.[48]

However, it is clear from the plummeting expenditure on occasional charity, shown in Fig. 8, that estate based charities were being phased out.

This fall in expenditure can largely be attributed to the poor law, especially if it we consider that the Ballinasloe Union Workhouse opened on 1 January 1842. Bermingham, who had been elected as a poor law guardian, was sceptical about its capacity to deal with the number of poor who sought refuge within its walls. In a letter to Clonbrock on 13 January he stated that he had

> attended the accommodation of paupers last Saturday. It is awful, the destitution, and the house is not ready to accommodate all those who apply, it is damp and was, in my opinion, opened too soon – they are very properly sending back to the electoral division the paupers – it will be a great tax unless all landlords shall provide for their own paupers out of the house – one young woman was admitted on Saturday – with five children. She was dead on

48 Clonbrock rental and accounts, 1842 (NLI, Clonbrock papers, MS 19,611).

Monday so here is five children at once chargeable to the electoral division
of Killane at least £20 a year and yet you know a house and acre of land
would have given them enough to eat with the mother's labour it is an ill
advised measure.[49]

By March, however, Bermingham appears to have overcome his fears regarding the
readiness of the workhouse and the case of Biddy Maguire from Kilglass, adjacent to
the demesne, illustrates the transition from localized, landlord-controlled estate charities to the centralized workhouse system based on the poor law. During December
1839–40 she received £4 8s. 6d. in charity spread over sixteen instalments throughout
the year. The following year she received £2 5s. in eleven instalments, 10s. of which
was paid to 'nursetenders' to care for her while she was in fever. However, in 1842,
just over two months after the workhouse opened, there is only one payment to her,
on 10 March, when 2s. 6d. was paid 'to take Biddy Maguire to the poor house'.[50] The
petition against the poor law in 1838 warned that it was 'calculated to wither the
purest sentiments of benevolence' and for Biddy Maguire, at least, this seemed to be
the case.

Another factor in the decline of some charities on the Clonbrock estates was the
retirement of Thomas Bermingham as land agent in February 1843. He was replaced
by Charles Filgate, Bermingham's former colleague on the neighbouring Mahon
estate, who appeared intent on cutting expenditure. On assuming his position he
disallowed Catholic holidays to the estate's labourers, which had been permitted by
Bermingham, and discontinued many of his improvement projects and his austerity
may have influenced his management of estate charity. Unfortunately, Filgate's
surviving accounts do not provide personal information about those in receipt of
charity, so it is not possible to study estate charity in detail after Bermingham's retirement in February 1843. Bermingham's departure marked a continued fall in the
amount expended on 'occasional charities' but it would be somewhat unfair to lay all
the blame for this at Filgate's door, as the necessity of having to pay the poor rate
must have curtailed the agent's ability to dispense charity. In 1843, the Poor Law
Amendment Act released occupiers on holdings valued at less than £4 from paying
the poor rate and the responsibility for their payment fell to the landlord. That year
£175 was paid in poor rates and this accruing expense would have done little to
promote estate charities and may explain why 'occasional charities' fell as low as £15
in 1844 (see Fig. 8).[51]

There is a contradiction in this chapter; the poor law did not initially undermine
landlords power at local level yet it did, nevertheless, have a considerable effect in
weakening the paternal relationship between Clonbrock and his tenants by diminishing his capacity to dispense charity. This capacity was further diminished with the
introduction of the Medical Charities Act in 1851 which brought all dispensaries
under the remit of the poor law and heralded an end to Clonbrock's donations to

49 Bermingham to Clonbrock, 13 Jan. 1842 (ibid., MS 35,727). 50 Clonbrock rental and
accounts, 1839–42 (Ibid., MSS 19,607,19,609,19,611). 51 Ibid., MSS 19,615–6.

those located on his estate. However, landlords like Clonbrock who had opposed the poor law soon came to accept it, as the Ballinasloe board of guardians, on which he served in the ensuing decades, was largely controlled by the landed interest. In 1842 the boards of guardians of the Ballinasloe and Galway unions were recorded as having the highest number of elected magistrates in the country.[52] Landed control was further tightened when tenants with holdings valued at less than £4 were disenfranchised in the following year by the Poor Law Amendment Act.

While it was not immediately apparent that there was a threat to landed power there was an indication that it was beginning to weaken. Peter Gray has argued that the political excitement in the run up to poor law elections in the pre-Famine period has been underplayed. This, he argues, was particularly evident before the introduction of the Poor Law Amendment Act in 1843 when tenants on holdings of £4 or less were entitled to vote in the elections and that the 'political revolt against landed control [in the 1880s] had been prefigured in the contested poor law union politics of the pre-Famine period'.[53] Essentially a Trojan horse had been permitted to enter the citadel of landed power and while the initial danger was neutralized, the inherent threat of a wide franchise was to remerge later in the century as their positions of dominance on the poor law boards were challenged once again.

Roberts has argued that in early Victorian England 'no social outlook had deeper roots and wider appeal than what twentieth-century historians call paternalism'. The literature that influenced this outlook came from a wide array of authors who published philosophical treatises, novels and magazine columns. Names such as Edmund Burke, Walter Scott and Benjamin Disraeli, and publications such as the *Quarterly Review* and the *Edinburgh Review* all contributed to the creation of this paternalist *zeitgeist*. Interestingly the catalogues for Clonbrock library for the early Victorian period have survived and works by these authors and numerous issues of the magazines were all to be found at Clonbrock.[54] Thomas Bermingham's *The social state* was also present on the shelves and it, along with his other works, can, without difficulty, be said to have contributed to this *zeitgeist*.

This contribution has argued that paternalism as a social outlook informed how the Clonbrock estates were managed during the 1830s and early 1840s. It has shown, through a study of estate charity, how 'the gift' symbolized and reaffirmed the deferential dialectic with its contrasting elements of identification and differentiation. It played an important role in legitimizing landed power and for these reasons, among others, both Bermingham and Clonbrock resisted the introduction of the poor law. They understood its role in copper fastening the paternal relationship but despite their efforts to resist it, the centralized model of the workhouse won the day. Howard

52 O'Brien, 'The establishment of the poor law unions', p. 114; Clonbrock became chairman of the Mountbellew union in 1851 following its creation by the poor law commissioners in 1848. 53 Gray, *Irish poor law*, p. 340; O'Brien, 'The establishment of the poor law unions', p. 114. 54 Clonbrock library catalogues, 1807–c.1850 (NLI, Clonbrock papers, MSS 19,947–9).

Newby has argued that one of the consequences of the rise of charitable organizations in the nineteenth century

> has been increasingly to deform the gift by rendering it more bureaucratically
> organized and impersonally dispensed on a less localized and less discrimi-
> nating basis. The gift has thus become less effective as a means of social
> control, and its use has become less appropriate to the exigencies of a hier-
> archy characterized more and more by rational-legal authority.[55]

There is no doubt that Clonbrock had lost something very valuable once the poor
law was introduced. Workhouses were not designed to foster identification with the
landlord but toward the state and given the harsh conditions that existed in these
institutions it is doubtful if they fostered identification on any level. Clonbrock lived
until 1893 so he would, in time, come to realize the loss of power which this act
entailed when his family lost control of the Mountbellew board of guardians in the
latter part of the century. It could, without exaggeration, be described as the first in
a series of measures that would topple Clonbrock and his class from what, in 1844,
appeared to be an unassailable position of power.

---

55 Newby, 'The deferential dialectic', p. 162.

Pecuniary assistance for poverty and emigration: the politics of landed estate management and philanthropy in mid-nineteenth-century Ireland

JOANNE McENTEE

In 1838, a memorandum signed by 452 tenants on the Shirley estate in Monaghan was presented to their landlord Evelyn P. Shirley (1812–82). It expressed a 'sincere thanks for your constant and unvarying attention to the temporal improvement, comfort, and prosperity of your tenantry on this property'.[1] Such an unbridled effusion of gratitude by the tenantry towards their landlord in response to perceived positive estate management policies and practices, on a superficial level at least, may point towards a philanthropically motivated landlord. However, the motives behind the apparently benevolent policies upon a deeper analysis proved multifaceted. This essay is not concerned with philanthropic landlords per se. Rather it seeks to gain a greater understanding of how seemingly philanthropic gestures facilitated and supported an estate management policy which was aimed ultimately at increasing order on the estate.

Members of the landed class often adopted an active role in dispensing charity in their localities. Some elites were inspired to help the needy due to the possession of a compassionate disposition or out of a sense of duty. Traditionally landed families were expected to perform acts of charity in pre-welfare societies. David Spring argued that the social leadership role frequently adopted by the landlord was a traditional one highlighting the long-standing patriarchal nature of the position in rural society.[2] Indeed, The Drapers' Company in Londonderry took an active philanthropic role during the nineteenth century, while the Farnhams' charity accounts attest to the breadth of their involvement and the relatively significant amount of financial assistance they dispensed in their locality.[3] During the early 1830s, many rural dispensaries and medical institutions benefited from the philanthropy of wealthy locals. Private subscriptions to the Cavan dispensary, amounting to £40 5s., were derived from several individuals and it was believed that such beneficence and

---

1 'To Evelyn P. Shirley Esq., our good and respected landlord', Sept. 1838 (PRONI, D3531/P/2) 2 David Spring, *The English landed estate in the nineteenth century: its administration* (London, 1963), p. 182. 3 Philanthropy papers, 1829–82 (PRONI, Drapers' Company papers, D3632/U) (NLI, Farnham papers, MS 11,492).

kindliness would continue indefinitely.[4] Linda A. Pollock described kindness within elite circles as the melding of 'goodwill, material aid and courtesy into a practical template for the tenor and structure of early modern social relationships', while also highlighting its associations with patronage culture.[5] In his *General report on the Gosford estates in County Armagh, 1821* William Greig, a Scot who was employed on Lord Gosford's estate in the capacity of surveyor and valuator, argued that 'endeavours should be used to liberalize their [tenants] minds by good offices and acts of kindness'.[6] While undoubtedly some landlords assisted the needy due to a genuine desire to alleviate conditions for the poor, an opportunity to reorganize and reorder estates often proved a welcome by-product. Through altruistic actions, both male and female members of the gentry and aristocracy were able to instil in the lower orders a sense of obligation and a feeling of dependence.[7] The 2nd earl of Leitrim's comment regarding English charity to Irish paupers reveals an awareness of the potentially powerful political support that displays of charity could harness:

> The people of England have come forward nobly (as they always do when charity is in question) to assist the poor Irish, and I hope that the subscriptions that have been raised in England to so great an amount, will have the effect of conciliating the minds of the Irish, and of attaching them to the people of England.[8]

Consequently estate management policies often embraced a tenant welfare component during the mid-nineteenth century. Patrick J. Duffy explained how land agents up to the 1850s often acted as 'welfare officers' for the tenantry.[9] In relation to the Shirley estate, Duffy argued that the 'hundreds of petitions [received from tenants] in the 1840s point to the important role played by the estate in providing a minimal amount of social welfare, at a time when central and local authorities made little contribution in this area'.[10] In turn, many tenants expected the landlord to provide for all their needs and wants.

To date several studies have focused on landlord assistance during periods of extreme distress such as those by Christine Kinealy, David Fitzpatrick, Patrick J. Duffy and Gerard Moran, whose work sheds much light on landlord involvement in

---

4 *First report from his majesty's commissioners for inquiring into the condition of the poorer classes in Ireland, with appendix (A) and supplement*, HC 1835 (369), appendix b, p. 231.   **5** Linda A. Pollock, 'The practice of kindness in early modern elite society', *Past & Present*, 211: 1 (May, 2011), p. 124.   **6** William Greig, *General report on the Gosford estates in County Armagh, 1821* (Belfast, 1976), p. 167.   **7** Jessica Gerard, 'Lady bountiful: women of the landed classes and rural philanthropy', *Victorian Studies*, 30:2 (1987), pp 183–4.   **8** Letter from the 2nd Earl of Leitrim to Austin Cooper (head agent), 7 July 1822 (NLI, MS 36,064/12)   **9** Patrick J. Duffy, '"Disencumbering our crowded placed": theory and practice of estate emigration schemes in mid-nineteenth century Ireland' in Patrick J. Duffy (ed.), *To and from Ireland: planned migration schemes c. 1600–2000* (Dublin, 2004), p. 86.   **10** Patrick J. Duffy, 'Assisted emigration from the Shirley estate 1843–54', *Clogher Record*, 14:2 (1992), p. 15.

emigration schemes.[11] However, landed provision of assistance during more relatively stable economic periods to a petitioning tenantry requires a more in-depth analysis to ascertain the following; in particular, estate motives and aims in granting pecuniary assistance to tenants; the content and style of tenant petitions; the decision-making process adopted by landlords and agents in determining which tenants were 'deserving'; and finally, what factors influenced the demise of this almost symbiotic and customary relationship between landlord and tenant. The sociologist Eric R. Wolf questioned whether peasants were attached to traditional notions of order or whether they enjoyed 'tactical power' or 'leverage', which emerged from external social processes, allowing them to engage in collective action in their own interests.[12] Through an investigation of financial assistance provided by the landlord to tenants, this essay will analyse whether tenants exercised some agency or tactical leverage in influencing the landlord's answer to requests for pecuniary relief and emigration assistance across three decades in mid-nineteenth century Ireland. The section which addresses trends in the provision of pecuniary relief will be structured chronologically, while the subsequent section dealing with emigration will follow a thematic structure.

Estate policy and practices on several estates were analysed for this study. Estate papers from the Farnham Estate, Cavan and the Shirley Estate, Monaghan provided the richest sources. The remainder of source material for the study was derived from the Leitrim papers, the Westport papers and the Drapers' Company papers.

PECUNIARY ASSISTANCE

In an increasingly modernizing and centralizing world, confusion seemed to exist among the tenantry in relation to who exactly was responsible for their physical and economic welfare (if not themselves). Struggling tenants frequently petitioned the landlord for pecuniary assistance. Some landlords acquiesced to such requests,

---

11 Christine Kinealy and Tomás O'Riordan, 'Private responses to the Great Famine: documents' in Donnchadh Ó Corráin and Tomás O'Riordan (eds), *Ireland, 1815–70: emancipation, famine and religion* (Dublin, 2011), pp 95–128; David Fitzpatrick, *Irish emigration, 1801–1921* (Dublin, 1990); Duffy, 'Assisted emigration', pp 8, 10; see also Patrick J. Duffy, 'Emigrants and the estate office in the mid-nineteenth century: a compassionate relationship?' in Margaret E., Crawford (ed.), *The hungry stream: essays on emigration and famine* (Belfast, 1997), pp 71–86; Gerard P. Moran, *Sir Robert Gore Booth and his landed estate in County Sligo, 1814–76: land, famine, emigration and politics* (Dublin, 2006); see also Gerard P. Moran, *Sending out Ireland's poor: assisted emigration to North America in the nineteenth century* (Dublin, 2004); Duffy, *To and from Ireland: planned migration schemes*. **12** Samuel Clark and James S. Donnelly, Jr (eds), *Irish peasants: violence & political unrest, 1780–1914* (Madison, 1986), p. 14; see also Eric R. Wolf, 'On peasant rebellions', in Shanin Teodor (ed.), *Peasants and peasant societies: selected readings* (London, 1987), pp 367–74; Eric R. Wolf, *Peasant wars of the twentieth century* (London, 1973); T.M. Devine, *Clanship to crofters' war: the social transformation of the Scottish Highlands* (Manchester, 1994).

although some agents did not feel that the solution to the eradication of poverty among the tenants was in giving money to the poor, believing they would 'only squander it upon tobacco and such like'.[13] Petitions from tenants could be made in person or come in the form of a written request. Many of the Farnham tenants submitted their requests to the landlord at a biweekly meeting held on the estate for estate management purposes. These applications were subsequently entered into a ledger. Applications made by post to Lord Farnham were not acceptable as Phill Reynolds discovered in 1850.[14] The Shirley estate officials received written supplications. Informal face-to-face requests for assistance were not always welcomed by members of the landed family. The wife of Colonel Clements debated the most expedient method to 'get rid' of such uninvited guests. Believing that the simple dispensing of money to paupers would set an undesirable precedent, she instead appeared to favour humouring the crowd by 'promising to remember their wants, and shaking hands all round, the[y] gradually went home through the day'.[15]

PECUNIARY ASSISTANCE AND THE POOR LAW: THE RELATIONSHIP BETWEEN ESTATE AND STATE, 1830–9

Prior to the introduction of *An Act for the more effectual relief of the destitute poor in Ireland* or the Irish Poor Law in 1838, the government appeared content to let landed proprietors maintain primary responsibility for the welfare of their tenantry. Oftentimes landlords themselves recognized this fact. In 1837 William Sharman Crawford (1780–1861), radical politician and agrarian reformer, revealed how even the religious were dependent on landed assistance:

> I regret that it should be necessary for you to make solicitation to the landed proprietors for assistance in relieving the poor of your parish. Why is it necessary? Because you have no legal power of assessment founded on just principles as respects landlord and tenant. And why have you not that legal power? Because the nation does not energetically call for it.[16]

However, in some quarters a collaborative effort between government and landlord attempted to tackle the matter of poverty in Ireland. During the early 1830s, Edward Smith-Stanley, 14th earl of Derby, was in communication with the marquess of Sligo

---

13 'Causes of complaint stated, and certain alterations suggested in reference to the management of the Shirley Estate', Trench, 11 July 1843 (PRONI, Shirley papers, D3531/S/55). **14** Summaries of applications (NLI, Farnham papers, MS 3,118). **15** A.P.W. Malcomson, *Virtues of a wicked earl: The life and legend of William Sydney Clements, 3rd earl of Leitrim, 1806–78* (Dublin, 2008), pp 347–48. **16** William Sharman Crawford, Crawfordsburn to Whyte and Revd J[effry] Lefroy, 8 July 1837 (PRONI, Whyte papers, D2918/8/82).

regarding the relief of the poor.[17] The prevalence and seriousness of the problem of poverty in Ireland resulted in a specially appointed commission to investigate the matter. Described by Niall Ó Ciosáin as 'the most substantial and comprehensive examination undertaken of pre-Famine society', *The royal commission on the condition of the poorer classes in Ireland* (1833–6) – usually referred to as the Poor Inquiry – highlighted the 'great poverty' and 'wretched and miserable' condition of the poor in Monaghan and Cavan.[18] The 1841 census subsequently provided a unique insight into the problem of poverty through surveyor, administrator, and under-secretary for Ireland, Thomas Larcom's (1801–79) production of 'a social survey, not bare enumeration'.[19]

Requests made for assistance on the Farnham estate in the early part of the decade were generally granted. In 1834 single payments were given, ranging from 5s. to Joseph Briggs and £5 to Widow Martin, while a weekly payment of 1d. was to be made to Widow Reilly for an unspecified period of time. However, by the mid-1830s a reluctance to dispense money gratuitously was becoming more evident on the Farnham estate. Tenants who had previously received assistance such as Philip Sheridan and Margaret Coony [sic] (who was informed that she had obtained £5 in 1832) were told no more money would be forthcoming. Even widows, who previously were favoured for assistance, by 1835, were also refused assistance. Yet in certain instances money continued to be given to the needy – even to those who had 'no claim'. Whether or not to grant assistance did not appear dependent on the whim or the mood of the landlord on the day the request was submitted. For example on 6 April 1835 Widow Stephens received assistance, while Jane Cosgrave was declined. Such an occurrence may indicate that the previous behaviour of the tenant was taken into account by the landlord during the decision-making process. In the following year, tighter control of the system continued with the landlord clearly stating that he would not grant assistance if family members were employed. As Catherine Wilson's husband was in employment, the landlord refused to hand out any charity. In reply to requests for assistance in 1837 'no' appeared to be Lord Farnham's favourite answer: out of seven requests for relief only three petitioners received money.[20] The Leitrim estate took a similar stance in the same year. Lord Leitrim's clarification on the matter is telling; 'When I say that I am feeding them, I do not express myself quite accurately, for I do not give them food gratuitously, but I give them what is better both for them and for me – I give them work, for which I pay them to enable them to

17 Letter from Howe Peter, 2nd marquess of Sligo, Westport to E.G. Stanley, Dublin Castle, 2 Jan. 1831 (TCD, Special collections; MS 6403); Letter from E.G. Stanley, Dublin Castle to Howe Peter, 2nd marquess of Sligo, 7 Jan. 1831 (TCD, Special Collections; MS 6403) **18** Niall Ó Ciosáin, 'The poor inquiry and Irish society – a consensus theory of truth', *Transactions of the RHS*, 20 (2010), p. 127; *First report from his majesty's commissioners … poorer classes in Ireland*, 1835, p. 260; 254. **19** *Report of the commissioners appointed to take the census of Ireland for the year 1841*, HC 1843; E. Margaret Crawford, *Counting the people: a guide to the censuses of Ireland, 1813–1911* (Dublin, 2002), p. 20. **20** Seven requests for assistance and all met with the answer 'no', 1837. All references from the 'Summaries of Applications', 1837.

buy food'.[21] Tenants, therefore, had to prove themselves deserving or worthy before assistance was given.

Developments on estates reflected deliberations at government level in relation to the welfare of paupers. Following the rejection of the Whately Commission's report (which 'offered assistance to Irish landlords, chiefly through aiding the removal of their "surplus" estate populations, while denying any direct welfare assistance to any but the most "incapable" categories for poor'),[22] a more modest and 'simplistic solution' based on the English workhouse system was enacted in Ireland, the aforementioned Poor Law (Ireland) Act 1838, which was extended in 1843.[23] 'Irish property must support Irish poverty' was the maxim of the day.[24] In 1838 W.S. Clements called for gentry involvement on poor law boards in his paper entitled 'The present poverty of Ireland'.[25] Poor law reformer and administrator, George Nicholls (1781–1865), highlighted the important relationship between landlords, tenants and welfare claiming that 'the connexion between the inheritor and the occupier of the soil being one which must influence if not control the whole system of society'.[26] He maintained that

> It is of use also by interesting the landowners and persons of property in the welfare of their tenants and neighbours. A landowner who looks only to receiving the rents of his estate, may be regardless of the numbers in his neighbourhood who are in a state of destitution, or who follow mendicancy and are ready to commit crime; but if he is compelled to furnish means for the subsistence of persons so destitute, it then becomes his interest to see that those around him have the means of living, and are not in actual want.[27]

The poor law altered the nature of landlord-tenant relations with respect to the provision of welfare. Many landlords and agents retained a significant measure of control over entitlements to assistance through their membership of Boards of Guardians and relief committees. However, by indirectly assisting their impoverished tenantry through the payment of poor rates directly to their union Board of Guardians, landlords were deprived of the disciplinary force they had previously exercised on their tenants with respect to the granting of financial aid on a one-to-one basis. Thereafter the relationship between the estate and the state, with respect to the alleviation of poverty, assumed a new form. In 1849 the *Nation* maintained that since introduction of the poor law a landlord no longer could 'do as he pleases with his

21 Letter from Lord Leitrim, Great Cumberland Place to Lady Leitrim, Killadoon, 29 July 1836 (NLI, Leitrim papers, MSS 36,034/44). 22 Peter Gray, *The making of the Irish poor law, 1815–43* (Manchester, 2009), p. 341. 23 Virginia Crossman, *Local government in nineteenth century Ireland* (Belfast, 1994), p. 44. 24 Ibid., p. 45. 25 James Quinn, 'Clements, William Sydney', DIB (*http://dib.cambridge.org/viewReadPage.do?articleId=a1735&searchClicked=clicked &quickadvsearch=yes*) (10 Mar. 2012) 26 George Nicholls, *A history of the Irish poor law* (New York, 1967), p. 97. 27 Ibid., p. 190.

own property ... because a landlord cannot eject a host of paupers without placing part of their burden upon neighbouring properties, and thereby injuring an independent portion of the community'.[28] Therefore the law also had an important effect on the rent collection process adopted on many estates.

Lord Farnham's resolve with respect to granting assistance to needy tenants continued to harden as the decade came to a close. The succession of the evangelical 7th Baron Henry Farnham as landlord in 1838, coupled with the introduction of the poor law, may have contributed towards this more resolute stance which had been occurring on the estate since the middle of the decade. The poor law did not provide a statutory right to relief for those in destitution, therefore why should the landlord? In that year petitioners were frequently redirected to their immediate landlord for assistance.[29] Financial assistance was frequently used to encourage tenants to quit the estate, as in the case of Jas O'Connell who, after he requested relief, was informed that the late Lord Farnham had previously given him £1 to quit the estate. By the end of the decade, Lord Farnham appeared only to give assistance to those who would genuinely use it for the purpose they requested. Thomas Mill's request for the price of a coffin to bury his wife in 1839 was rejected as an earlier request for money that had been granted had not been spent appropriately.

PECUNIARY ASSISTANCE BEFORE AND DURING
THE GREAT FAMINE – THE 1840S

During the early 1840s many Farnham supplicants continued to receive a negative response from the landlord. Others were simply advised to dispose of their interest. As Oliver MacDonagh explained, a tenant's interest in his holding referred to his right to claim monies when a new tenant took over the property for the time and effort he expended on the farm while in his possession. In effect it 'implied a degree of co-possession between the lessor and the lessee'.[30] The selling of one's interest in their holding was part of the practice of tenant-right which functioned on many estates, in a variety of forms, throughout Ireland. The tenant's right to receive recompense for the time and money they invested in the upkeep of their farm did not translate into an automatic right to sell to either the highest bidder or individual of their choice. Some tenants were told they must sell their land to a neighbouring tenant.[31] Only those with a 'claim', or deemed 'worthy' were entitled to receive help from the landlord. Requests made in 1844 reveal an increasing awareness amongst tenants of the need to be perceived as deserving in order to benefit from the bounty of the estate. Such a shift is most apparent in requests for clothing. By 1844 instances are

28 'The Shirley Extermination', *Nation*, 22 Sept. 1849. **29** Summaries of applications (NLI, Farnham papers, MSS 3,117–18) **30** Oliver MacDonagh, *States of mind: a study of Anglo-Irish conflict, 1780–1980* (London, 1983), pp 45–6. **31** Summaries of applications (NLI, Farnham papers, MSS 3,117–18)

evident of tenant appeals being carefully drafted, adopting the language of the poor law, and including information on the size of their family (Philip Fitzsimons), previous acts of loyalty to the landlord – for example being a member of militia – (John Johnston), and their status, such as 'poor widow'(Alice Johnston). In 1845, requests made to Baron Farnham included appeals for assistance after properties were maliciously burned. Once again no pattern is evident as to why a landlord would approve a request or decline it. Requests for assistance, such as blankets, were also declined if it was felt family members could assist instead. Tenants on the Shirley estate also requested bed clothing during this period.

In Monaghan there is also evidence of tenants providing examples of their obedience and worthiness to the landlord in petitions. 'That your petitioner is in the greatest extremity for want of bedclothes to cover himself and his family. He had paid all rents and sold his oats in order to clear off all rents'.[32] Similarly, on the Westport estate, individuals in a dangerous state of illness who were deemed to be 'an object very worthy of relief' were given wine for medicinal purposes.[33] Unsurprisingly, requests for assistance and clothing continued during the Great Famine (1845–50). As in previous years, the estate continued to give money directly to those in need such as 5s. to Catherine Kirk, £1 to Ann Walsh and her daughter, and 2s. 6d. to Jas Murphy.[34] However, a change was beginning to occur. In 1846 when Bernard McCaul, whose wife was poorly and with five small children to support, was granted 5s., he was also advised in future to apply to the local relief committee. Others did not receive any assistance from the landlord but were told to go to the relief committee directly. Patrick Mahon was advised to apply for employment from the public works, while John Thompson was advised to go to his father for support. Tenants like Michael Briody and Patt Reilly were told to sell up in 1847. Others were simply told that they had no claim. While it is not revealed in the papers what exactly 'no claim' referred to, some of the comments made with respect to tenant requests suggests that those who complied with estate rules and displayed good behaviour were considered to have a claim. It is not unconceivable that those who belonged to the same Church as the landlord may have received more leniency than their Roman counterparts, although there is no clear evidence to support this. When John Hague requested assistance the landlord replied that the tenant and his family had no claim. He continued 'I have already found them extremely troublesome. He must apply to the Butlers Bridge relief committee', and in relation to another tenant simply stated 'he has nothing to expect from me'.[35]

---

32 Petition of James Callen, Box upper to William Steuart Trench Esq., 27 Feb. 1845 (PRONI, Shirley papers, D3531/P/1).   **33** Note from Mr Burke to G. Hildebrand, Monday, 3 Aug. 1842 (NLI, Westport papers, MS 41,032/6); a bottle of Claret at Westport house for the young nun at the Convent of Mercy (NLI, Westport papers, MS 41,032/5); Letter to 'My dear George' (presumably Clendining), sender's name illegible, 13 Oct. 1842; Note from Thomas Hamilton Burke to Hildebrand, 20 Dec. 1842 (NLI, Westport, MS 41,032/5). **34** Summaries of applications (NLI, Farnham papers, MS 3,117–3,118)   **35** Ibid.

Why did tenants go to the landlord for assistance rather than go directly to state sponsored resources such as relief committees and the local workhouse? This circumvention of the state system may either point towards a lack of appreciation on the tenants' part of their entitlements under the poor law system, or, alternatively, may reveal a continued reliance on semi-feudalistic patterns and the patriarchal bond between landlord and tenant. The landlord may also have been among several others who were approached for help or simply proved the most convenient and local port of call. Alternatively, the stigma which many attached to entry to the workhouse, coupled with the 'Gregory clause' which stated in the Poor Law Act of 1847 that anyone holding at least a quarter of an acre was exempt from receiving relief, may have deterred many from seeking help from the state. Culturally, an expectation seemed to prevail in certain quarters that the onus for relief rested with the landlord. In 'A new song on the rotten potatoes' (1847), landlords were advised to take care of their tenants, while tenants were encouraged to turn to their landlords 'and see what they'll do'. Not only were landlords expected to shoulder the burden by the tenants, but they were also to be forced to do so if unwilling through the withholding of corn or meal for the payment of rent. A resolute stance was encouraged in the face of landlord intransigence: 'If then to your wishes they will not comply,/Then tell them at once that you'd rather die, ... Sure they can't tyrannize or attempt to prevail/To make you to part with either corn or meal'.[36] Consequently, tenants were in position to exert a measure of tactical leverage with respect to this demand from their landlords.

NON-CHARITABLE REQUESTS DURING THE 1850S

Requests for assistance continued to be received on estates during the 1850s. However, it was during this decade that a noticeable change in the type of requests for assistance is in evidence; requests no longer were simply related to extreme poverty. In 1850 the Farnham tenants began to ask the landlord for assistance to purchase stock. When John Wilton submitted this request, the surprised landlord replied that it was 'a very extraordinary application. I have no intention of complying with it'.[37] However, estate policy seems to have changed over the subsequent years with several tenants receiving financial aid for the purchase of stock over the remainder of the decade. In 1858 Mr McPartlan received the price of an ass, while two years later Patt Smith obtained £1 10s. towards the purchase of a pony. Financial assistance was also forthcoming to James Conaughty who received 10s. to buy seed potatoes and Ann Hogg who was granted £2 towards her daughter's marriage. In respect to the latter, although not clarified, presumably the money was requested to

---

36 Georges-Denis Zimmerman, 'A new song on the rotten potatoes' (1847), *Songs of Irish rebellion: political street ballads and rebel songs, 1780–1900* (Dublin, 1967), pp 237–8. **37** Summaries of applications (NLI, Farnham papers, MS 3,118).

go towards a dowry and not simply the cost of the wedding itself. One tenant, William Mee, sought money to buy a cot and was allowed one pound in his rent for it.[38] Thus, a variety of requests for monetary assistance continued to bombard the landlord. It is unclear whether these were loans that had to be repaid as no record of repayment exists – such as the Shirley loan book (1827–45) for an earlier period. The emergence of such non-typical requests may point towards either desperation or a new found confidence on the part of the tenant. Regardless of the motivations for such unorthodox requests, the fact that the landlord granted assistance in such instances may suggest an altered remit for estate assistance during the relatively more prosperous decade of the 1850s.

Throughout the 1830s, 1840s and the 1850s, landlords were frequently approached by their tenants for financial assistance for a variety of purposes. The introduction of the poor law in 1838 did not automatically alter this traditional landlord role. The catastrophe of the famine which occurred in the country only a few years after the introduction of the new law and before a comprehensive understanding of the latter's functions and operation was appreciated, resulted in confusion at a local level with regards to whose responsibility it was to provide direct assistance to the many starving and poverty stricken tenantry. During the 1850s when relative stability returned, tenants continued to seek financial assistance from their landlord in order to improve their circumstances. The provision of money to their tenantry over these economically pivotal decades resulted in some landlords having simply to sell up their estates, a process made somewhat easier through the introduction of the Encumbered Estates Acts of 1848 and 1849. Some landlords attempted to retain their properties and reduce costs in the long term by actively reducing the number of tenants on their estates through the process of assisted emigration.

EMIGRATION

During the early nineteenth century the population of Ireland rose exponentially. Tallies in the 1821 census suggested a total of 6.8 million inhabitants, a figure which dramatically climbed over the subsequent twenty years to a staggering 8.5 million.[39] Many estates experienced the negative effects of overpopulation, such as extreme poverty and competition for land, and the alleviation of the problem became a pressing concern for landlords and agents alike. At this time, as Patrick Duffy noted, 'the idea of overpopulation as an "encumbrance" on society, restricting improvements in moral and social order and civilization, was fashionable in colonial discourse'.[40] Overcrowding became synonymous with disorder. Therefore, it was imperative to remove surplus peoples from the estate to achieve optimal conditions for order. Although a number of individuals, such as the Revd Mr Duffy in

38 Ibid. **39** Cormac Ó Gráda, *Ireland: a new economic history, 1780–1939* (Oxford, 1995), p. 6. **40** Duffy, 'Disencumbering', p. 80.

Monaghan, did not believe emigration would sufficiently solve the problem of competition for labour and small holdings, for some landlords emigration was perceived the only solution.[41]

The 1841 census of Ireland was the first census of the country to provide information on emigration, with the 1851 census following suit.[42] Thereafter, emigration records could be found in the *Agricultural Statistics* commencing in December 1856.[43] Although in theory perhaps a relatively simple solution, in practice emigration from estates proved more problematic for all parties involved. The financing of emigration schemes proved a contentious matter between the state and the estate. Prior to the Famine, the Shirley agent expected the government to assist with the emigration of cottiers from the estate.[44] Yet, government intervention in the area was minimal, with an 1847 report revealing that a mere 306 individuals received emigration assistance from a total of sixteen unions between 1844 and 1846.[45] During this period at least 180 landlords and philanthropists offered some form of assistance to more than 80,000 emigrants.[46] Landlord assistance towards emigration did not simply cover the cost of the ship journey. Duffy listed basic passage money, landing money, clothing, luggage, and arrears write-offs as part of the estate's assistance towards would-be emigrants.[47] Other costs for the landlord could include 3rd class rail fares for travel to ports and money for provisions for the voyage.[48] In 1849 the Shirley agent Morant spent £9 9s. on shoes for tenants emigrating from the estate. Between 1841 and 1851 the population of the Shirley estate fell by forty-four per cent – from 18,600 to 10,200, with emigration accounting for 15–18 per cent of this number.[49]

Irish society was well versed in the notion of moving for work or to provide a better quality of life for those who remained at home. Many unmarried, young males migrated for temporary work – either to Dublin or Meath during harvest season, or England or Scotland during the summer season.[50] Permanent upheaval however was an entirely different prospect and one which required significant psychological and emotional adjustment if any real attempts were to be made to improve quality of life. Although contemporary sources often emphasized the disdain of the Irish towards emigration, it is clear from the number of petitions received at some estate offices

41 *Third report of the commissioners for inquiring into the condition of the poorer classes in Ireland* [43], HC 1836, p. 17. **42** *Report of the commissioners appointed to take the census of Ireland for the year 1841,* HC 1843 [504], xxiv. **43** *Agricultural statistics, Ireland. Tables showing the estimated average produce for the year 1856; also the diversity of weights used in buying and selling corn, potatoes and flax in Ireland; and the emigration from Irish ports, from 1st Jan. to 31st Dec. 1856,* HC 1857, session 2 (2245) **44** Ibid., p. 90. **45** *Emigration (Ireland). Summary of a return of the number of persons who have emigrated at the expense of the different poor law unions in Ireland, in the years 1844, 1845 and 1846,* 1847 (255) **46** Fitzpatrick, *Irish emigration,* p. 19. **47** Duffy, 'Disencumbering', p. 91. **48** Summaries of applications, Patrick Dempsey, 1836 (NLI, Farnham papers, MSS 3,117–18); 'Australian Emigration' 10 Aug. 1849, railway fares from Dundalk to Drogheda (PRONI, Shirley papers, D3531/P/1). **49** *Third report of the commissioners ... poorer classes in Ireland,* 1836, p. 102. **50** *First report from his majesty's commissioners ... poorer classes in Ireland,* 1835, p. 314.

that many tenants wished – even pleaded – with the landlord to go.[51] On one occasion eight men petitioned the Shirley agent on behalf of another tenant who wished to be entered on the emigrants' sheet. Patrick Garvey, a tenant on the Shirley estate, informed the Devon Commission that many of his neighbours were offering to emigrate, but unless Trench the agent assisted them, they would be unable to go.[52] Trench also informed the same commission that in consequence of the landlord offering to pay most of the passage money, a large number of tenants proved agreeable to emigration.[53] The Shirley Manorial Court book is peppered with requests for assistance to America, most notably in the year 1849.[54]

Although evidently many tenants actively begged for assistance, others attempted to bargain with the estate in order to receive financial aid. Ruth-Ann M. Harris suggested that many negotiated for emigration assistance depending on their observation of changing estate polices.[55] Duffy commented that many of the Shirley tenants' petitions demonstrated a shrewd awareness of their bargaining power with respect to the landlord's desire to obtain peaceful possession of holdings.[56] Trench and the landowning class, on the other hand, frequently referred to a degree of 'native cunning' in the tenants' behaviour with respect to negotiations with estate authorities. This canniness identified by the agent reveals the powerful – even innate – negotiating skills some of the tenants possessed in their bargaining with their lord. Trench and Kincaid were convinced that many of their pauper tenants had hidden resources, with Trench suggesting that some of them who were newly clothed kept their 'rags' for begging in America.[57] At the same time a destitute tenant had little choice but to accept the landlord's offer of emigration.[58] Through consideration of estate-driven and tenant-driven emigration from a small sample of mid-nineteenth-century Irish landed estates, this section of the essay will examine whether tenants exercised any measure of tactical leverage in the decision-making process and consider to what extent did 'philanthropy' feature as part of an estate's emigration policy.

ESTATE MANAGEMENT AND ESTATE-DRIVEN EMIGRATION

Duffy described estate-driven emigration as being fundamentally antagonistic to the tenantry, even to those who were relatively healthy, young, or behind in rent

---

51 Margaret Dixon McDougall, *The letters of Norah on her tour through Ireland* (1882), p. 16; 20; Alexander Innes Shand, *Letters from the west of Ireland 1884* (Edinburgh, 1885), p. 98.   **52** *Reports and minutes of evidence … in respect to the occupation of land in Ireland*, p. 925.   **53** Ibid., p. 934.   **54** Manorial Court Book (D3531/M/6/1).   **55** Ruth-Ann M. Harris, 'Negotiating patriarchy: Irish women and the landlord' in Marilyn Cohen and Nancy J. Curtin (eds), *Reclaiming gender: transgressive identities in modern Ireland* (London, 1999), p. 214.   **56** Duffy, 'Disencumbering', p. 95.   **57** Ibid., p. 103.   **58** R. Dudley Edwards and T. Desmond Williams (eds), *The Great Famine: studies in Irish history, 1845–52* (Dublin, 1956), p. 336.

payments. Many, understandably, were apprehensive about the immense distances which would separate them from their loved ones (such as Australia) and about the limited information which was available about life in foreign lands.[59] Estate-driven emigration functioned as a part of estate management policy and was often motivated by a desire to check the 'surplus' population, while simultaneously facilitating a re-organization of estate lands through consolidation.[60] Lord Dufferin spoke of a landlord 'weeding his property of men whose want of energy, or skill, or capital renders them incapable of doing their duty by their farms' and his right to 'replace them by more suitable tenants'.[61] Trench's 1852 comment in relation to emigration from the Bath estate in Monaghan supported this assertion:

> The great and marked differences between the emigration off this estate and that which is purely voluntary, is that in our case none but paupers are going. We have not lost one single man I should wish to keep ... Other estates where no assistance is given (and where emigration has at all set in) retain their paupers, whilst all the respectable tenants are moving off.[62]

During the 1860s, the 3rd Earl of Leitrim decided to tackle the Ribbon problem on his estate by sending some of its most active adherents to America.[63] However, emigration was not simply used to rid estates of undesirable tenants. Good behaviour in the eyes of the estate authorities also increased the chances of a tenant receiving the requested assistance.[64] Characters and recommendations were frequently sought by emigrating tenants. Therefore, it was important for tenants to be perceived in a positive light by their landlords in order to obtain a positive reference.[65] Despite their power in this regard, landlords could not always control who left their estates. Harriet Martineau observed how 'landlords disliked autumnal emigration as respectable farmers leave then paying out of cash they received for their crops', while spring emigration was disliked by priests as it attracted the poorest tenants who were 'the priest's peculiar people'.[66]

Tenants who frequently fell into the category of 'surplus' to the estate's requirements were uneconomic tenants such as cottiers and young females, undesirable tenants, and those who were insolvent.[67] With respect to the latter, emigration proved a much coveted means of escape from the vicious cycle of poverty and

59 Duffy, 'Disencumbering', pp 96–7. **60** Ibid., pp 89–99. **61** Isaac Butt, *The Irish people and the Irish land: a letter to Lord Lifford, with comments on the publications of Lord Dufferin and Lord Rosse* (Dublin, 1867), p. 213. **62** Duffy, 'Disencumbering', p. 90. **63** Malcomson, *Virtues of a wicked earl*, p. 206. **64** Letter to Morant, Shirley House, Carrickmacross from Margaret Cassidy for emigration aid £2 10s., 18 Apr.1846 (PRONI, Shirley papers, D3531/P/1). **65** Summaries of applications (NLI, Farnham papers, MSS 3,117–18). **66** Harriet Martineau, *Letters from Ireland* (London, 1852), p. 206. **67** Duffy, 'Disencumbering', p. 89; Summaries of applications (NLI., Farnham papers, MSS 3,117–18); Letter to George Morant Esq., Lough Fea from Davis London, 27 June 1853 (PRONI, Shirley papers, D3531/C/3/8).

indebtedness. Desperate tenants often relied entirely on the goodwill of their land-lord for assistance during their time of need. While emigration costs usually fell on the landlord, it still proved a more attractive alternative to many than supporting the pauper through the poor law rate. On the Farnham estate emigration assistance was only forthcoming to tenants who 'quit the land', gave up 'entire possession', or gave up possession quietly.[68] Emigration was also used to prevent sub-division of estates.[69] Similar to some of the responses tenants received in relation to their requests for relief, some tenants were told to sell their land to a person approved of by the land-lord before any assistance for emigration was dispensed. Martin W. Dowling stated how tenant-right helped organize emigration from estates. By the start of the nine-teenth century it was widely recognized by landlords and agents 'that tenant-right exchanges were fuelling the much-desired emigration of smallholders' and that a real connection existed between emigration, indebtedness, and the sale of tenant-right.[70] Consequently, the payment of a tenant's emigration costs was not simply a gesture of goodwill on the landlord's part. The practice of tenant-right on a range of Irish estates facilitated the process. The relationship between emigration and tenant-right sales afforded landlords and agents an easy method to rid the estate of undesirable tenants.[71] On the Shirley estate, the agent felt that with help from the estate, most emigrants could get 'something for their interest or goodwill'. He further maintained that the 'whole expense of exporting those who are willing, but unable to emigrate' fell on the landlord.[72] Although the Drapers' agent firmly believed that only emigra-tion could effectively dismantle rundale communities, in effect this could only be carried out through supplementation of emigration costs due to the often inadequate amount achieved from tenant-right sales.[73]

TENANT TACTICAL LEVERAGE AND TENANT-DRIVEN EMIGRATION

According to Duffy, tenant-driven emigration involved tenants desiring to emigrate as a result of deteriorating conditions and repressive estate regulations.[74] While tenants often received either a prompt acceptance or rejection to their appeal for emigration assistance, sometimes tenants displayed a limited measure of tactical leverage. Tenants could refuse to emigrate although previously entered on the emigration list. In 1849 twenty-eight out of a total of 335 Shirley tenants refused to

68 John Brownlee (1832); Patrick Fitzpatrick (1835); Bridget Farrelly (1836), Fitzpatrick family (1848) Summaries of applications (NLI, Farnham papers, MSS 3,117–118). **69** Letter to William S. Trench Esq. from Peter Duffy, Ardragh, Mar. 1845 (PRONI, Shirley papers, D3531/P/1). **70** Martin W. Dowling, *Tenant right and agrarian society in Ulster, 1600–1870* (Dublin, 1999), p. 130. **71** Ibid., p. 132. **72** 'Causes of complaint stated, and certain alterations suggested in reference to the management of the Shirley estate', Trench, 11 July 1843 (PRONI, Shirley papers, D3531/S/55). **73** The policy of subsidization ceased in 1854, since the 'times have considerably changed'. Dowling, *Tenant right*, pp 131–2, 212. **74** Duffy, 'Disencumbering', pp 96–7.

emigrate when the time to depart arrived.[75] It is not stated in the records how such tenants were subsequently treated by estate officials, although some newspaper reports later that year highlighted the 'extermination' that had just occurred on the Shirley estate where approximately 1,000 persons had been evicted from their holding.[76] Therefore, tenants may have been confronted with a basic choice in certain instances – emigration or eviction.

Although ultimately the power rested with landlord and agent when deciding who should receive assistance to emigrate, landlord replies proved more propitious when tenants met certain conditions. On the Farnham estate some factors existed which impeded tenant success. Tenants who previously had received financial help from the landlord were sometimes refused when they requested money to emigrate. Ann Kells' request to send her daughter to America was not granted with the comment that 'her mother received help from Lady Farnham'.[77] Tenants deemed to have 'no claim' were also bypassed. As noted earlier having a claim may have been related to compliance with estate rules or good behaviour. Tenants who sought aid to travel to America were also less fortuitous. During the mid-1840s the 7th Baron Farnham became adamant that he would not pay the passage of any more tenants from his estate to travel to America. It is not clear from the records why he adopted this policy. Although the landlord appeared firm with respect to America, his stance did not stem the amount of requests for assistance.[78] This highlights the importance of shared knowledge among the tenants. Although the landlord appeared to adopt an intransigent position on the matter, allowances still continued to be received by a few lucky tenants. In 1846, for example, Lord and Lady Farnham granted £10 to Widow Adams to travel to America. In the subsequent decade Farnham continued to state his objection to financing emigration. In contrast, he did seem willing to finance passages to other destinations such as John Kirke's request to go to Scotland in 1846 for which he received £1 from the landlord. In the following year he gave the same amount of money to finance the emigration of a family to Jersey, and in 1853 provided assistance to A. Patterson to emigrate to Australia. Even if the disposition or the inclination of the agent or landlord on the day the request was submitted is taken into account, it remains difficult to account for instances in which one tenant received help and others did not. Such discrepancies may suggest that decisions were not arbitrary or economically based, but rather were guided by tenant character or perhaps even gender.

Tenants who were refused assistance could be offered a variety of explanations from the landlord. In 1847 Mr Merryman was advised that the landlord was

75 Emigration list for Australia, 16 May 1849. Original list of persons who applied to be sent to Australia from the Shirley estate 1849 (PRONI, Shirley papers, D3531/P/1). **76** 'The Shirley Extermination', *Nation*, 22 Sept. 1849; 'Evictions in Ulster', *Nation*, 15 Sept. 1849. **77** Summaries of applications (NLI, Farnham papers, MSS 3,117–118). **78** Ibid. 1845 Trainer; 1846 Ann Mulligan, George Folles, Anne Reilly and John Armstrong; 1847 John Comisky; 1849 Margaret Porter and Widow Reilly; 1851 Matilda Hart; 1855 John Montgomery; 1857 Mr Kemp.

unwilling to give any more help. In 1850 Henry Magill's request was met with a curt 'certainly not', while in 1857 Widow Tweedy's application was rejected as 'the application did not come in the usual way'.[79] Some tenants revealed an awareness of estate policy with respect to the financing of tenant emigration and attempted to increase their tactical leverage by informing the landlord that they were willing to give up possession if they, in turn, received assistance to emigrate.[80] What may be termed 'pseudo leverage' also existed, whereby tenants would attempt to negotiate with the landlord for assistance when in actual fact they had nothing to bargain with. In 1847 Widow Griffith offered to give up her land in return for emigration assistance. It later transpired that she had already been evicted.[81] Impoverished tenants in reality had little to bargain with. The most they could hope to offer their landlord in return for financial assistance was a prayer. In return for granting £2 5s. for emigration costs a landlord could receive a prayer gratis.[82] It remains unclear whether tenants shared their approaches for petitioning the landlord with each other and whether a generic formula existed. It would be interesting to learn how the traditionally evangelical Farnham landlord received the gift of a Romanish prayer. The Marquess of Sligo appeared to dislike such devotional effusiveness and their 'appeals to the almighty on all trifling occasions'.[83] Once they had emigrated, some tenants wrote to their landlords to thank them for the financial assistance they provided and for organizing the travel itinerary. In 1887 Mr Richard Powell, Lord Sligo's agent, commented on how he had kept up correspondence with many of his tenants who had emigrated to America.[84] Shirley emphasized the positive reports he received from his tenants who had emigrated: 'Of those who emigrated to Canada, Australia, and the United States, generally good accounts were afterwards received'.[85] Emigration from the estate to Britain is not referenced on this occasion. However, this source must be approached with caution due to a possible propagandist motive behind the author's intentions. Tenants may have communicated with their previous landlord due to a genuine feeling of gratitude or to ensure that family members left behind were to remain in favour with the landlord. Consequently it would appear that estate-driven emigration could be utilized to punish those who failed to comply with estate rules, reward tenants of 'good' character, and rid estates of uneconomic or surplus individuals. In effect it served a variety of purposes, all aimed at increasing order on estates. Tenant-driven emigration depended on whether the landed authorities deemed the

79 Ibid.   **80** Duffy, 'Assisted emigration', p. 45.   **81** Ibid.   **82** Shirley Estate Emigration Ticket, no. 16, for Patt Loughran signed by Mr G. Smith to Mr Thomas Elliott, 11 Waterloo Road, Liverpool, 26 Apr. 1844 (PRONI, Shirley papers, D3531/P/1); Duffy, 'Assisted emigration', p. 45; Letter from Thomas Mc Connon to George Morant Esq., Thursday Mar. 27 (PRONI, Shirley papers, D3531/M/6/1).   **83** Letter to Mrs Roycroft, Attyreece, Westport, from the 3rd Marquess of Sligo, Westport, 15 July 1872 (NLI, Westport, MS 40,997/2).   **84** George Pellew, *In castle and cabin; or, talks in Ireland in 1887* (New York; London, 1888), p. 192.   **85** *On 'tenant right' or 'good will' within the barony of Farney and County of Monaghan in Ireland* (London, 1874), p. 18, 26 June 1874 (Warwickshire County Record Office, Shirley papers, CR464/165 (2)).

petitioner deserving of the landlord's favour. Compliance with the landlord's wishes and 'good' behaviour were thus rewarded with 'philanthropic' gestures. Less than exemplary tenants were left to turn elsewhere in their search for assistance. The only real tactical leverage that a tenant could exert was perhaps by providing evidence that they were deserving. Whether evidence or displays of deference and compliance with estate rules were genuine or fabricated will remain unknown.

CONCLUSION

The 1838 address from the Shirley tenantry to their benevolent landlord mentioned at the beginning of the essay continued as follows; 'we are well convinced of the advantages of attending to your kind and excellent suggestions altho' [sic] to our shame and loss we have been as yet but too negligent in putting some of them into practice, but we hope still to profit by them'.[86] This statement reveals a tenantry conscious of their obligations in the interdependent landlord-tenant relationship. The tenants stressed their positive intentions regarding the fulfilment of the landlord's wishes, though it would appear some of the tenantry may have been a long way off from the landlord's desired aim. It was imperative to keep the landlord in good favour for future requests. A blend of deference and respect for social tradition and tenant tactical power existed on Irish landed estates at this time and set the framework and parameters for landlord-tenant interactions. Some astute tenants may have displayed a modicum of leverage through performing and acting as deferential and compliant tenants in order to have their needs met. Tenants were aware of the politics of estate philanthropy and that they could benefit from its benevolence once a docile demeanour was adopted. The importance of religion in nineteenth-century Ireland and its influence on estate management policies should also be noted. Both the Maxwell and the Shirley families were members of the Church of Ireland, employed moral agents, and presided over a tenantry the majority of whom were members of the Roman Catholic faith. The 7th Baron Farnham, in particular, was a well-known evangelicalist. However, the extent to which religion actively influenced the decision making process of landlords with respect to tenant petitions is difficult to determine. It is important to reiterate that altruistic motives undoubtedly were present for some individuals who fulfilled such obligations as part of an estate management policy. As Duffy noted, the private correspondence of Trench suggests a degree of philanthropy in his approach to the emigration schemes.[87]

However, 1838 also saw the introduction of the poor law to Ireland, a development which significantly altered traditional landlord-tenant relations with respect to tenant welfare. Landlords lost the leverage they held over the tenantry – dispensing favours to favourites, punishing recalcitrants, and ultimately exercising a significant

---

86 'To Evelyn P. Shirley Esq.' (PRONI, Shirley papers, D3531/P/2). **87** Duffy, 'Disencumbering', p. 97.

amount of non-contractual power over their tenatry. However, estate coffers, specifically the annual payment of the poor rate, continued to provide much of the financial assistance demanded for the relief of the tenantry.

Ultimately, estate philanthropic gestures veiled a rather complex process of negotiation and consent in the daily lives of both landlord and tenant. However, increasing intervention from the state as the nineteenth century progressed gradually eroded this interdependent relationship, a development that ultimately led to the disintegration of landlord power and the demise of the landed estate.

'Guinness is good for you': experiments in workers' housing and public amenities by the Guinness Brewery and Guinness/Iveagh Trust, 1872–1915

LINDA KING

We have the greatest pleasure in announcing this morning the most splendid act of private munificence that has been contemplated and carried out in our time by any Englishman. SIR EDWARD CECIL GUINNESS GUINNESS, the head of the great Irish firm of brewers ... has placed in the hands of three trustees, LORD ROWTON, MR. RICHIE and MR. PLUNKETT, the sum of a quarter of a million sterling to be held by them in trust for the 'erection of dwellings for the labouring poor'.[1]

The story of how Edward Cecil Guinness Guinness (1847–1927) established the Guinness Trust, London and Dublin Funds in 1890 has been frequently acknowledged as one of the most generous philanthropic donations in British and Irish history. Providing housing and ancillary facilities for the working poor of both cities regardless of employer, the Dublin Fund was renamed the Iveagh Trust in 1903 and centred its activities in the Liberties area of the city.[2] In Dublin the work of the Trust commenced with the building of two blocks of dwellings at Thomas Court (1892), adjacent to the Guinness Brewery on James' Gate, and containing 118 flats. Three larger blocks of 336 flats followed at Kevin Street (1894–1901), a short distance south of St Patrick's Cathedral. The Guinness/Iveagh Trust's third scheme at Bull Alley, between Christchurch and St Patrick's Cathedrals and in the vicinity of the Guinness brewery on James' Street, was the most ambitious project undertaken by either Dublin or London Trusts. Between 1901 and 1904 it provided 250 flats in eight architecturally distinctive, five-storey, T-shaped blocks on Patrick and Bride Streets. To this were added twenty-six shops, a six-storey hostel to accommodate 508 homeless men

1 'The dwellings of the poor', *Times*, 20 Nov. 1889, emphasis original. By this time Edward Cecil Guinness was the richest man in Ireland. 2 The Liberties area was Dublin's industrialized centre and the industries established there tended to be those that could take advantage of water, the area's greatest resource. This resulted in a growth of textile manufacturing in the seventeenth and eighteenth centuries, overtaken by alcohol production in the eighteenth and nineteenth centuries. As the nineteenth century unfolded the number of alcohol manufacturers diminished due to the increasing dominance of the Guinness Brewery and its acquisition of smaller concerns.

(1905) and a community centre and children's care facility (1915). This group of buildings occupy the perimeter of a site enclosing a central courtyard with gated access that is accessible from the surrounding four streets. Adjacent to these were added a public swimming pool with twenty-seven private baths (1906) built opposite the hostel, and a public park with park-keeper's house (1903) occupying the area between the Bull Alley complex and St Patrick's Cathedral. An indoor market for local traders displaced by the complex (1906) was built some distance away on Francis Street.

In some ways the expression of such civic generosity in this particular area was not unexpected; it followed a pattern of substantial philanthropic gestures by the Guinness family dating back to the second Arthur Guinness (1768–1855) who had made several donations to the maintenance of St Patrick's Cathedral.[3] However, the establishment of the Guinness/Iveagh Trust,[4] which provided in total 680 flats and ancillary facilities in Dublin alone, was ambitious in gesture and physical scale beyond any donation the family had previously made. Unusually, the initial intention was to 'reach the very poorest of the labouring population' – as opposed to the artisan worker favoured by other housing schemes – although this aspiration was not achieved.[5] Of the initial donation of £250,000 made collectively to the Dublin and London funds, £50,000 went to Dublin supplemented by an additional *c.*£367,000. This brought the total donation close to £617,000 or almost €81 million in contemporary terms.[6]

Yet, in spite of the centrality of the Guinness Brewery and family to Irish cultural history there is little substantive research on the Guinness/Iveagh Trust schemes beyond short appraisals within architectural texts and volumes on cultural history.[7]

---

3 Arthur's son, Benjamin Lee Guinness (1798–1868), father of Edward Cecil Guinness, continued in the same spirit, financing the rebuilding of St Patrick's Cathedral in 1856 with a contribution of £150,000 and began the restoration of the adjacent Marsh's Library. Edward Cecil Guinness's brother, Arthur Edward (1840–1915, Lord Ardilaun from 1880), finished the library restoration and financed the construction of a new wing for the Coombe Lying-in Hospital (1877). Arthur Edward's most famous philanthropic gesture was the purchase of a 30-acre site at St Stephen's Green from local inhabitants which he had landscaped and handed over as a city amenity (1882). Edward Cecil Guinness donated the back garden of his Dublin city centre home, Iveagh House, to University College Dublin (1908) and it is now a public garden. **4** I collapse the Guinness Trust, Dublin Fund and the Iveagh Trust together with this descriptor to avoid confusion around the provenance of individual buildings by virtue of the organization's change of name in 1903. **5** 'The dwellings of the poor'; the city's poorest were excluded from the Trust by virtue of the fact that they would have been in casual employment and therefore not able to make the necessary advance rent payments. **6** F.H.A. Aalen, *The Iveagh Trust: the first hundred years* (Dublin, 1990), pp 27, 50. The conversion of the original donations is approximately €80,719,182: I'm very grateful to James Kavanagh, Economic Analysis and Research Division, Central Bank of Ireland, for providing this information. The additional monies for Dublin involved the clearance of slums occupying the Bull Alley site, the landscaping of St Patrick's Park and the building of the Iveagh Market and Iveagh Play Centre. **7** Short

The most significant contribution is the pioneering research of F.H.A. Aalen. He analyses the Guinness/Iveagh Trust within broader surveys of Irish housing, urban development and planning legislation and was commissioned by the Trust to write its commemorative publication in 1990.[8] This essay focuses on the Bull Alley scheme and expands contextualization of the project to consider the ideological and architectural antecedents of the Trust.[9] The ebb and flow of philanthropic discourse between London and Dublin in the late nineteenth and early twentieth centuries is of particular importance here as Dublin was, at that time, part of the British Empire. The Trust was administered from London until 1903 and at the time of its establishment Edward Cecil Guinness was largely domiciled in the English capital. In establishing the Trust he sought advice from London-based philanthropists, including his friend Lord Rowton, followed closely the pioneering projects of American banker and diplomat George Peabody (1795–1869) and his London-based Peabody Donation Fund (1862–), and employed London-based architects for the Bull Alley complex. The architectural practice comprising Nathan Solomon Joseph (1834–1909), his son Charles Sampson Joseph (1872–1948) and partner Charles James Smithem (d.1937) was one of the most prolific and experienced in the design of block dwellings and worked for a number of London's philanthropic and semi-philanthropic trusts in addition to various municipal authorities.[10] The distinct architectural treatment of the Bull Alley complex – reflecting a hybrid of popular, contemporary styles – provide an unusual typology within Irish architecture, although this is commonplace in Britain. It is argued here that the Dublin buildings are emblematic of the philanthropic discourse that permeated British society in the nineteenth century and are an imported archetype modified for local circumstances. In so doing, this essay is mindful of Aalen's comments that the history of working-class housing provision in Dublin needs to be placed in the 'wider British context' to be fully understood.[11] This essay will explore these narratives while also demonstrating how the Bull Alley buildings were the culmination of almost two decades of architectural experimentation in Dublin that began with housing

architectural references to the scheme can be found in Annette Becker et al. (eds), *20th-century architecture: Ireland* (Munich and New York, 1997), pp 92–3; Seán Rothery, *Ireland and the new architecture: 1900–40* (Dublin, 1991), pp 38–41. For historical approaches see: Jacinta Prunty, 'Improving the urban environment: public health and housing in nineteenth-century Dublin' in Joseph Brady and Anngret Simms (eds), *Dublin through space and time (c. 900–1900)* (Dublin, 2001), pp 207–11 and Jacinta Prunty, *Dublin slums, 1800–1925: a study in urban geography* (Dublin, 1998), pp 142, 176–7. **8** Aalen's *The Iveagh Trust* is a slim but densely packed volume with specific and contextual information and remains the most substantial study of the complex to date. **9** This contribution evolved from my unpublished MA dissertation 'Progressive housing: the role of two industrial families in the development of philanthropic architecture in Dublin', National College of Art and Design (Dublin, 1994). **10** The practice operated under two different names during the period of this study: N.S. Joseph and Smithem (1886–98) and N.S. Joseph, Son and Smithem (1899–1904). **11** Aalen, 'Health and housing in Dublin', pp 279–304. Prunty, 'Improving the urban environment', also makes a similar point, p. 207.

provided by Edward Cecil Guinness specifically for Guinness workers. While the Brewery and Trust have always sought to maintain distinct identities and while housing in the Guinness/Iveagh Trust was open to all workers regardless of employer, Edward Cecil Guinness's personal involvement ensured that there was a relationship between these various projects.

ARCHITECTURAL AND IDEOLOGICAL ARCHETYPES:
LEARNING FROM LONDON

The Guinness/Iveagh Trust is the only large philanthropic trust to have been established in Ireland and provides a localized example of what John Nelson Tarn has described as the 'second wave' of philanthropic and semi-philanthropic housing societies that became commonplace in British cities during the nineteenth century.[12] It has similarities with several pioneering London experiments but the strongest ideological and architectural comparisons can be made with the housing complexes and public amenities provided by the Peabody Donation Fund; the work of heiress Angela Burdett Coutts (1814–1906); and the provision of the semi-philanthropic 4% Industrial Dwellings Company (1885–), for whom the Bull Alley architects, N.S. Joseph and Smithem, also worked. In harnessing contemporary middle-class anxieties around health, sanitation, class mobility, societal agitation and social improvement, combined with genuine altruism and strong religious faith, these philanthropic organizations provided housing solutions reflective of such concerns at a time when municipal authorities were wrestling with housing provision.[13] Tarn contextualizes such motivations against the backdrop of mass industrialization:

> A society newly rich, attempting to recompense the people out of whom its wealth was made for the inconvenience – the inhumanity – of their homes and indeed their lives. The haughty sanctimonious, the earnest evangelical, the apostles of self-help, the prophets of socialism: all were motivated by a deep and abiding sense of guilt, of a peculiarly Victorian kind.[14]

In London much philanthropic endeavour focused on the East End of the city which experienced 'the full flowering of social investigation as armies of reformers, "slummers" and missionaries beat a heroic path to the heart of darkness' and here early prototypes for working-class block housing were established.[15] Susannah Morris suggests: 'The housing problem was therefore considered to be one of the most major

12 John Nelson Tarn, 'The Peabody Donation Fund', *Architectural Association Quarterly* (Winter 1968/9), p. 33. Tarn's seminal volume on this subject is *Five per cent philanthropy* (Cambridge, 1973).   **13** Dublin Corporation had begun to provide housing in 1887 but in a reactionary, piecemeal way hampered by inadequate legislation.   **14** Tarn, *Five per cent philanthropy*, p. 31.   **15** Drew D. Gray, *London's shadows: the dark side of the Victorian city* (London, 2010), p. 118.

public problems of its day, which threatened to harm the physical, moral, social, and even economic health of society.'[16] Morally, there was particular concern about families sharing cramped conditions that would necessitate children and adults sleeping in the same beds; pragmatically, typhoid and cholera affected all classes, de-stabilizing middle-class confidence in the benefits of putting physical distance between themselves and the working classes.[17] Dublin experienced several outbreaks of Asiatic Cholera in the nineteenth century and typhoid was prevalent throughout the 1870s and 1880s, including an outbreak within the staunchly middle-class Pembroke Estate (1879). However, middle-class industrialists had an additional concern: the effects of poor housing conditions on productivity.

By the mid-nineteenth century, Britain had formulated three models of privately funded housing provision for the urban working classes: the endowed or charitable trust established as a consequence of the benefaction (including Peabody and Guinness) or bequest (Samuel Lewis, 1901 and William Sutton, 1900);[18] the subscription charity which raised monies through patrons' donations (for example, the Society for Improving the Condition of the Labouring Classes, 1844); and the model-dwelling company, run as a limited-liability company which raised capital from investors (for example, the 4% Industrial Dwellings Company, 1885).[19] The third – and often the second – model provided a modest dividend on investment; capped around 4–5 per cent they embodied a provision that Tarn famously described as '5% Philanthropy' and by virtue of this return for investors these organizations can be categorized as semi-philanthropic.

Amid this rush of developments, a number of distinct architectural and ideological paradigms emerged. The building of cottages or terraces of houses proved expensive and the majority of companies focused on the block dwelling form so that the number of people displaced by slum clearance could – notionally at least – be re-housed in high-density replacement schemes. Blocks consisted of five or six storeys built in parallel rows, as per the Guinness/Iveagh Trust housing at Kevin Street,[20] or

16 Susannah Morris, 'Changing perceptions of philanthropy in the voluntary housing field in nineteenth- and early-twentieth-century London' in Thomas Adam (ed.), *Philanthropy, patronage and civil society: experiences from Germany, Great Britain and North America* (Indiana, 2004), p. 143. 17 Ruth McManus, *Dublin 1910–40: shaping the city & suburbs* (Dublin, 2002), p. 428. The British housing reform movement of the nineteenth century stemmed from the investigation into public health issues in the wake of cholera and typhoid outbreaks in the 1830s by the first secretary to the Poor Law Board, Edwin Chadwick. His *Report on the sanitary conditions of the labouring population and on its means of improvement* (1842) firmly established the link between poor housing and inadequate sanitation in the context of public health and was a landmark in mobilizing the rapidly expanding middle classes into philanthropic and charitable activity. 18 These organizations are still operational and all but the Iveagh Trust have changed their names recently. The Peabody Donation Fund is now known as Peabody; the Guinness Trust became The Guinness Partnership (2007); the Samuel Lewis Trust is now the Southern Housing Group (2001). 19 Morris, 'Changing perceptions on philanthropy', p. 144. 20 The Birkenhead Dock Company were probably the first to provide block buildings for workers in 1847, Tarn, *Five per cent philanthropy*, p. 4.

1 Peabody Square, Greenman Street, Islington, London, 1865, Henry Darbishire for
Peabody Donation Fund. Courtesy: http://greenmanstreet.wordpress.com/
category/history/plans-and-images/

utilized the Peabody principle of four perpendicular blocks forming a square as
evident at Bull Alley. The eclectic range of styles typical of nineteenth-century
British architecture was reflected in the elevations of the housing solutions. Mid-
century 'Italianate' designs were favoured by early Peabody schemes, although these
were routinely criticized for their 'barrack-like' appearance and contemporary
reports describe a 'cross between the reformatory and the workhouse ... Everything
about the buildings ... has been made as dull-looking and heavy as it could be'.[21]

Mid- to late-nineteenth-century schemes often included neo-Gothic references
(as preferred by Coutts) or referenced Dutch revival styles through the use of red
brick, distinctive triangular and curvilinear gables and mansard or dormer roofs, to
minimize the monumentalism of the structures. Yet, the designs were still relatively
austere despite attempts to soften these with a modest amount of applied decorative
detail. By the late nineteenth century many housing organizations deliberately tried
to shake off criticisms of institutional-like austerity and embraced a style loosely
referred to as 'Queen Anne' that had become popular for middle-class domestic
architecture. This hybrid of Dutch revival, Arts and Crafts, vernacular architecture,

21 *Telegraph,* 24 Dec. 1868, cited in Tarn, 'The Peabody Donation Fund: the role of a
housing society in the nineteenth century', *Victorian Studies* (Sept. 1966), 14.

coupled with the sporadic Art Nouveau flourish, was popularized by Scottish architect Norman Shaw (1831–1912) and featured good quality brickwork, multi-pane sash windows, varied fenestration, asymmetrical elevations and integrated decorative detail.

Of the earliest phase of block housing, architect Henry Astley Darbishire (1825–99) was the most prolific exponent through his work for Peabody. He evolved a template of four or five units, of one-to-three rooms per floor, accessed off a central staircase containing 'associated facilities' (lavatories and sinks shared between families). Pram sheds were available for tenants within an internal courtyard that doubled as a children's playground, and communal bathhouses were also provided. Edward Cecil Guinness, his architects and advisors, followed the work of the Peabody Fund very closely, modified extant Peabody plans, and in London, Guinness Trust housing was often built near or adjacent to existing Peabody schemes. The enclosed courtyard model, separating the block housing from its immediate surroundings and also evident in the Dublin Bull Alley scheme, was favoured by Darbishire and was the physical manifestation of the rhetoric of self-improvement and social control:

> The estates were cut off from the surrounding district by great iron railings, complete with gates, which were locked each night. Inside, men and women could live quiet lives and children could play in safety, not only from traffic but also from contamination with the undesirable people in the slums outside. Peabody tenants were expected to live improving lives, sober and clean, thrifty and honest.[22]

Physical separation was complemented by a strict system of monitoring the behaviour of residents ensuring that social order was imposed and maintained. The Guinness/Iveagh Trust adopted the staff structure of Peabody, ensuring that resident superintendents were ex-military and porters had a practical trade.[23] These men enforced a strict code of conduct for tenants, including temperance and a rota of cleaning communal spaces. Peabody had stipulated that his donation was dependent on maintaining the 'virtues of moral character and good conduct' and while excluding the very poor, favoured a 'respectable poverty' defined by the artisan who could afford regular rent payments.[24]

In *Discipline and punish* (1977) Michel Foucault argues that architectural forms became more politicized in the late eighteenth centuries as a consequence of the plague that gripped seventeenth-century Europe.[25] He suggests that the segregation of people into ill and healthy – a consequence of quarantining a plague town and its inhabitants – gave rise to cultures of surveillance from which 'disciplined' societies

22 Tarn, 'The Peabody Donation Fund', p. 32. 23 Ron Lear, 'My goodness' (n.d., n.p.), courtesy of the Guinness Trust. 24 Tarn, 'The Peabody Donation Fund', p. 15. 25 Michel Foucault (Alan Sheridan, translation), 'Panopticism', *Discipline and punish: the birth of the prison* (Middlesex, 1977), pp 195–228 and Paul Rabinow (ed.), 'Space, knowledge and power', *The Foucault reader: an introduction to Foucault's thought* (Middlesex, 1984), pp 239–56.

emerged, controlled through stringent organizational and surveillance systems. Of these, the Panopticon – the prison that allows inmates to be observed at all times – is the most emblematic structure. Foucault argues that this technological system, comprising architectural form and human intervention, was adapted to suit a variety of needs, including military barracks, the form of which, with its stacked, high-density units, can be seen as an antecedent of model block housing.[26] The ultimate aim of the panoptical system was control of the working classes '. . . to strengthen the social forces – to increase production, to develop the economy, spread education, raise the level of public morality'.[27] In considering the architectural typologies examined here, Foucault's analysis is particularly pertinent as he makes reference to the fact that 'charities' (and philanthropic organizations can be included in this definition) have had a long-standing interest in developing such technologies with the express purpose of 'moralization' but also with an eye to economic development and the neutralization of social agitation.[28] In nineteenth-century London such threats to the social order included the rise of trade unionism, while in Dublin there was an additional layer of anxiety reflective of the social unrest heralded by the rise of the Home Rule movement and the growing popularity of Parnell. For a staunch Unionist like Edward Cecil Guinness such societal shifts may have provided some degree of concern.

Yet, situated within the city and exposed to myriad changes, trust housing could not be as tightly controlled as the model or industrial village concept that also found favour in Britain, Europe and the US in the eighteenth and nineteenth centuries and with which it shared some ideological commonalities.[29] The model village was the romanticized alternative to the congestion and revolutionary influences of the industrial city and provided cottage-type housing in a rural environment. Built around the factory of the industrialist, panoptical systems dominated and close monitoring of the workforce stretched from housing across a range of ancillary services – including schools, churches, libraries – and of these Cadbury's Bourneville (1895) and Lever's Port Sunlight (1890) would be particularly well known. The latter two schemes also had considerable influence in popularizing Arts and Crafts and 'Queen Anne'-inspired architecture as a template for workers' housing of all forms as locally sourced materials (for example brick and stone), combined with vernacular forms (including sash windows, dormer roofs), satisfied Victorian ideas of the domestic and pictur-esque. Due to its relative lack of industrialization Ireland did not experience this phenomenon to the same extent as mainland Britain although model villages were built by the Malcolmsons, at Portlaw, County Waterford, around their cotton mill (1830s); and by the Richardsons in Bessbrook, County Armagh (1852), around their linen-weaving factory. These 'benevolent dictatorships' exerted almost total control over tenants and flexed a level of authoritarianism that was a constant reminder of

---

26 Foucault, 'Panopticism', p. 215.   27 Ibid., p. 207.   28 Ibid., p. 212.   29 See Vittorio Gregotti (ed.), *70 Rassegna: company towns: themes in architecture* (Bologna, 1997) for analysis of a range of models across Europe and the United States.

the links between industrial productivity, moral conduct, maintaining a home and the penalties for non-conformity.

In providing cottages grouped in picturesque clusters model villages can also be likened to the earlier archetype of the 'estate village' built by local aristocracy for their rural employees. Both typologies have similarities in that they were forms of corporate architecture where the elements of the parent building (factory or house) were modified for the smaller buildings creating recognisable designs that linked across all provision. It is argued here that the later provision of the Guinness and Iveagh Trusts operated on this level in evolving a recognizable corporate style that visually connected its housing projects. In Dublin the housing was not explicitly connected to the brewery, and in fact brewery workers were excluded from applying to the scheme for the first ten years of the trust's existence;[30] the prominent display of the name of the benefactor on the exterior of the buildings in an area intrinsically linked to both the brewery and other philanthropic gestures by the Guinness family suggest that the buildings were likely to have been connected back to the source of the benefaction by the public. In this way an implicit but highly visible link between the Trust, the Brewery and Guinness family philanthropy was maintained and this has undoubtedly contributed to the common misconception that Guinness/Iveagh Trust flats were exclusively for Guinness workers.[31] The breadth of facilities provided by the Trust at Bull Alley also aligns it more closely to the model village concept than typical trust provision in mainland Britain.

HOUSING, HEALTH AND PRODUCTIVITY: HOUSING INITIATIVES OF THE GUINNESS BREWERY

By the end of the nineteenth century Dublin had some of the worst slum conditions in the United Kingdom and the Liberties area of the city was particularly impoverished. The dominance of one-roomed tenement flats was of particular concern and mortality rates for Dublin were the highest in the British Isles and amongst the highest in Continental Europe or the US.[32] As industrial employers, Guinness and Pim (the textile manufacturers) were particularly vocal in recording the links between health and housing as a matter of public record and the city already had a short history of privately-funded workers' housing provision.[33] For the most part this followed the cottage model and complexes include Pim's Cottages, Harold's Cross,

---

30 Guinness Archives: GDB/1004–11/0017, John Lumsden, *Report on the inspection of dwellings occupied by the employés (sic) and pensioners of A. Guinness, Son and Co. Ltd*, 17 Nov. 1900 to 17 Jan. 1901, p. 12. **31** See, for example, Neil Hegarty, *Dublin: a view from the ground* (London, 2007), p. 227. **32** Joseph V. O'Brien, *'Dear, dirty Dublin': a city in distress, 1899–1916* (Berkeley, CA, 1982), p. 22. **33** See, for example, Frederick W. Pim, *The growth of sanitation in Dublin* (address given to the nineteenth annual general meeting of the Dublin Sanitary Association, 27 Mar. 1890); while Edward Cecil Guinness gave evidence at the royal commission on the housing of the working classes (1884).

2 Belview Buildings, Dublin (1872–1980), for Guinness Brewery.
Photo: author's own (*c.*1980).

built beside the company's textile mill (1844 and 1864); the Watkin, Jameson, Pim and Co. Ltd houses adjacent to its brewery, Ardee Street (1860s); and the Great Southern and Western Railway cottages, library, dispensary and dining room at Inchicore (1850s).[34]

In 1872 Edward Cecil Guinness financed the Belview Buildings (1872–1980) for brewery workers. Comprising austere, yellow-brick, three- and two-storey blocks – in one perpendicular and two parallel rows – and four cottages, these were situated beside the brewery at School Street. Reputedly designed by the brewery's engineer, Samuel Geoghegan (1845–1928/9), seventy-three units were provided – some with deck access – and the buildings were entered through iron gates off the street,

---

34 Nonetheless, the overall provision in the city was modest. Pim provided 36 one- and two-storey, yellow-brick cottages; Watkins, 87 one- and two-storey, yellow-brick cottages; GSWR built 149 two-storey, red-brick, granite and concrete cottages.

creating a contained environment similar to the Coutts and Peabody schemes.[35] Some 180 families or c.350 people were housed and the complex was well received, with one witness at the Royal Commission on the Housing of the Working Classes (1884) commenting that they were: '... most wonderful ... To my mind they are the best buildings I have seen'.[36] Some of the more distinctive features of the complex were that each flat had separate facilities and a communal bathhouse was provided for residents' use.[37] Although the Belview Buildings provided a much higher standard of accommodation than most and despite claims that they increased the healthiness of the tenants,[38] they were out-dated and in need of improvement as early as 1889.[39] Their location may have contributed to their deterioration as the complex was tucked away between brewery buildings at a distance from the main thoroughfare of James' Street. In 1905 Arthur Hignett, the engineer-in-chief at the Guinness Brewery, commented that:

> Attention should be drawn to the moral atmosphere in the neighbourhood of the Bellevue [sic] Buildings. The streets, dark corners and gateways, appear to be the regular nightly resort of 'corner women'; and the foul language and behaviour of such women and drunken men are such that respectable married men refuse to live in the neighbourhood *even rent free*.[40]

Between the establishment of the Belview Buildings and the founding of the Guinness Trust, Edward Cecil Guinness became an enthusiastic supporter of the Dublin Artisans' Dwellings Company (DADC, 1876–1979), a semi-philanthropic organization based on the 5% philanthropy model, which supplied a total of 3,379 housing units for approximately 16,000 people.[41] Its preferred architectural prototype was the cottage for the skilled or artisan worker although it also built a number of block dwellings, including Echlin Street (1878) and Crampton Quay (1891), the latter

35 Guinness Archives, GDB/C009/0386 'The housing question: Belview, Thomas Court and opinions from Mr Gowan'. Housing with deck access is a cheaper model of provision as many units can be accessed from the one balcony. 36 Stanley Raymond Dennison and Oliver MacDonagh, *Guinness, 1886–1939: from incorporation to the Second World War* (Cork, 1998), p. 127. 37 The brewery dispensary was also on the site from 1870 until it moved in 1901. At the time of their construction the only other block tenements in the city were the New Model Dwellings (c.1868): six red-brick, four-storey tenement houses comprising fifty units on the corner of Meath and South Earl Street in the Liberties built by the Industrial Tenements Company (1867). They quickly degenerated into slums, partly as a consequence of having only six external latrines, Aalen, 'The working-class housing movement in Dublin, 1850–1920', pp 142–3. 38 Prunty, 'Improving the urban environment', p. 208. 39 Dennison and MacDonagh, *Guinness, 1886–1939*, p. 129. 40 Guinness Archives, GDB/ENOI/0059, 'Workmen's dwellings: general matters' (1905), emphasis Hignett's. The buildings were later reserved for members of the brewery Fire Brigade and became the subject of many Corporation summonses for breaches of public health throughout the 1930s before being handed over to Dublin Corporation in 1941. 41 King, *Progressive housing*, p. 16.

3 Rialto Buildings, Dublin, 1883, C.H. Ashworth for Guinness Brewery.
Photo: L. King (2012).

built around a courtyard with deck access. Strict codes of conduct were enforced on all tenants and many of the schemes were centred in the Liberties area. The establishment of the DADC was informed by legislation in 1868 and 1875 that permitted local authorities to demolish unsanitary housing for private companies to develop, provided the number of replacement units matched those demolished.[42] By the late nineteenth century the DADC board, investors and trustees read like a who's-who of Dublin industry and included several members of the Pim family and both Edward Cecil Guinness and Arthur E. Guinness. In 1913, a member of the Pim family commented at the Local Government Board of Ireland Housing Inquiry: 'Nearly all the people who were interested in industrial progress at the time shared in this company'.[43] Another witness at the Inquiry – Revd P.J. Monahan – commented that Powers Distillery, another Liberties industry, had an 'arrangement with' the DADC that in exchange for a 'fixed certain sum' its houses were let to its employees, suggesting that other industrialists might have had similar arrangements.[44]

42 For more detailed discussion of the DADC see Prunty, 'Improving the urban environment', pp 195–207. The acts were: Artisans' and Labourers' Dwelling Act (1868) and the Artisans' and Labourers' Dwelling Improvement Act (1875), otherwise known as the 'Cross Act'. **43** Local Government Board for Ireland, *The report of the departmental committee appointed by the Local Government Board for Ireland to inquire into the housing conditions of the working classes in the city of Dublin* (London, 1914), p. 185. **44** Ibid., p. 119.

By the turn of the century it was estimated that approximately one-third of all Guinness employees were living in DADC buildings, which would have eased the pressure on the brewery to provide more housing for its workers.[45]

Eleven years after his first foray into workers' housing provision Edward Cecil Guinness commissioned the DADC to build eighty-seven units in three austere, red brick, three-storey blocks for Guinness employees at Rialto Court, near the brewery on James' Street (1883). The flats were clustered around a central staircase exposed to the elements, reflecting contemporary beliefs that fresh air dissipated disease. These were also constructed some distance away from a main thoroughfare. Designed by C.H. Ashworth, architect to the DADC, they were sold at a loss to the DADC in 1885 after criticism by Rowton.[46] Notably, Alfred Barnard in his appraisal of breweries across Britain (1889) mentions both Belview and Rialto as 'villages', 'colonies' and 'townships' erected by Guinness. His comments seem to have been influenced by the fact that additional facilities, including medical supervision, recreational grounds and a 'flourishing cooperative store', were provided.[47]

Federico Bucci has argued that the provision of housing by any industrialist is a 'paternalistic project' reflecting a desire to exact total control over a workforce and that this is inherent in the relationship between 'Protestant ethic' and the 'spirit of capitalism'.[48] He argues that the factory system – defined by the 'functional relation of surveillance and discipline' – inevitably spills over from the workplace into other 'territories', including that of the workers' private lives. While many Dublin industrialists realized that good health was integral to maintaining an industrious workforce, none matched the facilities provided by Guinness, which included educational programmes, social clubs and free medical assistance. A brewery doctor ensured that there was a constant monitor of how the quality of housing affected individual productivity levels and Dr John Lumsden, medical advisor to the brewery and the head of Guinness' social and medical services, regularly documented his concerns on the links between poor sanitation, housing and health.[49]

Lumsden undertook a detailed analysis of Guinness workers' housing between November 1900 and January 1901, which provides an illuminating comparison between the living standards in early Guinness housing projects, Dublin's philan-

---

45 Aalen, 'The working-class housing movement in Dublin', p. 145. **46** The DADC extended the complex with the addition of two-storey cottages in 1890 that served to integrate the complex visually into its surroundings. Critics claimed that the rents were too high and the buildings were too far from the brewery (although this distance was a quarter of a mile), Dennison and MacDonagh, *Guinness, 1886–1939*, p. 128. **47** Alfred Barnard, *Noted breweries of Great Britain & Ireland, volume I* (London, 1889), p. 42. **48** Federico Bucci, 'Territories of surveillance' in Gregotti (ed.), *Company towns*, p. 64. **49** John Lumsden, 'The history of medical and social services in James' Gate 1894 to 1943' (unpublished manuscript), p. 55, Guinness Archives, GDB / C004.9 / 0002.09. Comment is made on the loose-leaf document that 'This was never printed, but typescript copies were bound.' Lumsden's tenure spanned 1894 to 1943 and he was particularly concerned with the spread of tuberculosis.

thropic and semi-philanthropic housing organizations, privately owned tenements, and the Guinness Trust units that were in the midst of construction. Addressing the company board directly, he noted that 33 per cent of employees lived in 'ideal' self-contained artisans cottages which were in the main owned by the DADC and the Corporation; 10.5 per cent in artisans' tenement buildings also owned by the same organizations; 19.8 per cent in self-contained houses; 0.6 per cent in private tenement buildings; 8.5 per cent in old cottages 'unfit for human habitation' and 24.2 per cent in similarly problematic tenement houses. He concluded, in relation to the latter: 'The very large majority of these houses in my experience are dens of disease, are so impregnated with filth and so utterly rotten they should be regarded as unfit for human habitation and dealt with as dangers to public health.'[50] Lumsden gives scant mention of the Belview Buildings, noting that 'recent improvements and re-construction' were 'excellent' but otherwise he had not been 'satisfied with the general condition of the people' living there.[51] By comparison, he had visited two or three employees who had just moved into Guinness Trust buildings in Bride Street, observing that the buildings were nearly as perfect as anything he could imagine, concluding that they were 'admirably managed'.[52]

Lumsden's record of the visits is revealing as to the complex relationship between philanthropy, surveillance and employment. His aim was '... to gain knowledge of its [brewery] houses and manners of your [the board of the brewery] people', indicating a perceived entitlement to survey all workers' accommodation although most were privately rented. However, by the time the report was published the assumption of an employer's entitlement to view their employees' accommodation was being challenged; Lumsden notes that he was denied access to only one house by the 'gate porter who holds strong socialist views ... He held that it was no business of an employer how or where his servant lived'.[53] The report consistently emphasizes the benevolence of Guinness as an employer, making clear the links between generous working conditions and subjugation: '... as a class I look upon our men, as a most respectable and well conducted body of operatives, they are proud of their employment, always ready to listen to the advice and amenable to reason', they were aware that amongst their peers they were '... better paid and better cared for employés [sic] of a firm that treats them so well'.[54] In emphasizing the links between health, housing and productivity he called on the board to provide more purpose-built housing for employees:

> If the firm could only see their way to erect more tenement buildings or self-contained cottages, similar to those already in existence ... I am convinced our people would flock to them ... Thus the heartfelt gratitude of many employés [sic] would be earned, the mortality returns would be diminished,

50 GDB/1004–11/0017, J. Lumsden, *Report on the inspection of dwellings occupied by the employés (sic) and pensioners of A. Guinness, Son and Co. Ltd,* 17 Nov. 1900 to 17 Jan. 1901, pp 9–10. **51** Ibid., p. 44. **52** Ibid., p. 12. **53** Ibid., p. 4. **54** Ibid., pp 8–9.

greater contentment and happiness made possible, less sickness, want and misery would be evident and a stronger community, physically, mentally and morally would in time be developed.[55]

Lumsden's concluding suggestions that 'an inspector of dwellings be appointed' and that allowances, including sick pay and medical provision, be withdrawn from any employee '... who, after due notice has been given, continues to reside in a house condemned as insanitary and unsatisfactory by the firm', were rejected by the board until such time as the supply of suitable dwellings was adequate.[56]

THE GUINNESS TRUST LONDON AND DUBLIN FUNDS: IMPORTED INFLUENCES AND MODIFIED ARCHETYPES

This modest experiment with housing for brewery employees is significant in that it enabled Edward Cecil Guinness to test and modify established housing archetypes before beginning work on the Bull Alley site. Benjamin Lee Guinness had attempted to develop this area as early as 1865, Edward Cecil Guinness and Arthur Cecil had unsuccessfully tried to turn it into a park in celebration of Queen Victoria's golden jubilee in 1887, and Dublin Corporation were keen to clear the site of the warren of tenement houses, brothels, pubs, abattoirs and open markets that were routinely criticized.[57] Housing provision directly tied to an industrial concern was partisan and favoured the artisan worker as opposed to the very poorest who were not in steady employment. In founding the Guinness Trust, Edward Cecil Guinness took the model of benefaction established by Peabody, but broadened the scope for application to all workers. Rents were kept modest but were still not affordable for the poorest, typically the casual worker, a demographic that had to wait some decades to be catered for by the large-scale municipal housing projects that emerged during the early decades of the Free State.

The Guinness Trust, London and Dublin Funds, produced its first housing complexes in 1891 and for the first ten years a multiplicity of solutions were employed before a distinct architectural treatment began to emerge that identified the complexes in both London and Dublin as emerging from the same source. In Dublin the DADC built the first Guinness Trust housing at Thomas Court on the

---

55 Ibid., p. 19.   **56** Ibid., pp 19, 50. Lumsden also suggested annual prizes be awarded for 'houses kept in an exemplary and creditable manner' which was adopted.   **57** Benjamin Lee Guinness had formed the St Patrick's Building Company in 1865 with the intention of clearing and landscaping the Bull Alley area but died before this could be achieved. Between 1871 and 1878 local distiller Henry Roe employed the Gothic Revivalist George Edmund Street to 'restore' the dilapidated nearby Protestant cathedral of Christ Church. This ensured that there were two grandiose, religious monuments to the generosity of two of Dublin's most successful industrial families, which book-ended one of the worst slums in the city.

4 Thomas Court flats,
Dublin, 1892, Meade and
Company for the
Guinness Trust, Dublin
Fund. Photo: L. King
(2012).

periphery of the Belview Buildings site (1892), comprising two three-storey, red-
brick blocks of – mainly – single-roomed units with shared facilities.

Designed by Meade and Company building contractors, with revisions by
Ashworth as architect, the blocks had enclosed stairwells and attempts were made to
soften the elevations with the inclusion of triangular gables and modest decorative
detail. Yet, these were also considered to be unsuccessful and were sold to the DADC
at a loss in 1895 after criticism by Rowton.[58] The buildings were then acquired by
the brewery for its own workers around 1901 and were managed as part of the
Belview complex before being handed over to Dublin Corporation at a substantial
loss in 1939.[59] The Dublin Trust built only one more complex before Bull Alley
commenced: Dublin architect R.J. Stirling provided three parallel rows of five-storey

---

58 Aalen, *The Iveagh Trust,* p. 23. As the Iveagh Trust archive is not accessible to the public
it is difficult to establish detail around some decisions made by the Trust. **59** Guinness
Archives, GDB/EN01/0059,'Workmen's dwellings: general matters'. The Belview Buildings
were valued at £11,473 in 1879 and £975 in 1939; Thomas Court was valued at £7827 and
£3248 for the same dates.

5 Kevin Street flats, Dublin, 1894–1901, R.J. Stirling for the Guinness Trust. Photo: L. King (2012).

blocks and a bathhouse at Kevin Street in mostly small, two-room units where facilities were shared.

A variety of elaborately shaped gables and heavily projected doorways distinguish the elevations from Thomas Court but otherwise the blocks are rather crudely resolved. The first Guinness Trust complex in London, at Brandon Street (1891–1967), Walworth, was substantially larger. Nine five-storey blocks containing 190 tenements were designed by N.S. Joseph and Smithem/N.S. Joseph, Son and Smithem – with similar elevations to Thomas Court – but which were virtually indistinguishable from the designs of other housing trusts within the London area. The rhetoric of social improvement typical of the model village concept was very much evident: the complex included a range of ancillary facilities including a crèche for working mothers run by Lady Iveagh and a clubroom containing games and reading materials.[60] Seven more complexes were completed in London (1892–1901) using a number of architectural firms: Draycott Avenue, Chelsea (1892), and Vauxhall Walk, Lambeth (1894–1975), both by Mervyn McCarthy; Columbia Road, Bethnal

60 Frederick Mulally, *The silver salver: the story of the Guinness family* (London, 1981), p. 35.

6 Fulham Palace Road flats, Hammersmith, London, 1901, N.S. Joseph, Son and Smithem for the Guinness Trust. Copyright: Robert Freidus/George P. Landow. Courtesy: http://www.victorianweb.org/art/architecture/homes/48.html (2011).

Green (1892), by F.L. Pilkington; and Lever Street, Finsbury (1893), Page's Walk (1895), Snow's Fields (1897), and Bermondsey and Fulham Palace Road, Hammersmith (1901), all by N.S. Joseph, Son and Smithem. All followed a template of five- or six-storey brick blocks built in parallel rows – except for Draycott Avenue which was built around a courtyard – connected by decorative archways, bathhouses (with reclining baths) and clubrooms. Although the architectural styles were some-what disparate, prominently displayed decorative cartouches stating the date of completion and name of the Trust formed a strong visual link between the complexes. Snow Fields and Fulham Palace Road share the closest stylistic features with the Bull Alley buildings.

The treatment of the facades, terminal gables and prominent chimneystacks establish a distinct corporate style of architecture distinguishing the housing of the Guinness Trust from other London-based philanthropic trusts. Many of these complexes have been demolished while those surviving have been radically altered and dormer stories removed, ensuring that the Dublin scheme is the most architecturally faithful to the original designs of the Guinness/Iveagh Trust complexes.[61]

ARCHITECTURAL INNOVATION AND THE RHETORIC OF SELF-IMPROVEMENT: THE BULL ALLEY COMPLEX

As the Kevin Street flats were under construction, Edward Cecil Guinness began buying land and clearing the Bull Alley site at personal expense.[62] The warren of streets and alleyways was cleared, roads were straightened and new and modified street names bestowed. By the time N.S. Joseph, Son and Smithem were employed to work on the scheme the principal partner had accrued considerable experience in designing trust housing influenced by his mother, a charity activist in the East End of London.[63] N.S. Joseph became a driving force behind the 4% Industrial Dwellings Company (IDC, 1885–), a Jewish-run, semi-philanthropic organization established by Lord Nathan Rothschild. Rothschild was a merchant banker and Britain's first Jewish MP and it was through the IDC that his theories on workers' housing were put into practice.[64] The IDC focused activities in the Spitalfields area of London's East End where the population largely consisted of Jews fleeing Eastern Europe and Russia, and Irish immigrants. The company was non-sectarian and early projects included formidable looking block dwellings of which the Brady Street Dwellings, Spitalfields (1890–1978), are typical examples. Similar to the Peabody model, IDC elevations were severe as external decorative detail was sacrificed to provide a high standard of internal fittings and private facilities for all units. Internal staircases, open to the elements, provided access to four units on each landing and a resident superintendent enforced a policy of free access to each home. The *Irish Builder* voiced its disapproval that an Irish architect had not been chosen to design the scheme and, in the process, wrongly attributed the designs to N.S. Joseph's nephew, Delissa Joseph, an architect famous for work on London's underground system. It commented: 'It is rather regrettable that Lord Iveagh should have again thought it necessary to go across the water in search of an architect. Was there no practitioner here capable of

---

61 The removal of dormer stories, at Snow Field's, for example, was to 'allow more daylight into the courtyard' while Fulham Palace also had one block removed: Gillian Aver, the Guinness Trust, letter to author, Apr. 1994. **62** He did so with powers he acquired under the Dublin Improvement (Bull Alley Area) Act of 1899; see Aalen, *The Iveagh Trust*, p. 27. **63** Sharman Kadish, 'Joseph, Nathan Solomon (1834–1909), *Oxford dictionary of national biography* (Oxford, 2004) [http://www.oxforddnb.com/view/article/74454, accessed 13 Apr. 2012]. **64** The company changed its name to the Industrial Dwellings Society in 1952 and is still operational as the IDS, maintaining over 1,400 properties, many of which occupy the original late nineteenth early twentieth-century buildings.

7 Patrick Street Flats and shops, Dublin, N.S. Joseph, Son and Smithem for Iveagh Trust, 1901. Photo: L. King (2012).

meeting his lordship's views?'[65] Local expertise was employed and the Dublin firm of Kaye-Parry and Ross, who had substantial experience in the design of bathing facilities, were assigned to oversee the scheme's construction.[66]

The five-storey Guinness/Iveagh Trust flats were built in two stages lining Patrick Street (1901) and Bride Street (1904), negating the original proposal of four parallel blocks typical of the London complexes. The one-, two- and three-roomed units, accessed from enclosed internal staircases, provided a range of accommodation with both associated and self-contained facilities, the latter reserved for what the *Irish Builder* referred to as a 'superior class of tenants able to pay for their own separate laundry, balcony and conveniences'.[67] The publication also claimed that this demographic embraced a substantial number of Guinness Brewery and Jacob's Biscuits Factory employees and that a number of those displaced by the construction of the buildings had not been re-housed in the scheme as they could not afford the rents of the new dwellings.[68] While the buildings did not cater for the poorest of the working

65 *Irish Builder,* 30 Jan. 1901. Joseph is recorded as advising on modifications to the Belview Buildings in 1899 during discussions to erect 'Workman's dwellings' at 'Christchurch Fields', Guinness Archives, GDB/C006/0085, Board minutes, London, volume 1, but it is not clear if this work proceeded.   **66** *Irish Builder,* 16 June 1906, credited Kaye-Parry and Ross with the design of the baths, p. 484. It's not clear how much input the Dublin company had in the design as the publication sometimes mistakenly credited Irish designers over British. **67** *Irish Builder,* 6 Apr. 1907.   **68** 'Housing reform', *The Irish Architect and Craftsman,* 20

classes, families earning more than 25s. per week were also disqualified from applying and, as had become commonplace with trust housing, the tenants were closely supervised and monitored.[69]

The Bull Alley development marks a notable architectural shift for the firm away from the barrack-like structures typical of its early work towards a more eclectic aesthetic influenced by populist styles that defined London's late nineteenth-century housing provision. The 275-foot long elevations of Patrick and Bride Streets use a vibrant red brick, feature cut stone dressings at ground floor level, incorporate decorative panels in coloured-concrete, have sash windows of varying sizes and shapes, and display striking gable ends terminating in coloured concrete cartouches stating the source of benefaction and date of completion.[70] Decorative brickwork and copper domes top the entrance doorways of the stairwells – a popular local motif in distinguishing significant public buildings – indicating the importance the Trust attached to the complex in the context of urban planning, and sinuous Art Nouveau style railings encircle the complex.[71] The overall aesthetic of the buildings has more in common with the architectural firm's mature work for the 4% Industrial Dwellings Company, Chelsea Borough Council, and City of Westminister Council as can be noted in, for example, the Grosvenor Estate, Vincent Street, 1903, the building of which ran concurrently with the completion of the Bull Alley project.[72] In 1898/9 Joseph's son Charles joined the practice and this appears to have been the catalyst for shifting the company's rather ponderous aesthetic towards a lighter Queen Anne inflection.[73]

Joseph and Smithem provided two more buildings at Bull Alley. The hostel on Bride Road is a miniaturized version of a 'Rowton House', the 'poor man's hotel' concept that Lord Rowton had successfully established in Britain. Six storeys high with a more austere elevation than that of the flat buildings, it was built in an E-shape formation with cubicles arranged off central corridors, divided by wooden partitions, eighteen inches from the ceiling. Superintendents were located on each floor, gambling and drinking alcohol were strictly forbidden and meals could be bought at cost. A dining room, a reading room, library, smoking room, tailor, shoemaker, laundry and barber's shop were also provided, underlining the contemporary discourses on cleanliness, education and social enrichment.[74]

Sept. 1913, p. 418. **69** Aalen, *The Iveagh Trust*, p. 68; Guinness Archives, GDB/C004.9/0002.09, 'History of the medical and social services in James' Gate, 1894–1943, by Sir John Lumsden', p. 58. **70** Seán Rothery comments that the gables demonstrate the influence of Scottish Art Nouveau architect, Charles Rennie Mackintosh, in *Ireland and the new architecture*, p. 40. **71** As Art Nouveau had little impact in Ireland, this detail is most unusual. Similar railings can be found in the company's work for 4% IDC and London City Council (LCC). **72** Work for the 4% IDC includes the Evalina Mansions (1901) and Navarino Mansions (1905); work for Chelsea Borough Council includes Sir Thomas More Dwellings, Beaufort St (1903). **73** *The Builder*, 19 June 1909, 'Mr Joseph' (obit.). For comments on shifts of style in workers' housing provision, see A. Stuart Gray, *Edwardian architecture* (London, 1985), pp 22–3. **74** A mix of permanent flat

8 Vincent Street Flats, Pimlico, London, N.S. Joseph, Son and Smithem for London City Council, 1903. Copyright Derek Harper. Courtesy: http://www.geograph.org.uk/photo/1449939 (2009).

More ambitious, but in keeping with nineteenth-century anxieties of public health, was the provision of a public swimming pool and private reclining baths, at a time when Dublin had only one other such facility at Tara Street (1886–1986). Teresa Breathnach, in an assessment of the steam or 'Turkish Bath' popular amongst the Victorian middle classes, argues that bathing was another middle-class reaction to outbreaks of cholera and typhoid, but that memory of the Famine must also be considered as a catalyst for similar provisions in Ireland:

> The bath was regarded as a tool for the moral and physical advancement of society and was seen to play a part in the civilization of the 'masses', and in turn in the maintenance of the status quo. This was not simply about the shaping of their own class culture, but also about the control of others, an assertion of middle-class dominance.[75]

As principal Guinness medical officer, bathing had been of concern to Lumsden for some years. The Belview Buildings were provided with reclining baths for women and children and were opened up to all employees and their families in 1903. By July of that year it was noted, with some concern, that the facility, which could accom-

accommodation with temporary hostel accommodation had already been tried, albeit unsuccessfully, by Dublin Corporation at Benburb Street (1887). **75** Teresa Breathnach, 'For health and pleasure: the Turkish Bath in Victorian Ireland', *Victorian Literature and Culture*, 32:1 (2004), pp 162–3.

9 Iveagh Hostel, Bride Street, Dublin, N.S. Joseph, Son and
Smithem for Iveagh Trust, 1901. Photo: L. King (2012).

modate up to 100 people per week, had no clients some weeks and a maximum of
eleven on others.[76] The Iveagh Baths were erected on land donated by Dublin
Corporation and unlike the flats or hostel were intended as a public amenity
providing bathing facilities (reclining baths, showers and foot baths), a 65 x 30 foot
swimming pool for leisure and exercise, and a viewing gallery at mezzanine level,
which ensured the pool was popular for local sporting competitions. The building is
recognizably similar to both the flats and the hostel but the asymmetrical frontal
elevation is the most striking of the three: featuring a bold archway topped with
decorative panels, a copper dome and cut-stone dressings, Seán Rothery suggests that
it is typical of an English Art Nouveau style formulated by Charles Harrison
Townsend (1851–1928) who designed the striking Bishopsgate Institute (1895) and
Whitechapel Art Gallery (1896) in London's East End.[77]

The two-and-a-half acre park between the Bull Alley buildings and St Patrick's
Cathedral displaced the numerous street traders who operated stalls in the immediate
area and, protected by royal charter, an alternative site had to be provided. The Iveagh
Market (1906) was built at some distance from the other facilities at the edge of a

76 Guinness Archives, GDB/PE03.01/0350, 'Women's baths, Belview'.   **77** Rothery,
Ireland and the new architecture, p. 34. The building was sold to Dublin Corporation in 1951,
after having been on loan to the municipal authorities for some years. The Corporation
cited falling numbers and structural damage before deciding to close the baths in 1985. The
building is now a privately owned leisure centre with very little remaining of the original
internal design.

Linda King

10 Iveagh Baths, Bride Street, Dublin, N.S. Joseph, Son and
Smithem for Iveagh Trust, 1906. Photo: L. King (2012).

DADC estate (1882) on nearby Francis Street and reflects another dimension to the
discourse on health and hygiene: the selling and disposal of foodstuffs. This particular model had been championed by Burdett Coutts who provided a Gothic-revival
style indoor food market (1869–86)[78] for local traders at Columbia Market, Bethnal
Green, placed at a distance from her housing provision at Columbia Square (1859).
Part of Burdett Coutts' motivation was 'to harness the disorder of the streets', and
similar pleas to provide an alternative to outdoor trading were commonplace in
Dublin by mid-century.[79] An enclosed fruit and vegetable market had been built at
Mary's Lane (1892), designed by Spencer Harty and replacing the notorious Old Pill
Lane market, while the Pim family had invested in an enclosed, arcaded market at
South Great George's Street (1881), designed by Lockwood and Mawson. The Iveagh
Market, designed by a British architect living in Dublin, Frederick G. Hicks, is Neo-
Classical in design and therefore radically different in style to the other buildings. It

---

78 These are the dates the building was operational as a market. The building's original
purpose proved unpopular as local traders preferred to sell outdoors and it was subsequently
turned into warehouses and workshops. It was demolished sometime between 1958 and
1961: see http://archiseek.com/2012/1869-columbia-market-dwellings-london/ [accessed:
05.05.12].   **79** Susan Lewis 'The artistic and architectural patronage of Angela Burdett
Coutts' (PhD, Royal Holloway, University of London, Jan. 2012), p. 20; *Irish Builder*, 1 Feb.
1859. Edel Sheridan argues that Dublin markets came under scrutiny from the seventeenth
century onwards as a cause for concern: 'Designing the capital city: Dublin, *c.*1660–1810' in
Brady and Simms (eds), *Dublin through space and time*, p. 78.

11 Iveagh Market, Francis Street, Dublin, FG Hicks for
Iveagh Trust, 1905. Photo: L. King (2012).

specialized in the sale of old clothes and bric-a-brac in the front section of the
building – which contained some enclosed units similar to those in a contemporary
shopping centre – and the sale of fish and foodstuffs at the rear. A disinfecting
chamber and washhouse to launder goods were provided and on completion the
building was handed over to Dublin Corporation, which had the responsibility of
monitoring the city's markets.

The final building of the complex, The Iveagh Play Centre (1915), provides the
fourth elevation of the Bull Alley site and was conceived as a community centre and
educational facility designed by Dublin-based architects McDonnell and Reid. It was
influenced by the People's Palace, Mile End, East London (1887), a facility established
for the working classes to which Edward Cecil Guinness had donated monies. It
combined popular entertainment with education, technical tuition and entertainment in the form of a concert hall, library, swimming pool, gymnasium and winter
garden.[80] Known locally as the 'Bayno' – from the word 'beano' meaning feast – the
Iveagh Play Centre similarly consisted of an assembly room, gymnasium and class-
rooms, providing skills training and after school care and meals – buns and cocoa –
for local children from the ages of three to fourteen. Architecturally, its Flemish
Baroque design bears no resemblance to the other buildings in the complex but its

80 For a contextual study of the origins of the People's Palace, see: Simon Joyce, 'Castles in
the air: the people's palace, cultural reformism and the East End working class', *Victorian
Studies*, 39:4 (Summer, 1996), pp 513–38.

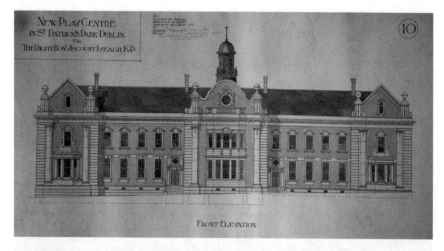

12 Iveagh Play Centre, Bull Alley, Dublin, original drawing by Mc Donnell and Reid for
Iveagh Trust, 1906. Photo: L. King with permission of the Iveagh Trust.

appearance is in keeping with the grandioseness of its British archetype. The Play
Centre was based on an earlier project founded by Edward Cecil Guinness on Francis
Street (1909), the popularity of which inspired the construction of the larger
building. The Play Centre remained in high demand until the 1950s when the city
centre became heavily depopulated in the wake of the Corporation's suburban
housing schemes.

   The range of facilities provided at Bull Alley and the rhetoric of social improvement they reflected were extraordinary within philanthropic provision generally and
are more typical of – and in some cases exceed – provision within the model village
concept. Almost all the buildings are still in use and broadly in the manner for which
they were intended. The housing and hostel have undergone substantial refurbish-
ment and units are much sought after, the baths were privately sold (1990) and now
comprise – substantially altered internally – a leisure centre, while the Play Centre
was sold to Dublin Vocational Education Committee (1977) and became the
Liberties College. The Market has been the only casualty: sold off by the
Corporation *c.*2000 and rejected for conversion into a hotel, it is now derelict.

CONCLUSION: GIFT GIVING AND ITS CONSEQUENCES

As others have argued, the study of philanthropy is a complex weave, reflective of
personal and societal concerns that have broad cultural impact. The motivations of
nineteenth-century industrial philanthropists have long been problematized and it
has often been argued that the establishment of the Guinness/Iveagh Trusts 'bought'
titles for Edward Cecil Guinness and eased his passage through Victorian society; the

fact that he was made Baron Iveagh (1891), Viscount Iveagh (1901) and Earl of Iveagh (1919), certainly supports this thesis.[81] In choosing to make a public announcement in the press and establishing a housing trust bearing his name while he was still alive, Edward Cecil Guinness replicated the actions of Peabody, combining genuine civic concern with the desire for public recognition. While this strategy was not unusual in the nineteenth century it was not without disapproval and the American bene-factor was criticized at his own funeral for his 'ambition' and 'ostentation' in this regard.[82] From an historical distance, it is impossible to be clear as to an individual's exact intentions, whether they were acting in their own interest, altruism or both. Depending on perspective, the Bull Alley scheme can be alternately 'read' as symbolic of working-class containment or, conscious of the area's extreme poverty, segregation in support of the rhetoric of self-improvement.[83] This theory is supported by local folklore; in 1980 one resident offered: '... to get one of these places [Iveagh Trust flat] your father would have to be an artisan ... they [the flats] compared as palaces against living in the slums of Dublin'.[84] Edward Cecil Guinness's donation was incredibly generous, the facilities he financed had a positive and lasting impact on the fabric of Dublin life, but the emphasis on social conformity that trusts like Guinness/Iveagh espoused ensured that access to quality housing, leisure, educational and trading facil-ities came at a price for individuals and society. Marcel Mauss argues that gift giving always has a 'contractual' exchange value and that with the acceptance of a gift are expectations of a reciprocal payment: 'In theory such gifts are voluntary but in fact they are given and repaid ... the transaction itself is based on obligation and economic self-interest'.[85] Mauss' comments have a particular resonance with regard to philanthropic gestures as he states:

81 In 1903, King Edward VII visited the hostel, then under construction, while in 1911 King George V and Queen Mary visited the Francis Street play and education centre, which may have had some bearing on Edward Cecil Guinness's accolades. **82** Robert Winthorp, philanthropist, politician and friend criticized Peabody for not having '... a pre-eminent measure of that sort of charity which shuns publicity, which shrinks from observation, and which, according to one of our Saviour's well-remembered injunctions, "doeth its alms in secret"', cited in Morris, 'Changing perceptions of philanthropy', p. 50. **83** Prunty argues that nineteenth-century urban Dublin produced 'geographical segregation' emblematic of 'social stratification and class self-consciousness' and that each social group was 'anxious to place an indisputable distance between themselves and those beneath them, further enforcing class distinctions', 'Improving the urban environment', p. 167. **84** Department of Irish Folklore, UCD, Urban Folklore Project, NFC_2002_201–4, Móna Ní Ailbhartaigh, interview with Ambie Collins, Iveagh Trust, New Bride Street, 26 Mar. 1980. **85** Marcel Mauss, translated by Ian Cunnison, *The gift: forms and functions of exchange in archaic societies* (London, 1966), p. 1. While Mauss was primarily concerned with the history of gift exchanging and contemporary systems in Polynesia, Melanesia, and north-west America, he notes '... the same morality and economy are at work, albeit less noticeably, in our own societies, and we believe that in them we have discovered one of the bases of social life', p. 2.

> The gift not yet repaid debases the man who accepted it, particularly if he did
> so without thought of return ... charity wounds him who receives, we must
> always return more than we receive; the return is always bigger and more
> costly.[86]

These observations are particularly interesting when the implicit and explicit
connections between the Guinness Brewery, Edward Cecil Guinness, and the
Guinness/Iveagh Trust are considered. It is impossible to ascertain the exchange
value of this philanthropic gesture but at the very least the buildings were the visible
and constant reminder of the munificence of an individual benefaction as linked to
a specific industrial concern and a popular commodity. The architectural evidence
of this relationship can be understood as suggesting an innate understanding of brand
identity and corporate advertising in an age before such concepts were formally
articulated. Barry Berdoll comments that by the end of the nineteenth century 'business and industry also began to assert claims through the manipulation of
architectural imagery, exploiting the urban prominence of buildings such as factories
and warehouses with a nascent sense of advertising' and cites breweries as being one
of the industries most prone to this strategy.[87] In outlining the 'kindness of the late
Lord Iveagh', the interest he took in 'his men' and the recognition of this by
employees and 'the general public in Ireland', Lumsden reflected on almost fifty years
of service to Guinness, stating: 'The "human touch" as a matter of "good business"
and the "employer's conscience" have never been lost sight of, and I venture to think,
quite apart from the humanitarian standpoint, it has been a splendid advertisement.'[88]

The Guinness/Iveagh Trust Buildings and the Guinness Brewery bookend a
compact area of Dublin's city centre, providing permanent and monumental
reminders of Dublin's premier industry. The Bull Alley buildings are conspicuous –
unlike the Belview, Rialto, Thomas Court and Kevin Street buildings – and
concretize specific nineteenth-century values and anxieties, imported into a city that
was on the cusp of seismic change and social and political revolution. Post-
Independence, different perspectives on block housing emerged and this model of
housing became the domain of the poorest in society. Nonetheless, the work of the
Guinness/Iveagh Trust and the Guinness Brewery serve as a visible and tangible
reminder of the influence of philanthropy on the development of municipal housing
strategies in the move towards a welfare state.[89]

---

86 Ibid., p. 63.   **87** Barry Bergdoll, *European architecture: 1750–1890* (Oxford, 2000), pp 275–
6.   **88** Guinness Archives, GDB/C004.9/0002.09, Lumsden, 'History of the medical and
social services in James' Gate, p. 1.   **89** The Iveagh Trust continued to build. Projects
include the Iveagh Gardens – 136 cottages – in Crumlin (1926–36) and 112 sheltered units
in Rathmines (1960–73). Recently it has focused on maintaining and improving the original
buildings but has also taken ownership of some new building programmes including the 50-
unit Eleveden House, Cork Street (2010), 130 units at Clongriffin, north Dublin, 110 units
at Applewood, Swords. The organization currently houses 1088 people: *The Iveagh Trust,
annual report*, 2010, p. 10. The Guinness Trust, London, is now the Guinness Partnership and
operates nationally. It has provided 60,000 homes for 120,000 people.

'A person of the second order': the plight of the intellectually disabled in nineteenth-century Ireland

OONAGH WALSH

INTRODUCTION

Medical history has proven itself to be an exceptionally rich field for social constructionists. The belief that the mad, for example, are made, not born, has underpinned many major works in the history of psychiatry.[1] This approach permeates much of the broad field of medical history, with the development of each specialism – obstetrics, psychiatry, and surgery in particular – analysed by sociologists and historians in terms of ulterior social and cultural motives, with scientific and technical advances often a barely acknowledged footnote. Issues of authority and control lie at the heart of the engagements, with mental health regarded as perhaps the most obvious area in which patient autonomy might be subject to the overwhelming power of the physician.[2] But even within this often-rancorous and well-trodden field, significant gaps remain. Despite two decades of substantial research in international psychiatric history, intellectual disability remains a relatively neglected field.[3] This may be partly explained by the powerful attraction that madness holds for the general as well as the academic population, succinctly noted by Roy Porter: 'madness continues to exercise its magic, but mindlessness holds no mystique'.[4] There is arguably a certain glamour attached to some mental illnesses, which is underpinned by a cultural belief in the

---

1 Michel Foucault's works, especially *Histoire de la folie à l'âge classique* (Paris, 1972), are the most important, but polemics including Thomas Szasz's *The myth of mental illness* (New York, 1974, first pub. 1960) also had a formative influence upon the academic anti-psychiatry movement. 2 Perhaps the two most influential early works in this regard are Andrew Scull's *Museums of madness: the social organization of insanity in nineteenth-century England* (New Haven, CT, 1979) and Elaine Showalter's *The female malady: women, madness and English culture, 1830–1980* (London, 1987). Both works provided a new scholarly framework within which to evaluate institutional histories, and influenced a generation of sociologists and historians. 3 A number of groundbreaking works have been published including David Wright and Anne Digby (eds), *From idiocy to mental deficiency: historical perspectives on people with learning disabilities* (London, 1996), Mathew Thomson, *The problem of mental deficiency: eugenics, democracy and social policy in Britain, c.1870–1959* (Oxford, 1998), and David Wright, *Mental disability in Victorian England: the Earlswood Asylum, 1847–1901* (Oxford, 2001). But given the numbers of 'mental defectives' in workhouses, asylums and the community at large, historical studies are surprisingly rare. 4 Quoted in Wright, *Mental disability*, p. 3.

association between insanity and creativity, but mental handicap is a different matter. The dichotomy is clearly expressed in popular culture: the term 'crazy' can be positively applied to an ambitious, if reckless, individual, but the playground insult 'retard' has no positive connotations.

The contrast in attitude towards the mentally ill and the mentally deficient is apparent from historic efforts to accommodate and treat the respective groups. At its most cruel, the distinction between the two was reduced to a relatively simple equation: the mentally ill had a mind and lost it, the mentally deficient never had a mind to begin with. In early nineteenth-century Ireland, when asylum physicians as well as the State optimistically believed in the likelihood of large-scale cures of the insane, the incurable mental defectives were a problematic cohort. Mental deficiency was in some ways more easily accommodated in the pre-industrial era, with those individuals who survived their early years (a perilous time, when neglect or indeed active ill-treatment saw high mortality rates) finding a place in communities as the 'village idiot'.[5] But as the nineteenth-century State became increasingly interventionist, creating and making compulsory basic standards of education and medical care, those who were deemed incapable of benefiting from either became increasingly marginalized. The rise of the institution further accelerated the division of citizens into productive and dependent populations, and government investment was geared towards maximizing the former and minimizing the latter. The primary impulse behind the huge expansion of the district asylum system in Ireland was curative, and each institution operated on the understanding that their goal was to return patients to society as productive members. Within this rubric, the intellectually disabled were deemed problematic, and a general belief in their unvarying condition ensured that few philanthropists or reformers placed emphasis upon their training or education. But the second half of the nineteenth century saw the first recognition that this cohort deserved, and required, specialist treatment, and the early initiatives were undertaken by voluntary groups. This chapter seeks to examine the development of institutions for the care of the intellectually disabled in nineteenth-century Ireland, and looks at the respective roles played by the State and voluntary institutions in shaping primary care systems.

INSTITUTIONAL CARE: THE STATE

A note on terminology. The terms 'idiot', 'imbecile', and 'feeble-minded' are used in this paper as a reflection of their use in Victorian and Edwardian records. They are

5 Although it is important not to romanticize this period, as Foucault had a tendency to do: his interpretation of the 'Ship of Fools' in his *Histoire* as carrying beings with universally recognized wisdom and insights was an allegorical ideal, not an historical reality. There is no evidence to suggest that the intellectually disabled were treated with a greater degree of humanity, but more accurate to state that the growth of institutional care made them a more conspicuous group.

not interchangeable; 'idiocy' and 'imbecility' in particular generally referred to children, and the feeble-minded were a category deemed educable to a reasonable standard by reformers, often in contrast to the former group. In Ireland, however, idiots in particular were included in legislation relating to insanity, leading to a delay in the development of specialist provision. Moreover, it limited an understanding of their specific needs, as they were conceptualized in terms of the potential danger they represented, and not the manner in which they might be integrated into mainstream society.[6] I am dealing here for the most part with the first two categories, and with individuals who were believed to be mentally incapable from birth or early childhood. The feeble-minded were quite a separate category, and were a source of great anxiety for the State and philanthropists alike at the end of the nineteenth century. Often 'indistinguishable' from the majority of the population, they were regarded as potentially highly disruptive elements. This was the cohort often referred to as 'moral imbeciles' in order to distinguish them from 'congenital idiots and imbeciles'. The 'feeble-minded' could 'pass' as normal, but contained the potential to weaken the national stock through unregulated reproduction. They were regarded as immoral, and as most likely to engage in low-level crime. Although reformers often attributed their criminal tendencies to economic and indeed nutritional deprivation, the general response was to deal with them punitively: many found themselves the inmates of borstals and industrial schools in the early twentieth century. Idiots and imbeciles were on the contrary more frequently categorized under a variety of terms intended to refer to shared physical characteristics that suggested mental incapacity. Thus 'mongol' and 'cretin' were used to describe children who were also 'mentally retarded', and their physical appearance was an important part of the diagnosis. I use the modern term 'intellectual disability' to refer to individuals, children and adults, who became the focus of attention from State and voluntary agencies from the mid-nineteenth century, and embraced a wide range of ability and disability.

Ireland had, in common with other European countries, well established folk and popular beliefs that explained intellectual disability. The most important of these is the changeling. According to myth, fairies stole babies from their cots, substituting their own unwanted, malevolent baby in place of the human child. These fairy offspring were recognizable by their physical appearance − always ugly, with disproportionately large heads, thin limbs, and dark, deep-set eyes. They made incessant, meaningless noise, had voracious appetites, and smiled vacantly or gleefully when the family suffered misfortune. The characteristics add up to a broad-brush description of many mentally and physically handicapped children, and, although overwhelmingly negative, permitted parents to accommodate the 'misfortune' of a profoundly handicapped child.[7] But as Catholicism took an increasingly firm hold on Irish

---

6 The Dangerous Lunatics Act applied to dangerous idiots as well as the mentally ill, ensuring that the asylum was the default institution for care in the nineteenth century.
7 C.F. Goodey and Tim Stainton, 'Intellectual disability and the myth of the changeling myth', *Journal of the History of Behavioural Sciences*, 37:3 (Summer 2001), p. 225.

culture, the conceptualization of idiots and imbeciles underwent a significant alter-
ation. Intellectually disabled children were now seen as deserving objects of
charitable support, and indeed as specific tests of Christian charity. Such individuals
were conceptualized, in modern parlance, as 'special': singled out by God, and a sign
of his Divine will. This re-evaluation was expressed in popular terminology that
persists today. The intellectually disabled were often described as 'touched' – the full
term is 'touched by the hand of God'. Older people will still say 'God Bless the
Mark', referring to someone who has been 'marked' as different by God. And the
term 'Duine le Dia' or person of God, commonly used to mean the intellectually
disabled, suggests a favoured elite and an entitlement to the protection of the able-
bodied population because of, not in spite of, their mental incapacity.

This does not imply, however, that the intellectually disabled were a privileged
group in Irish society. Although their presence provided individuals with the opportunity to demonstrate charity and forbearance through their support of a
demonstrably helpless group, the reality was that they were more often the objects of
abuse and mockery. Idiots were especially vulnerable to ill-treatment, and to
exploitation. Those who were cared for by families at home had at least the protection of a recognized status, and could depend upon a shared community
responsibility for the less able (a social contract that tended to be broken rapidly once
parents died or became themselves dependent), but it was the so-called 'wandering
idiots' that suffered most:

> Again, the reference to the torture inflicted by children (and, it might be said,
> ill-disposed grown persons, too) on wandering idiots is merely a hint which
> no one would care to have amplified whose feelings have been harrowed by
> having witnessed the matter referred to. Finally, much might have been said
> as to evils resulting from idiots of both sexes being allowed to wander unpro-
> tected through the country – often a source of hideous immorality. Not
> unfrequently idiot females are known or suspected to be the subjects of rape,
> and the number of cases of this kind that come under the notice of the police
> is probably small compared with the total.[8]

This is not to say, however, that Irish institutional care provided an ideal solution,
or an especially high standard of treatment. Joseph Robins, on the contrary, argues
that those 'idiots at large' were better off homeless in the community, than in either
the workhouse, or the early specialist idiot and imbecile homes.[9] The experiences of
vulnerable children in Irish industrial schools and reformatories were certainly far
from ideal, with even the most optimistic inspectors noting instances of cruelty and
abuse.[10] Throughout the nineteenth century, institutionalized children endured

---

8 H. Trentham Butlin, 'The Lunacy Inquiry Commission', *The Medical Press and Circular*, 29
(Jan.–June 1880), p. 43. 9 Joseph Robins, *From rejection to integration: a centenary of service by
the Daughters of Charity to persons with a mental handicap* (Dublin, 1992), p. 28. 10 Jane
Barnes, *Irish industrial schools, 1868–1908* (Dublin, 1989).

appallingly high mortality rates, with the youngest suffering most. Even at the start of the twentieth century, there was a truly shocking death rate of over 40 per cent amongst children under the age of 24 months in the North Dublin Union's two nurseries.[11] Intellectually disabled children frequently suffered from chronic illnesses that included respiratory and heart ailments, and were more susceptible to infectious diseases than most children. But they faced additional problems in coping with the highly competitive environment of the workhouse, and often failed to secure even their meagre entitlement to food and care. It is painful indeed to imagine the lot of children who could not easily communicate, either to ask for help, or to complain about their treatment. One such child was sent from Roscommon workhouse to the Ballinasloe Asylum in 1891, with his condition reflecting his vulnerable state:

> He is an idiot child of about eleven years of age, and was brought under a charge of violently striking another inmate. His hair is matted and filthy, and his clothes in a ragged and filthy state. His stature is small for his age and he appears ill-grown, although free from any obvious physical malformation. His manner is fearful and timid, and he replies to questions with low incomprehensible sounds: I cannot detect any propensity to violence, on the contrary he seems eager to please.[12]

The treatment of idiots at home varied. Children in supportive households, however impoverished, were undoubtedly better off than in institutional care. But even with the best of intentions, it proved difficult to satisfactorily address the needs of such dependent children, especially in environments where the rest of the family were absent during the day. In 1879, Major William LePoer Trench presented his report on the state of the lunatic poor in Ireland, which became the basis for the Bill 'To Make Better Provision for the Lunatic Poor in Ireland'.[13] He included the plight of unregistered idiot children in his brief, and provided ample evidence of domestic neglect:

> I found [a] little boy, 14 years of age, an idiot, and he was perfectly naked, lying in a filthy bed, wretchedly neglected, unable from confinement to bear the light, and who ought to have been in an institution. That was a child lapsing into blindness from neglect. The next on the list is J.B., aged 16, another pitiable case – a congenital epileptic idiot lying on straw in a wretched room. He was whining and sobbing when I went in to see him. He was alone in the house, and the neighbours all stated that he ought to be looked after. He was lying naked, his limbs were contracted, his body filthy, and chilblains on

---

11 Catriona Clear, *Social change and everyday life in Ireland, 1850–1922* (Manchester, 2007), p. 115. **12** Case No. 3171, 13 Nov. 1891. **13** The Bill had its second reading in the House of Lords in July 1883, but soon became embroiled in a debate regarding the difficulties of funding appropriate provision for Irish pauper lunatics and idiots. *HL Deb*, 3 July 1883, vol. 281, cc160–8.

his feet. That gives an idea of the condition of these unregistered idiots at large.

> There is absolutely nothing done for them. I have found cases in my visitations ... where parents when they were obliged to go out to do their day's work, simply locked the imbecile children in. I have found them sometimes in a cabin in company with a pig, or a cat, or sitting over a fireplace without a fire in it in the middle of winter.[14]

The intellectually disabled were a highly vulnerable group in nineteenth-century Ireland, with no State and very limited philanthropic support. The majority were cared for by the family, with a substantial minority (estimated at one-fifth of the total idiot population) resident in workhouses.[15] In the first half of the nineteenth century, the district asylum system was also an important State means of care for idiots, imbeciles and mental defectives. The numbers varied from asylum to asylum, but at the Ballinasloe asylum, idiots and imbeciles accounted for between seven and ten per cent of admissions in the 1870s, out of an average annual intake of 110 patients per year.[16] Many of these individuals were repeat admissions: it proved a characteristic in the treatment of the intellectually disabled that they moved repeatedly between the local asylum and the workhouse, discharged and readmitted in a distressing pattern of evasion of responsibility. One child was shunted seven times between the workhouse and asylum at Ballinasloe over the course of several years, finally settling permanently in the asylum as a dangerous idiot.[17]

The idiotic population in asylums attracted official, as well as charitable, attention. The asylum inspectors made frequent note of their presence (most often to state that they should be housed elsewhere), and commented in particular upon the hardship faced by children who were placed in environments with often violent and unstable patients. The Ballinasloe asylum's annual report for 1882 reiterated the necessity to provide suitable accommodation – 'It is pitiful indeed to see these idiot children wander about the asylum grounds, with little prospect of an improvement in their condition' – and this was envisaged as being outside the asylum, rather than as a distinct element within it.[18] Because so many areas within the asylum required attention, little was done to improve their lot. The asylum authorities prioritized other

---

14 The plight of such children was a matter of continued debate. Trench's findings were presented by W. Neilson Hancock to the Statistical and Social Inquiry Society of Ireland, with the demand that provision follow the varied model already in place in England, including idiot colonies and boarding-out. 'On the Report of the Irish Lunacy Inquiry Commissioners, and the policy of extending the English Law for the Protection of Neglected Lunatics to Ireland', *Journal of the Statistical and Social Inquiry Society of Ireland*, 7, Part 55 (1878–79), pp 454–61. **15** The numbers of 'known idiots' varied significantly, owing not least to a reluctance on the part of parents to acknowledge such disability in their children. **16** Calculated from committal warrants, and the Register of Admissions of the Connaught District Lunatic Asylum, 1871–80. **17** Case No. 2477, first admission 24 Sept. 1882. **18** 31st Annual Report for 1882.

pressing issues, including salary arrears, overcrowding, the need for a post-mortem room, additional staff, and a long litany of vital improvements in the asylum's accommodation, in their correspondence with the Lord Lieutenant's office, with requests for additional funds to care for the intellectually disabled tagged on to other petitions. The group did not thus have a particular champion, and in an often chaotic environment, such inmates often became the target of abusive patients. One such delighted in 'tormenting' the idiots and the bedridden, and was also suspected of sexual assault.[19] The idiotic had food stolen from them, and were easily ousted from seats at the fire, and other favoured places. Difficulties with speech proved a further disadvantage, although staff made efforts to protect them: 'Nurse N. reported that she had instructed another patient to mind TN when he is in the ward: she tells me that the other patients move him from his place by the fire, and mock his attempts to remonstrate'.[20] There were some individuals who found security and fulfilment within the asylum, including one who became 'a most useful drudge to the carpenter, to whom he is inordinately attached, and accompanies around the asylum ready to do his bidding.' But such cases were rare enough to be specifically noted, and the more pressing needs of mentally ill inmates always took priority over the cases which could never be cured. There was however one area in which the asylum idiots were favoured over others, and which constituted a minor form of philanthropy within the State system. In common with other institutions, including orphanages, prisons, industrial schools, and residential homes for the elderly, Ballinasloe asylum received numbers of visitors who came to inspect the institution, and were taken on tours of the premises. Such visitors often left sums of money to buy treats, or to support improvements such as libraries for the inmates. The Ballinasloe Board of Guardians often dedicated this small fund to the idiots, noting rather poignantly that they were the inmates who were least likely to receive visits, letters, or parcels from home.[21]

One of the issues that hampered voluntary efforts on the part of idiots and imbeciles was that their numbers in Irish asylums were difficult to establish, not least because the classificatory systems used were so imprecise. 'Idiots' were prone to epileptic seizures, and occasionally appear in the records under both 'idiot' and 'epileptic' patients, leading to them being counted twice in the patient registers. Individuals were often represented as 'simple' and 'wandering in their thoughts' as part of committal evidence, but without any additional proof of mental inadequacy. Families were also reluctant to admit to a mentally defective offspring or sibling, and did not record numbers accurately in official returns. The publication of the 1889 royal commission on the condition of the blind, deaf and dumb marked an attempt to quantify the scale of the problem, but found that little notice of the group, or their numbers, had been taken since 1881: 'In Ireland nobody looks after them. So little are they looked after that no Department has even taken the trouble to have

---

19 For a discussion of the case, see Oonagh Walsh, 'A perfectly ordered establishment' in Pauline Prior (ed.), *Asylums, mental health care and the Irish, 1800–2012* (Dublin, 2012), pp 263–4. **20** Case No. 2841, 19 Oct. 1885. **21** Board of Guardians Minute Book, 14 July 1893.

them enumerated since the census of 1881... [when].... it was found that there were then 6,700 of these persons all over the country, a large proportion of them being children.'[22] However, by 1909 this figure had been drastically revised, suggesting a four-fold increase of known idiots and imbeciles: '... there are in Ireland 25,415 mentally defective persons, or 66.05 per 10,000 of the population, in addition to the 25,050 insane (56.18 per 10,000) already in institutions under certificates ... The numbers in proportion to the population are very much greater than in England and Scotland.'[23]

State provision for the mentally afflicted had expanded and improved greatly during the nineteenth century. The district asylums had been established to offer the most modern of treatments to the mentally ill, and with the specific intention of rehabilitating patients and restoring them as productive members of society. But they were highly unsuitable for the intellectually disabled, despite large numbers being committed as dangerous idiots under the Dangerous Lunatics Act. Incurable cases such as idiots and imbeciles were not regarded as fit subjects for admission to asylums, which had been established for the treatment of 'curable lunatics' only. The 'tranquilly demented', for example, were supposed to be cared for in workhouses (under the Poor Law Act of 1838), as were the harmless 'idiots and imbeciles'. Epileptics, if not violent, were intended for the workhouse or the 'epileptic wings' added to Irish asylum buildings throughout the nineteenth century. Despite this, large numbers of intellectually disabled individuals were inmates of the district asylums, often for protracted periods of time. The problem was exacerbated by the fact that the few institutions that existed for the care of feeble-minded, idiotic and imbecilic children could not accommodate adults, so many were admitted to the asylums once they reached the age of 14. Thus, despite the unsuitability of the environment, the intellectually disabled constituted a considerable percentage of the asylum population nationally, creating therapeutic problems that persisted until the mid twentieth century.

But the available alternatives were little better, and in some cases worse. Until the 1880s and 90s, when special schools began to be established in Britain, the primary locus of care for the intellectually disabled was the workhouse. The presence of idiotic and imbecilic residents was a constant source of anxiety for the workhouse inspectors who, while acknowledging the eligibility of this group for public support (most fulfilled effortlessly the poor law imperative of extreme poverty, and an inability to support themselves), also recognized that the workhouse could do little to improve their limited lot. In any case, education and training were not the primary purpose of the workhouse, nor was it envisaged as a place of permanent residence, or even an asylum in the sense of a refuge for the vulnerable. Rather it was more

---

22 *Report of the royal commission on the blind, the deaf and dumb, &_c., of the United Kingdom. 1889.* This Report embraced idiot and imbecile children, as many also suffered from sight and hearing problems. 23 W.R. Dawson, 'The Irish recommendations of the royal commission on the care and control of the feeble-minded', *Transactions of the Royal Academy of Medicine in Ireland*, 27:1 (Dec. 1909), p. 345.

accurately a place of last resort for those utterly without resources, succinctly summarized thus: 'For those on the fringes of society the workhouse was a central element of the mixed economy of makeshifts'.[24] And even here, in the company of those equally marginalized, the idiotic and imbecilic were subject to harsh treatment and liable to be discharged on spurious grounds. The 1876 Report of the Charity Organization Society had highlighted the problematic position of idiot and imbecilic children and adults in the workhouses, who had neither remedial education nor basic training for employment.[25] Indeed, it was clear from the evidence included in the Report that this group received even less than their miserly entitlement, especially with regard to food:

> ... no difference of opinion can exist as to the advisability of taking from the workhouses ... imbeciles and idiots, for whose proper management nearly all the conditions are there wanting; there being, moreover, neither suitable education for the children nor industrial occupation for the adults; and it being difficult to persuade the guardians that a more than usually nourishing diet is absolutely necessary for them.[26]

As the nineteenth century advanced, there was a growing conviction in any case that the overburdened workhouses and asylums offered poor value for money in terms of nursing idiots and imbeciles. There was insufficient room for the numbers of insane who clamoured for admission to the district asylums (or more accurately whose relatives did so) and to the workhouses, and the persistent presence of incurable intellectually disabled inmates put further pressure upon strained resources. Thus discussion focused upon the role to be played by philanthropists, who could be appealed to on the grounds that the state was already heavily committed, and in any case these pitiful objects were more deserving of charity. There was a general acceptance that there was no more money to be extracted from Irish ratepayers, who were already stretched by the demands of other dependent groups:

> Owing to the comparative absence of wealth in Ireland, the resources of benevolence are very limited, while, having regard to the poverty of the country as a whole, and to the fact that many of the ratepayers are themselves steeped in poverty, and already heavily burdened with lunacy charges, they cannot justly be expected to bear any further heavy impost for founding or supporting institutions for the training of imbeciles and feeble-minded persons.[27]

24 Virginia Crossman, 'The poor law in Ireland', *History in Focus* 'Welfare', Issue 14 (Winter 2008). 25 *Report of the Charity Organization Committee on the legal provisions in Ireland for the care and instruction of imbeciles, idiots, deaf and dumb and blind, with suggestions for amended legislation* (1876). *Journal of the Statistical and Social Inquiry Society of Ireland*, vii, part li, 1876/1877, pp 136–7. 26 'The education and care of idiots, imbeciles and harmless lunatics', *British Medical Journal*, 28 July 1877, p. 109. 27 *Royal commission on the care and control of the feeble-minded*, 1909, p. 229.

There was an increasing expenditure in Ireland on infrastructure, education, and health, in an effort to bring Ireland up to the prevailing mainland standards. This investment could be justified in terms of an anticipated reward in healthier, better-educated citizens, who would contribute to the nation's prosperity through employment. By contrast, the permanently dependent offered little return other than the promise of a life-long financial burden. Poor law expenditure rose towards the end of the century, despite the universally acknowledged misery of indoor relief in workhouses, and a scanty system of outdoor support.[28] Thus, the claims of a group that would never recover and contribute to the economy, nor had the claim of prior value, as in the case of the aged, were far down the list of welfare priorities for a care system under severe pressure.

PHILANTHROPY: VOLUNTARY INSTITUTIONS

The intellectually disabled became the object of philanthropic attention towards the end of the nineteenth century, as much by default as by deliberate intent. In the 1870s, a concerted focus upon this group emerged, and a significant effort, based on voluntary care, began to address them as a distinct body which might be capable of improvement. Debates over the perceived problem of mental disability were taking place, with the medical profession taking an active part: Ireland's care systems for idiots and imbeciles were firmly predicated upon a medical model, which was to have negative implications for their long-term care.[29] Concern for their position resulted in two influential reports, which identified the precarious existence of many, especially children, but with few suggestions as to how the problem might be approached. The *Report of the Charity Organization Committee on the legal provisions in Ireland for the care and instruction of imbeciles, idiots, deaf and dumb, and blind, with suggestions for amended legislation* of 1876 presented often harrowing detail of the impoverished position of children with learning difficulties throughout the country, while the *Report of the Charity Organization Committee on imbeciles, idiots and harmless Lunatics* of 1877 reflected a philanthropic concern for neglected children at home, and in workhouses. Each supported the arguments made in successive workhouse and asylum inspectors' reports regarding the necessity for separate accommodation for the mentally disabled. This period is also characterized by significant changes in poor law provision, which had a direct impact upon the large numbers of intellectually disabled children and adults in the poor law system. The 1861 *Report of the select committee on poor relief (Ireland)*, and the 1879 *Report of the Poor Law Union and Lunacy Enquiry Commission (Ireland)*, along with the annual poor law commissioners'

---

28 Virginia Crossman, *The poor law in Ireland, 1838–1948* (Dundalk, 2006), p. 50.   29 John Sweeney, 'The role of the Irish division of the Royal Medico-Psychological Association in the development of intellectual disability nursing in Ireland', *Canadian Bulletin of Medical History*, 28:1 (2001), pp 95–122.

reports reflected an unease regarding the lack of appropriate accommodation and treatment for the mentally defective, but were unwilling to suggest large-scale state provision, owing to the expense. A small number of idiots' colonies had been established in England, but proved costly to run, and the Irish commissions were reluctant to propose them for Ireland. It thus fell to private charity to fill the breach. In the case of the Catholic Church, there was a logic to their advance into this area: their growing role as providers of education in Ireland had brought them forcefully into contact with those who clearly found little benefit from a 'learning by rote' system.

Indeed, one of the most important influences on care for the intellectually disabled was the introduction of compulsory education in Ireland from the 1870s onwards.[30] For the first time, children with learning difficulties began to stand out from their increasingly literate peers, and schools complained that such children either 'derived no benefit from education', or were disruptive in the classroom. A basic standard of literacy was now regarded as an integral element in eventual economic independence, and employers increasingly expected their workers to be literate and numerate. It was also an essential part of every migrant's skills, and young men and women leaving Ireland knew that they were entering a market where the illiterate were badly disadvantaged. The intellectually disabled were perceived to be an increasingly problematic cohort who could not contribute to the domestic economy, or to the workforce, in any position that required basic numeracy or literacy skills. Moreover, it brought into even sharper focus the unsuitability of the district asylums for this group. No Irish asylum was required to provide any form of education. Although some did recognize the importance of training, which could include basic literacy skills, their efforts were focused upon recovering lunatics, and not in the provision of the specialist remedial teaching required by idiots and imbeciles. Finally, as the nineteenth century advanced, schools adopted a 'payment by results' system that led to a focus upon brighter children in the classroom, who could be intensively coached to secure high examination grades: the school received a 'bonus' payment for every successful candidate. The pressure that teachers were placed under to secure good results meant that slower children were at best ignored, and at worst excluded from schools completely.

But the outlook was not entirely bleak. National compulsory education also had an interesting, and positive, impact upon approaches to the education of the intellectually disabled. Although many children failed to flourish in mainstream schools, teachers found, and testified to the royal commissions on education, that they were in many cases capable of a substantial improvement in their general condition if they received special education. With help – and indeed the language used persisted well into the twentieth century, including phrases such as 'sheltered' accommodation, and

---

30 The national system of education began in 1831, but it was principally towards the end of the century, through the compulsion of the 1880 School Attendance Act, that Ireland achieved high levels of literacy. Donald H. Akenson, *The Irish education experiment: the national system of education in the nineteenth century* (London, 2012 (1970)), p. 9.

'special' assistance – it was argued that 'slower' children could master the fundamentals of reading and writing, and, perhaps more importantly, they could be trained up in repetitive tasks, and under instruction make a contribution to the economy in areas such as laundry work, basket weaving, and basic domestic and agricultural tasks. It was recognized that such improvements required the investment of a considerable degree of time and effort, but it was spurred on by an increasing tendency of schools to exclude children with learning difficulties, sending them home on often spurious charges of disruption and inattention.

PROTESTANT INTERVENTION

The question of whether harmless idiots and imbeciles could be productively trained did not go unnoticed by the medical profession. In 1869, the first philanthropic institution for their care was established in Palmerston, Co. Dublin by Dr Henry Hutchinson Stewart, a staunchly Protestant medic (his father as well as his wife's father were clergymen) with a strong social conscience. As a doctor working in North Brunswick Street in Dublin he had noted the plight of intellectually disabled children in the inner city, and the lack of appropriate educational and training facilities for them. He established 'The Stewart Institution for Idiots' which became in 1879 'The Stewart Institution for Idiotic and Imbecile Children', offering a sophisticated regime that included hydrotherapy, occupational therapy, and an early engagement with sensory therapy. Stewart had significant experience with the treatment of mental illness – a private asylum of his own establishment shared the original site of the idiots' institution – and it was his realization that the intellectually disabled were languishing in such large numbers in the asylums that prompted the creation of his Institution. It was established along classic asylum moral therapeutic principles (despite the impossibility of his charges regaining their 'senses'), in a beautiful wooded setting, with forty acres of parkland for the diversion and entertainment of the inmates. Daniel Hack Tuke noted its ample provisions on a visit to Ireland in 1875, and bemoaned the fact that it was the only specific institution for the care of idiots in Ireland: 'A large mansion at Palmerston, in the neighbourhood of Dublin, was in 1875 ... being adapted to the requirements of an asylum ... Let us see how far the opportunities meet the want, and what becomes of those idiots and imbeciles for whom no distinct provision is made.'[31] The institution targeted Dublin's inner city populations, and sought to serve those whom the doctor had seen 'in states of utmost neglect, denied that opportunity for communion with their fellow man that is the right of all'.[32] Stewart personally believed that the children would benefit to the greatest extent through removal from their families, many of whom were impoverished and with limited resources to educate an intellectually disabled child. In this he

---

31 Daniel Hack Tuke, *Chapters in the history of the insane in the British Isles* (London, 1882), p. 161.   **32** Flyer advertising the opening of 'The Stewart's Institution for Idiots', 1869.

followed the general trend towards the establishment of 'colonies' of intellectually disabled children in England in particular, and set a pattern of segregation that continued until the second half of the twentieth century in Ireland.

Stewart's was established on non-denominational lines, and catered for a tiny minority of the country's total population of intellectually disabled. The first intake consisted of only 12 children, a tiny drop in the vast ocean of potential candidates, who ranged across the full spectrum of impairment from total mental incapacity to mere learning difficulties. But its opening provoked a swift and antagonistic response from Catholic Church leaders, who saw in Stewart's the ever-present threat of Protestant evangelism. Late nineteenth-century Dublin was a veritable battleground for souls. The city sustained an enormous philanthropic effort that catered for all denominations, and almost every conceivable subject, including distressed gentlewomen, unmarried mothers, prostitutes, disabled servicemen, indigent labourers, and groups at every possible stage of the human lifecycle from pre-natal (homes for unmarried mothers) to the afterlife, in the form of cemetery associations.[33] Although some organizations were free from any religious influence, the majority were not, and if they lacked an explicit link with a specific denomination they were underpinned by a broadly Christian philosophy and outlook. Most reflected a religious perspective (all of the larger bodies had clergymen as ex-officio committee members), and several were explicitly evangelical. Thus any new charitable endeavour was subject to intense scrutiny until its targets, and its territory, had been identified. Children's charities tended, especially in the early years, to attract more generous subscriptions. The plight of helpless infants, especially those 'crippled' in some way, was far more heartrending than the elderly, and few could resist an appeal to help 'heaven's special child'.[34]

Irish intellectual disability care emerged from this environment of competitive philanthropy, in which a priority was placed upon the removal of idiots and imbeciles from society, but their actual treatment and care was a secondary consideration. Even Stewart's Institution, established by a skilled physician, placed more practical emphasis upon removing children from unsuitable or neglectful environments, than upon training or rehabilitation. This is noteworthy, as Dr Stewart was an experienced alienist with a substantial private as well as public practice, and one who adopted a medical model (based on his private asylum) for his idiots' institution. From the mid nineteenth century idiots and imbeciles in England became part of a sophisticated classificatory system, underpinned by the work of individuals including John Langdon Down. Down developed both a scale of intellectual ability, to distinguish between idiot children, and a practical system for training the 'higher' ranking

---

33 An indication of the number and scale of exclusively Protestant female philanthropic endeavour in Dublin in 1910 is evident in the 91 separate organizations listed in Oonagh Walsh, *Anglican women in Dublin: philanthropy, politics and education in the early twentieth century* (Dublin, 2005), pp 213–19. **34** Paul Longmore, '"Heaven's special child": the making of poster children' in Lennard J. Davis (ed.), *The disability studies reader* (4th ed., New York, 2013), p. 35.

individuals.[35] Drawing upon both medical and anthropological writings, Down's classifications became the accepted standard for specialist institutions, and despite some modern criticism of 'an overtly "racist" taxonomy of mental disability that stigmatized those with trisomy 21 for the next century', his work, and his name, were synonymous with this group until the 1970s. [36] In Ireland, debates about idiocy and imbecility were equally intense, especially with regard to how such individuals should be maintained. However, the medical and scientific approach characteristic of many institutions in England and Scotland did not transfer to Ireland. Rather, the driving issue was that of State versus private responsibility, and an increasing faith in the importance of segregating the mentally sub-normal from the remainder of the population.

Stewart's Institution, the first philanthropic home for the intellectually disabled in Ireland, proved both a success and a failure. Its success lay in providing a model for care which, if it did not achieve its initial objective of training children to a standard that they might earn their livings in a supported environment, proved convincing enough to be followed by other bodies including the Catholic St Vincent's Homes in Dublin and Limerick. It consolidated a belief that segregation was the appropriate method for dealing with such children, and was held up as an example of what might be achieved through philanthropic means. The reality of the inmates' existence was somewhat different, however. On Dr Stewart's death, the institution declined to a degree, and the early optimism about making the children productive members of society faded away. The institution faced a greater demand than it could cope with, funds were erratic and unreliable, and the training programmes did not result in the semi-independent citizens that had been envisaged. By 1901 the home was overcrowded, and had a population of long-stay inmates who were entirely dependent. The Census returns show that the age range of the idiot residents was from 7 to 68 years, with the majority in their twenties.[37] Only a minority were under the age of 14 (29 out of 91), despite the institution's commitment to the education and training of the young. Thus, the institution was unable to accept many new admissions, and had the responsibility for caring for admissions for the remainder of their lives.

CATHOLIC EFFORTS

The Catholic Church's role in intellectual disability provision is interesting, and stands in sharp contrast to their virtual absence from the asylum system in the same period. The Daughters of Charity began to work voluntarily in the North Dublin Union workhouse in 1884, and were welcomed by poor law guardians because of their willingness to labour for virtually no pay (a token £20 to £30 per year). By the

---

35 Wright, *Mental disability*, Chapter 9. 'Down's Syndrome', pp 155–76.   36 Cited in Wright, *Mental disability*, p. 155.   37 Census of Ireland, 1901, Form 1, 'Return of Lunatics and Idiots in Public Institutions and Private Lunatic Asylums', for Stewart's Institution.

early twentieth century, they were firmly ensconced as administrators as well as nursing and teaching staff in the workhouse, and after the creation of the Free State took complete responsibility for the care of intellectually disabled children from the former North Dublin Union workhouse.

The vulnerability of mentally deficient children to proselytism had long been recognized. In 1878 the largely toothless 'Bill to Make Better Provision for Idiots, Imbeciles and Other Afflicted Persons in Ireland' included a 'conscience clause' – 'No pauper shall be sent to any hospital, institution, asylum or establishment under the provisions of this act, unless the same is under the exclusive management of persons of the religious denomination to which he belongs' – recognizing the particular problems faced by inmates who might not be able to articulate their opposition to conversion.[38] But the emphasis upon protecting the individual's soul, rather than mind and body, meant that more imaginative options were not explored. In England, for example, in addition to the colonies that were established for supported care, there were also philanthropic bodies that adapted the boarding-out system long utilized for lunatics in Scotland. In parts of England, the work of the Guardian Society facilitated an early model of 'care in the community' by placing mentally deficient children in approved family homes.[39] This model was not adopted to any substantial degree in Ireland, despite the fact that several charities, Anglican in particular, routinely placed orphan children with families until they reached the age of 14.[40]

Catholic Church attitudes in particular had a profound effect upon their conceptualization and treatment in the twentieth century. From the outset, there was a determined characterization of the intellectually disabled as child-like, regardless of their actual age or stage of development. They represented an unambiguous childish innocence, a still-prevalent representation that has caused a great deal of anger, denying as it does a fully adult identity. Idiots and imbeciles were conceptualized as eternal innocents, among the purest of God's creation. Because they could not reason, they could not sin. Incapable of adulthood, they were necessarily incapable of any taint of sexuality, or so the logic ran. Promotional literature published by the Daughters of Charity emphasized this element of innocence constantly, describing their charges as 'affectionate, entirely free from connivance or jealousy, and the most perfect expression of childish innocence'. The reality of course was that the inmates were complex individuals, and the wilful casting of them as a whole in an infantalized manner caused tremendous difficulties. As many reached adulthood, they often proved difficult to manage. Once they stepped beyond the rigid definitions laid

38 The Act empowered local authorities to fund the costs of maintaining several vulnerable groups in appropriate institutions via rates, but the more pressing problem of a lack of specialist centres was not addressed. *The Poor Afflicted Persons Relief (Ireland) Act, 1878.* **39** Louise Westwood, 'Care in the community of the mentally disordered: the case of the guardianship society, 1900–39', *Social History of Medicine*, 20:1 (2007), p. 61. **40** The Protestant Orphan Society, for example, paid board, lodgings and a clothing allowance to families who accommodated children, as well as an annual stipend to the head of the household. Protestant Orphan Society Records, National Archives of Ireland, 1045/5/5.

down for them, they often faced life back in the district asylums, admitted as dangerous lunatics, with no prospect of discharge and no specialist treatment. Descriptions of adults returned to the asylums are often remarkably similar, and cite 'the display of vicious propensities' as a precipitating factor in transfer. If they remained cheerful, malleable and indeed innocent and child-like, they often remained in the care of the Daughters until death (many intellectually disabled patients had chronic physical illness, and died young). But more complex ranges of behaviour could and often did mean expulsion – it seems everyone had to 'play the game' even if the rules were not clear to all. However, one rather poignant point that should be made is that the level of available care for such a vulnerable group was, despite the recommendations of successive royal commissions and reports throughout the nineteenth century, non-existent. The Catholic Church remained the single largest provider for the intellectually disabled for a century and a half,[41] and it was a responsibility that was not shirked, even as it moved away from a mildly reformist agenda that focused on the poor, to a more socially conservative stance in the twentieth century.[42]

The care of the intellectually disabled by nuns had a further internal logic. The presentation of these individuals as children, regardless of age, cast the sisters into the role of mothers, as pure embodiments of the Marian ideal – virgin births indeed. But because this particular role was unending, in that the patients would not recover and would require constant care, it was the fullest expression of a life of self-sacrifice, and a life in the service of individuals who could not understand the extent of the help they received. The Daughters of Charity emphasized this element in their own rare comments on their mission: 'It is a life of forbearance, one lived in the knowledge that those whom we help labour under such privations that gratitude is inexpressible: let that not deter us from our work, which is truly God-given.'[43] The care of the mentally ill was led by university trained physicians, who hoped that they would cure, or at least improve, the mental afflictions of their charges. Asylums vied with each other to record high cure, recovery and discharge rates, and the reputation of individual asylums rose and fell on the basis of these figures. But there were no such triumphs in the idiots' homes, a fact that underpinned the self-sacrificing nature of a nun's life. One might argue that in both cases ego was served – the asylum physician was praised for his skill in cure and treatment, the nuns for the fact that no cure was possible, but they persisted regardless. The intellectually disabled certainly needed the care offered by the Daughters of Charity, but one might also say that they offered in turn an exceptional opportunity to these women to fulfil their own religious mission.

In another important regard, the model of care adopted by Irish nuns for idiots

41 Robins, *From rejection to integration*.   **42** Tony Fahey, 'The Catholic Church and social policy', *The Furrow*, 49:4 (Apr. 1998), p. 146.   **43** Anon, 'Our mission', *The Sacred Heart Messenger* (Sept. 1899).

and imbeciles proved compatible with both their own self-sacrificing philosophy, and a medical approach that favoured the isolation of the mentally vulnerable. The tendency towards the segregation of idiots and imbeciles reflected the foundational principles of many orders, several of which were enclosed, with the absolute segregation from the outside world a highly visible statement of sacrifice by nuns. Orders such as the Carmelites exemplified the ideal that God's work was best carried out away from a potentially corrupting modern society, and that a withdrawal from the world was inherently spiritual. Removing those who could not care for themselves, and assuming a life-long responsibility for their welfare, underlined the value of the nuns' work. Thus, those who rejected the world, and those whom the world rejected, created communities of acceptance that prioritized spiritual and not material worth. Some critics of segregation have argued that it was merely a less brutal form of sterilization, given that one of the primary objectives was to prevent the undesirable from reproducing – '... histories of the eugenics movement show the degree to which this population labelled "feeble-minded" was at the top of the eugenic agenda, and how segregation was as much a eugenic control option as sterilization ... specialized custodial institutions for the mentally deficient were essentially manifestations of eugenically-driven social policy' – but this is to ignore both the complexity of social attitudes towards the mentally deficient, and the many expressions of concern about the quality of life for vulnerable individuals on the fringes of society.[44] Although those in the care of the Daughters of Charity had not chosen a life of celibacy, these two complemented each other: the virgin mothers and the eternal children, each supplying a Divine justification for their respective existence.

This characterization offered a unique advantage to the Irish intellectually disabled. Although their provision lagged behind that of the rest of the United Kingdom prior to Independence (and indeed well after – it was not until 1959 that the first Inspector for Special Education was appointed by the Minister for Education), and was unhelpfully driven by a battle for religious supremacy rather than the needs of the group, Ireland stood well in advance of the western world in her lack of engagement with practical eugenics, and a desire to limit the reproductive capabilities of the idiots and imbeciles. There was a concern regarding the heritable nature of idiocy in particular, and a substantial body of literature, penned by the asylum inspectors as well as individual physicians, concerning the dangers of uncontrolled marriage and reproduction by idiots, imbeciles and lunatics. But Ireland never engaged with the rhetoric and reality of eugenics with regard to mental incapacity, nor promoted ideals of racial or ethnic superiority, in the manner of other, arguably more advanced, countries. In this sense, the broad brush characterization of the intellectually disabled as harmless children, an effective refusal to acknowledge an adult sexuality, and a rigorous policy of segregation in institutions protected idiots and imbeciles from enforced sterilization and denunciation.

44 John P. Radford, 'Sterilization versus segregation: control of the "feeble-minded", 1900–38', *Social Science and Medicine*, 33:4 (1991), p. 450.

The mass sterilization campaigns of the Third Reich are a by-word for intoler-
ance and cruelty. But the earlier eugenics movement of the late nineteenth and early
twentieth centuries was equally repugnant, and arguably of a greater reach. Opinions
as to how the mentally 'undesirable' might be prevented from reproducing themselves varied substantially, but within respectable as well as extreme medical,
philosophical, and even philanthropic circles there was a unanimity of opinion as to
the necessity to control (by force or statute) the 'undesirable' from replicating themselves. Hereditary factors in the tremendous increase in institutionalized insane were
accepted by Irish asylum inspectors, with intermarriage regarded as an important
element in explaining the growth in the mentally ill. There had also been long-
standing concerns regarding the sexual exploitation of idiots and imbeciles at liberty,
a concern that was a recognition of their vulnerability as much as worry about the
'national stock'. In England, the discussion of what to do with 'defectives' was far
more explicit than in Ireland, and secured wider levels of support within high political circles.

But this is not to say that there was no concern in Ireland about the negative
impact of the intellectually disabled on society. Irish lay and medical figures shared a
wider British concern with children as the embodiment of national aspiration, and a
desire to promote good mental and physical health.[45] The creation of Na Fianna
Éireann in 1909 by Constance Markievicz was prompted by political developments,
but the rhetoric regarding health and purity was analogous to that of the Boy Scouts
and other, similar, organizations that made increasing divisions between the fit and
unfit. In part a development attributable to the widely perceived *fin-de-siècle* 'deca-
dence', each of these organizations promoted 'a healthy mind in a healthy body',
leaving aside those who possessed neither.[46] In the early years of the twentieth
century, low intelligence became increasingly associated with deviance, and as an
element to be controlled rather than changed. The Irish response to the potential
weakening of the national stock was simply to segregate, and protect the vulnerable
individuals as well as future generations:

> In addition to these [idiots and imbeciles 'at large'], there is one particular class
> well known in Irish workhouses, which I may specially mention. I refer to
> those women amongst the wastrels and ne'er-do-wells, who, through mental
> defect, are easily misled, and who spend their time in and out of workhouses,

45 As infant mortality rates slowly improved, children and indeed childhood itself was
reconceptualized. Children were now a national as well as a familial asset, and a range of
specialisms developed to address the emergent cohort. Interestingly, although child
psychiatry did not formally emerge as a discipline until the 1930s, its origins lie in this
period, as children came increasingly under scrutiny from a range of professionals. See
Alexander Von Gontard, 'The development of child psychiatry in nineteenth-century
Britain', *Journal of Child Psychology and Psychiatry*, 29:5 (Sept. 1988), p. 569. 46 Marnie Hay,
'The foundation and development of Na Fianna Éireann, 1909–16', *Irish Historical Studies*,
36:141 (May 2008), p. 53.

giving birth to illegitimate children, and thus perpetuating the social canker. I think that some means should be devised by which such women – on being proved mentally defective, although not certifiably insane – should be placed in institutions where they could no longer be the means of swelling the ranks of the submerged tenth.[47]

This wilful characterization of idiots and imbeciles as harmless, helpless children underpins, I believe, an important element in the Catholic Church's attitude towards mental disability, and mental illness. The Church's increasing dominance in post-Famine Ireland has been well documented, and her incursion into the formative realms of education and medicine (especially maternity care) is particularly important in understanding Irish society throughout the twentieth century.[48] But one of the very few areas in which little attempt at incursion was made was in mental health care. The district asylums remained largely under the control of non-denominational boards, and although it became common for Catholic priests to act as asylum board members from the early twentieth century, it was equally common practice for Protestant ministers to fulfil the same role. Most asylums had Catholic chapels on their grounds by the end of the nineteenth century, but the administration, staffing, and medical direction remained largely free from overt religious influence.[49] Why was the fate of so many vulnerable individuals (there were 17,000 inmates in district asylums in 1900, with an additional estimated 8,000 'lunatics at large') largely ignored by the Church, when it responded so vigorously to the perceived threat by Stewart's Institution to the souls of idiot children?

Part of the answer may lie in the often-complex and challenging behaviour of asylum patients, and the misunderstood nature of mental illnesses in the nineteenth century. Despite an increasingly scientific and medicalized interpretation of insanity in Ireland, that sought to dispel beliefs in demonic possession, many still feared the often unpredictable expression of mental illness, and were uncomfortable with the integration of former patients into mainstream society. Moreover, many patients were violent and unpredictable, and had few inhibitions. In particular, they were likely to express blasphemous thoughts – religious delusions were extremely common,

---

47 *Royal commission on the care and control of the feeble-minded*, p. 78. The 'submerged tenth' was a term used in the late nineteenth century to refer to a permanently impoverished population cohort who, despite general economic and social improvements, would never raise themselves above absolute poverty. 48 In 1851 there were 1,500 nuns of various orders in Ireland: by 1901 this had increased to over 8,000, against a total population that had almost halved to 4,400,000 in the same period. Maria Luddy, *Women and philanthropy in nineteenth-century Ireland* (Cambridge, 1995), p. 23. 49 There were however clashes over the role of religion, and religious worship in asylums. In institutions with substantial minority patient populations, and a tradition of evangelism, there were clashes at Board level with regard to the appointments of ministers and priests. Pauline Prior and D.V. Griffiths, 'The chaplaincy question: the Lord Lieutenant of Ireland versus the Belfast Lunatic Asylum', *Eire-Ireland*, 33:2 & 3 (1997), pp 137–53.

including beliefs that patients were Divine, or were the recipients of messages from God or the Devil – or to articulate sexually explicit hallucinations, and to attempt sexual assaults on fellow-inmates or nursing staff.[50] Nursing orders of nuns had traditionally placed limits upon the types of patients whom they could treat, and the environments in which they could work, and still retain the modesty necessary to their religious calling. Thus work in the district asylums was, I believe, potentially too great a challenge to their self-perception to be countenanced, despite the very great need for nursing care in these large-scale institutions. The intellectually disabled were a different matter. As long as the predominant characterization of 'eternal children' could be maintained, nuns could cheerfully assume life-long nursing responsibilities requiring substantial sacrifice with little obvious reward.

The plight of the intellectually disabled in nineteenth-century Ireland was indeed problematic. As society divided increasingly into productive and non-productive members, they found themselves on the margins of both State and philanthropic provision, cared for in institutions that failed to address their needs adequately. Although not mentally ill, they entered asylums; although not criminal, they were sent to industrial schools and to prisons. The voluntary bodies that sought to assist them imposed standards of behaviour and conceptualizations that ignored the complex reality of their abilities and limitations. Yet for all their inadequacies, the efforts made by Dr Stewart, the Daughters of Charity, and the individual staff in the district asylums at least began a process whereby the intellectually disabled began to be recognized by Irish society, and their needs partially, if far from wholly, addressed.

---

50 The threat of sexual violence against female nurses was common, and attempted assaults were frequently brought to the attention of the Board of Governors at Ballinasloe throughout the nineteenth century. See Oonagh Walsh, 'Psychiatric nurses and their patients: the Irish perspective' in Pamela Dale and Anne Borsay (eds), *Nursing the mentally disordered: struggles that shaped the working lives of paid carers in institutional and community settings from 1800 to the 1980s* (Manchester, 2014) for a discussion of the impact this had upon the status of the psychiatric nurse.

'Saver of the children': the National Society for the Prevention of Cruelty to Children in Ireland, 1889–1921

SARAH-ANNE BUCKLEY

The Society differs in its aim from all other Societies seeking the welfare of unhappy children, in that, whilst others seek to house and provide for the wanderer, homeless, destitute, it seeks to punish those worthless parents who make children wanderers, homeless and destitute, and to render other provision than their own home less necessary.[1]

The above quotation, taken from the first report of what was to become the first branch of the National Society for the Prevention of Cruelty to Children (NSPCC), the Dublin Aid Committee, is an apt illustration of the Society's focus in its early years. Parental responsibility, the vulnerability of children, derogatory and punitive language – these themes marked the early years as parents became the focus of the NSPCC and the State. This essay will look at the period from 1889 to 1921 in particular, to assess the early years of the Society, from its alumni and supporters to the number of branches opened. This examination will extend to an analysis of child neglect cases, the sentencing of mothers to inebriate reformatories and the transferral of children to industrial schools. Throughout, the importance of class and gender in cases will be addressed, as will the impact of the Society on the children it was protecting.

THE SOCIETY'S BEGINNINGS IN IRELAND

The Dublin Aid Committee, the first branch of the NSPCC in Ireland, was elected at a meeting in the lecture theatre of the Royal Dublin Society on 12 June 1889. In September, it began its work in Dublin and in 1890 became known formally as the NSPCC. Therefore, while the Dublin committee did not hold the title NSPCC until 1890, it was the same organization renamed. Following the opening of branches in Cork and Belfast in 1891,[2] Waterford in 1893, Derry in 1896, Kilkenny and Carlow

---

1 Annual Report of the Dublin Aid Committee (hereafter AR Dublin Aid Committee), 1889–90 (Dublin, 1890), p. 9. 2 The fourteen branches are as follows: Clonmel and District Branch; Cork District Branch; Dublin District and County Branches; Kerry Branch;

in 1897, Clonmel in 1899 and Athlone and Wexford in 1901, the branches reached fourteen in number by 1904. Yet, interestingly, it was not until 1956 that the Irish Society for the Prevention of Cruelty to Children (ISPCC) gained autonomy from the NSPCC and took control of the assets and responsibilities of the Society in the Republic. It is this author's contention that the transfer was a result of changes within the British NSPCC as opposed to pressure from the Irish branches. In 1953, the Liverpool SPCC became the last branch to integrate itself into the national group, and it appears in this period that the NSPCC was reorganizing and reinventing, hence the need to give autonomy to the ISPCC. Yet what is certain is that the connections between the Irish and British branches are critical throughout the nineteenth and twentieth centuries, but particularly in the earlier period.

By 1890, the year in which the first Irish branch of the NSPCC was founded, there were 34 SPCCs in the United States and 15 elsewhere. The movement had emerged in New York in 1874 after a landmark case in which a lawyer successfully used cruelty to animal legislation in a case of ill-treatment of a young girl.[3] Linda Gordon and other scholars have demonstrated the ferocity of the campaigns that ensued, emerging as they did from existing philanthropic endeavours. Following a visit to New York in 1881, Liverpool-based banker Thomas Agnew began lobbying for a British SPCC.[4] While the first President of the NSPCC, Reverend Benjamin Waugh, is synonymous with the Society's beginnings, it was Agnew who first proposed the setting up of the Liverpool branch.[5] With regard to Waugh's influence and the Society's beginnings Christine Anne Sherrington states that 'although the title of founder has been generally attributed to Waugh … it masks the coming together of different strands, the number of individuals involved, the coincidences and opportunism within the context of concern for the poor'.[6] One such individual was the social commentator Samuel Smith. Upon his return from America in 1881, Agnew told Smith of the NYSPCC, to which Smith replied: 'this is the very lever we want, the lever for which we have been waiting'.[7] In 1883, the Liverpool SPCC branch was opened.

The ethos of the Liverpool Society and its members is exemplified in a comment by Smith in 1883: 'no relief is to be found in any remedy which does not aim at

Kilkenny/Carlow/Queen's Co. Branch; Galway District Branch; Limerick/Clare District Branch; Mayo County Branch; Meath District Branch; North Louth/Monaghan/Cavan Branch; Waterford and District Branch; Westmeath/Kings Co./Offaly/Midland Counties District Branch; Wexford Branch up to 1950. There were changes in the period to some branches which had to be amalgamated due to financial concerns. **3** The connection between cruelty to animals and cruelty to children has been mentioned by a number of writers, see, for example, Harry Hendrick, *Child welfare: historical dimensions, contemporary debate* (Bristol, 2003) and Maria Luddy, 'The beginnings of the NSPCC in Ireland', *Éire-Ireland*, 44, 1&2 (Spring/Summer 2009). **4** For a history of the British NSPCC, see Christine Anne Sherrington, 'The NSPCC in transition, 1884–1983: a study of organizational survival' (PhD, University of London, 1984). **5** The Liverpool SPCC was the first branch opened and would remain autonomous from the NSPCC until 1953. **6** Sherrington, 'The NSPCC in transition', p. 64. **7** Ibid., p. 65.

producing individual virtue with independence; the proletariat may strangle us unless we teach it the same virtues which have elevated the other classes in society'.[8] It is also critical with regard to the set-up in Ireland as the ethos of the British branches was echoed. Throughout the 1880s, Smith wrote frequently about the poor in Liverpool, arguing that while Britain had sent men overseas to reform 'savages', they had not set their domestic scene in order. His references to the 'impulse of humanity' and responsibility were also mixed with indignation that middle-class gains secured by business and trade were now threatened by economic depression and could be further eroded by the 'thriftlessness and moral incapacity of the poor.'[9] Smith was not alone in his sentiments and for many in the middle and upper classes in the late nineteenth century the emergence of the SPCCs and the child-saving movement was seen as a long-awaited opportunity to reform the poor and attempt to inculcate middle-class principles in those who were amenable.[10] While there were still a minority of reformers who became involved in the NSPCC and comparable organizations to improve the lives of children and families, most appeared to be primarily motivated by a need to organize and regulate the lives of the poor, encouraging class-biased legislation and enquiries (for example the enquiries into the conditions of the working-classes) as a means of inculcating 'a sense of responsibility' in the working class.[11]

In nineteenth-century Ireland children, and in particular poor children, had come to the attention of religious organizations and the State under the auspices of education, health and welfare. Much of this attention was related to fears of proselytizing, the nationalist movement's recognition of the usefulness of children in its struggle and the fears prevalent in Britain surrounding the health and success of the British Empire. Childhood had been redefined and children had become a principal focus of State and voluntary efforts, through, for example, the introduction of compulsory schooling, changes to child labour laws and the focus on infant mortality. In Britain, continued emphasis on children as 'assets' and the 'children of the nation' related directly to fears for the Empire and population. Religion and proselytizing were crucial to the manner in which many educational and punitive institutions developed and expanded, as the battle to 'save the souls' of children caused divisions in philanthropic societies and political movements. These divisions would affect the development of feminism, and more crucially the actual care of children as Maria Luddy's work has shown.[12] The speed with which institutions and schools for children opened can be attributed to religious concerns as well as social need, as Catholic

---

8 Cited in Christine Anne Sherrington, 'The NSPCC', p. 61. **9** Ibid. **10** For a discussion of class and child neglect in Britain, see Hendrick, *Child welfare*. **11** Mary Tarbour, a British journal writer in the late nineteenth century, was a strong advocate of legislation to 'control' the working class. For a discussion of the motivations of those involved in the child protection movement at the end of the nineteenth century in Britain, see Sherrington, 'The NSPCC in Transition, 1884–1983', p. 63. **12** Maria Luddy, *Women and philanthropy in nineteenth-century Ireland* (Cambridge, 1995). Also Oonagh Walsh, *Anglican women in Dublin: philanthropy, politics and education in the early twentieth century* (Dublin, 2005).

orders established orphanages and schools to counteract what they saw as the proselytizing fervour of Protestant institutions. The fear of proselytism could be seen in
many areas, such as the debates on the setting up of reformatories for young offenders
in 1858, during which the Catholic hierarchy demanded that all boys and girls be sent
to schools of their own denomination. Yet the fears worked both ways, as during
debates on the formation of industrial schools, Ulster Protestants expressed fears that
working-class Protestant children could be ill-treated or stigmatized if they were ever
placed in Catholic industrial schools. Throughout the century, orphanages, 'ragged
schools', industrial schools and reformatories were set up to cater for orphaned and
deserted children, and, later, for neglected children. One of the key elements in
debates on the care of orphaned and neglected children revolved around the position of children in workhouses. For a variety of reasons, there was opposition by
groups and individuals to the placement of children in workhouses, most critically
the high mortality rates, lack of education and degrading conditions. Virginia
Crossman and, more recently, Anna Clark have examined the problems and control
of children under the Irish poor law. Both have demonstrated that institutionalization remained the primary choice for poor law guardians and the State by the end
of the nineteenth century, despite opposition.[13] While attempts had been made to
increase outdoor relief and boarding out, the easier workhouse option was chosen in
the majority of cases. From 1889, the NSPCC would advocate helping children
within the home through the threat of parental prosecution. Its role should therefore
be placed in the context of other child welfare reforms and initiatives occurring
throughout the nineteenth century.

PRINCIPAL CHILD PROTECTION AGENCY IN IRELAND

From its foundation, the Society was the principal child-protection agency operating
in Ireland. Child protection moved past previous attempts at reform and relief (the
operation of orphanages and 'ragged schools', for example), towards active lobbying
for legislative change. In short, the NSPCC utilized legislation to effect change
within the home. It becomes clear that throughout the nineteenth century, and especially from the 1880s, there was a shift in child welfare reform from a concern over

13 Virginia Crossman, "'Cribbed, contained and confined?": the care of children under the
Irish poor law', *Éire-Ireland*, 44:1&2 (Spring/Summer 2009), pp 37–61; Anna Clark,
'Orphans and the poor law: rage against the machine', in Peter Gray and Virginia Crossman
(eds), *Poverty and welfare in Ireland, 1838–1948* (Dublin, 2011), pp 97–114. See also Anna Clark,
'Irish orphans and the politics of domestic authority' in Lucy Delap, Benn Griffin and
Abigail Wills (eds), *The politics of domestic authority in Britain* (Basingstoke, 2009), pp 61–83,
Joseph Robins, *The lost children: a study of charity children in Ireland, 1700–1900* (Dublin, 1980),
Caroline Skehill, 'The origins of child welfare under the poor law and the emergence of the
institutional versus family care debate' in Gray and Crossman (eds), *Poverty and welfare in
Ireland, 1838–1948*, pp 115–26.

the rescue and reclamation of children through philanthropy to the active involvement of philanthropists and the State in moulding children and families through
education, social and health work. As part of an international 'child-saving movement', the Society's role is crucial to understanding the changing treatment of
children and families by the State and its agencies. Harry Ferguson argues that it was
between 1880 and 1914 that 'the modern concept of "child abuse" was constructed',[14]
and the NSPCC was at the forefront of this construction. Although the poor law had
restricted and questioned parental power (particularly that of fathers) from the 1830s,
the NSPCC deliberately advanced legislative reforms that increasingly involved the
State in the private lives of families. As the opening quotation elucidates, unlike
'other societies', the Society was focused on reforming parents through the threat of
prosecution, and as charity work took on a greater class consciousness and class fear
in the nineteenth century, the children of the poor became a primary focus.

An analysis of those involved in the early years is important in establishing how
and why the Society expanded so swiftly in Ireland. It is also integral to the issue of
the connection between the British and Irish branches, although at times this relationship was ambiguous, and it is impossible to ascertain why particular measures
were adopted and others were ignored. Emerging from the Dublin Aid Committee,
the Society was made up mostly of members of the Dublin elite. The first president
was the duke of Abercorn, and over the coming years the prominence of members
of the Anglo-Irish Ascendancy would be the norm in most branches, at least as
figureheads. The extent to which they were involved on a regular basis in activities
outside of fundraising cannot be ascertained here. The chairman of the Dublin Aid
Committee was T.W. Grimshaw, who would remain chairman of the Dublin branch
until his death in 1915.[15] Other members included the president of the Royal College
of Surgeons at the time, as this changed annually. All were influential figures in
Dublin at the time, and it appears from the subscription and membership lists that
support for the Society was in vogue in Ascendancy circles over the next twenty
years. In the first report of the Dublin Aid Committee, the following was included:

Be it known that by the recent Act of Parliament for the Prevention of
Cruelty to Children, every person –

Who illtreats, neglects, abandons or exposes a child
Who sends a child out to beg, though professedly to sell or perform

---

14 Harry Ferguson, 'Cleveland in history: the abused child and child protection, 1880–1914'
in R. Cooter (ed.), *In the name of the child: health and welfare, 1880–1940* (London, 1992), pp
148–9. **15** Cecil Thomas Wrigley Grimshaw remained as chairman of the Dublin branch
until his death. He was born in Ireland, was a medical doctor and served in the Royal
Dublin Fusiliers during the Boer War, during which time he kept a diary. The diary
recounts his experiences as a prisoner of war in Pretoria at the same time as Winston
Churchill. Later, he fought in the First World War, again with the Royal Dublin Fusiliers in
the Gallipoli campaign. He was killed in action there on 26 Apr. 1915. He had previously
served as Registrar General for Ireland.

Who sends one out under ten years old to hawk anything
Who sends one out to hawk after ten o'clock at night
Who employs a child under ten to publicly perform

IS LIABLE to three months' imprisonment with hard labour and £25 fine. After this notice proceedings will be taken against all such persons by the NATIONAL SOCIETY FOR THE PREVENTION OF CRUELTY TO CHILDREN.

All information was to be sent to the secretary, Mr Hamilton Leslie, 62 Dawson-Street, Dublin. At the end, it noted: 'The informant's name will be kept strictly private'. The inclusion of this section of the 1889 Prevention of Cruelty to Children Act was significant, as were later references to people's ignorance of the Act. It was a landmark piece of legislation, one driven by the Society in Britain, and its significance in the history of child protection is such that it was known by the NSPCC and other bodies as the 'Children's Charter'. The report also stated that 'one example made of those who commit a gross offence against a child reforms a neighbourhood'.[16] In clarifying the role of the society, the authors stated: 'It differs from the work of the Police ... It differs from the aims of the Public Prosecutor ... It does not seek the removal of children from their parents' into ideal circumstances ... It does not seek merely to punish'.[17] For many families over the coming years these differences would not be as clear-cut.

While the motives of individual members cannot be fully ascertained, qualifications for membership of the Society were purely financial: for patrons, a once-off payment of not less than £500; for a 'life councillor' a once-off payment of at least £100; for a 'life member', a once-off payment of not less than £10; for an annual member, a yearly subscription of at least £1; and for an associate member, a yearly subscription of not less than 5s. As was the norm for charitable and voluntary organizations, names and amounts of donations and subscriptions were printed in the annual reports. By March 1890, the committee had received £223 19s. 6d. in subscriptions and donations. £35 4s. 3d. of this was spent on advertising, indicating the importance of the press to the Society in the early days, and an inspector's salary is recorded as £55 5s. 9d.[18] By the 1930s and 1940s, this sum would range from between £250 and £350 per annum depending on the branch.[19] Not only did the Society thank the press at the end of most reports, in 1897 the Cork branch report contained a supplement with extracts from the *Cork Examiner, Evening Herald, Cork Herald, Cork Constitution,* and *Skibbereen Eagle* all praising the Society's work.

By 1911, the Society had 146 local 'organizations'. These were not all functioning branches but fund-raising groups and branches of the Children's League of Pity, which was principally a means of getting middle-class children involved in

16 AR Dublin Aid Committee, 1889–90, p. 9.   17 Ibid., pp 6–7.   18 Mr Francis Murphy was the first NSPCC inspector in Dublin, AR Dublin Branch NSPCC (ISPCC, Limerick). 19 In 2008, £300 in 1930 is calculated as £83,800.00, www.measuringworth.com

fundraising. The 'Lady Collectors' were also critical to raising funds up to the 1940s, but while flower days and other fundraising activities increased awareness of the Society's work, the bulk of the money in the early years came from subscriptions and bequests. In 1903, for example, contributions to the Dublin branch totalled £2,458, with £1,000 coming from a bequest left by the late Richard Hawkins Beauchamp.[20] Bequests were encouraged in the annual reports, but could not exceed £5,000 in cases of private property.

The expansion of the Society from 1889 to 1914 was notable, as measured in the number of new branches opened, the number of inspectors hired, the amount of money raised and the number of families investigated. In 1899, for example, the Dublin branch dealt with 2,067 children. In the following year this figure was 4,027, and by 1909 the branch had dealt with 18,450 cases. These had resulted in 1,435 prosecutions, 15,951 warnings, 736 otherwise dealt with, and 328 dropped. At this time, there is no question that many families were living in poverty and children were suffering neglect as a result. However, the question must be posed – to what extent did the Society merely punish parents for that poverty?

The earliest file in the NSPCC archive in Ireland dates from 1919. In the context of this discussion, it is necessary to look at the details it recorded. The following were all addressed on the investigation form which became standard practice in inspectors case-work – the child(ren)'s name(s), age(s), the address, the religious persuasion, the relationship to the accused, whether or not the child(ren) was illegitimate, whether or not the child(ren) was insured and for how much, were the parents living, where was the child(ren). Under the allegation section, the nature of the offence, the time of the offence and the locality were recorded. Following this, details of the accused and witnesses were recorded. Finally, the action taken, the result and how the child(ren) was dealt with were addressed. This first recorded case in one of the inspector's notebooks (as opposed to the generic file used) involved a 'neglect to provide' allegation. The father of two children was accused of deserting his family. The inspector recorded: 'it is alleged that he parted from his wife on good terms and promised to write and send money weekly for their support, but since then it is alleged that he has not written or sent any money'.[21] The file included a statement from his wife: 'his people were not satisfied to keep me and our children without payment and I came back to *** to live and reported my case to the inspector of the NSPCC Society who has since been endeavouring to trace my husband ... I hope you can get my husband arrested and dealt with for his cruel neglect.' The language of the woman is quite formal, almost as if she had been instructed on what terms to use. It appears to be in her own handwriting, as it is different from the inspector's

20 AR Dublin Branch NSPCC, 1903, p.7. In 1903, £1000 was worth the equivalent of £428,943.07 in 2008 using average earnings on www.measuringworth.com. Richard Hawkins Beauchamp was the nephew of William Hawkins Ball and Julia Ball. Most of the Ball estate was in the parish of Kilchreest, barony of Clonderalaw, County Clare, but they also held a townland in the parish of Kilmihil. Upon their death, as they had no children, they left the estate to Richard, who bequeathed this sum to the NSPCC. 21 Ibid.

entry, but she may have been told what to write and sign off on. The files in the 1920s and 1930s contain many desertion cases, as emigration resulted in many husbands not returning home. The Society would become a place for these women to use the British connections to track their husbands for maintenance.

Apart from the case-files, the inspectors' books (small notebooks kept to record case details) contain entries from 1920–1 which deal primarily with different 'types' of neglect, the placement of children in industrial schools, separation wives (wives of soldiers, often referred to as 'on the strength' because of their eligibility for state payments) and illegitimacy. In May 1920, a small card was sent by the Mother Superior in St Aidan's industrial school to the Wexford NSPCC Inspector:

> Dear Mr Sullivan,
> Many thanks for kind letter. I am happy to say the two children arrived today. The Police were busy. Thanking you most sincerely for your kindness to us. If you have any more children you won't forget St Aidan's.

I would argue that this quotation relates to both the acquisition of money and of a soul. The continuation of the capitation grant for industrial schools encouraged institutions to remain full.

How did the inspectors view their role? The *Inspectors' Quarterly* was a newsletter for officers of the NSPCC set up in 1913, and contained details on British and Irish branches. In its first edition, it advertised a meeting for officers in Ireland to be held in Cork. The newsletter included 'Hints' for officers, for example, the keeping and forwarding of all news cuttings from local papers on matters concerning children to the Central Office. In the second edition it stated that 'care should be exercised in calling a doctor to a case ... no child should be allowed to suffer, but an Inspector must exercise wide discretion and consult his Honorary Secretary in times of doubt, before incurring expense'. It also discussed a case in which 'inattention to instructions' led to a situation in which an inspector entered a child's religion as Protestant. The child was removed to an institution, but soon afterwards fell ill and was removed to a hospital where it was discovered that the child was a Catholic. It stated that the child had therefore been 'improperly placed in the wrong Home', demonstrating the importance of religious affiliation and fears of proselytism. The same volume recorded the retirement of Inspector Maher of Kilkenny, who had worked for sixteen years as an inspector. It stated that 'his best work has been done in warning neglectful parents, and he had only lost one case in court during the whole period he has been an inspector'.

The role of women in the NSPCC, and the gender bias of inspectors and those being investigated is worthy of further discussion here. Women did not act as inspectors in Britain until the First World War and in Ireland until the 1920s. This was perhaps due to the perception that inspectors needed to be viewed as strong, powerful and authoritarian – qualities not attributed to women generally in this period. These qualities were listed in the *Inspector's Directory*, as has been noted by

Maria Luddy in her article on the Society's beginnings in Ireland. What it demonstrates is that the inspectors were not benign figures, or even the equivalent of today's
social workers; families were wary of the inspector, particularly in working-class areas.

CLASSLESS?

Numerous scholars have demonstrated how, in the early years, child protection
workers viewed the mistreatment of children through their own cultural lenses, as
demonstrated by the focus on drunkenness, cleanliness and children working and
playing in the streets. As will be demonstrated, this focus did not expand to include
investigations of institutions (State and voluntary/charitable), child prostitution, child
abuse and neglect in upper-class homes (and in most instances middle-class homes)
and excessive corporal punishment in schools. The middle-class ideal of domesticity
that was highlighted through the emphasis on child neglect was impossible to achieve
for many families. Neglect and poverty were not the same, but many neglect cases
were as a result of poverty. This was particularly the case in Dublin city, where one-
fifth of the population of Ireland resided and the slums were described as the worst
in Europe. While previous child savers had focused on 'dependent' children, in
particular orphans and illegitimate children, the NSPCC was claiming the right to
intervene in all families and all homes.

George Behlmer argues that its 'interconnected roles as national pressure group
and local watchdog of parental conduct gave the NSPCC a philanthropic cachet that
fuelled spectacular growth'. Even though this is a fair assessment of the Society's
expansion, Harry Hendrick and Christine Anne Sherrington rightly criticize
Behlmer's later assertion of the Society as classless. Although correctly maintaining
that US reformers viewed cruelty to children 'as a vice of the inferior classes and
cultures which needed correction and "raising-up" to an "American" standard',
Behlmer's contention that 'no similar impulse coloured English child protection
efforts' is questionable. Maria Luddy's article on the Society's beginnings in Ireland
also addresses this issue with regard to the Society's official policy on investigations.
She states: 'the Society made it clear that cruelty to children was a classless crime, and
the Irish branch of the Society echoed this belief.' While this was the official stance
and the NSPCC occasionally asserted its status as saver of all children, there is an
obvious gulf between the Society's rhetoric and actions. In the sample cases and notes
up to 1921, almost all cases involved working-class or poor families. Also, in its focus
on the family rather than institutions, prisons or schools, the Society was consciously
deciding not to address corporal punishment, whipping of children for minor
offences or industrial and reformatory-school abuse. And in its shift from an
emphasis on cruelty to children to child neglect, the Society was, it appears, making
a decision to address only certain aspects of child welfare. As Hendrick points out, as
the Society gained experience, its early character and emphases changed and cruelty
remained an issue 'only within limited parameters'. The existence of cruelty to

children in society as a whole was a reality but it raised more questions than reformers felt they could contend with, since it spread beyond the behaviour of the poor. These and many other aspects of the NSPCC's policies make it difficult to view it as classless. Maybe the question should be why would the Society have been concerned with middle and upper-class families? Perhaps this had much to do with middle-class inspectors being uncomfortable with condemning parents of their own class? Had they initially focused on child neglect, the bulk of the work later on, perhaps the emphasis on working-class and poor families would be justifiable. Yet they had not – they had stated their focus was on cruelty to children, severe cruelty to children, in all homes. This makes it difficult not to view their work as class-based. There are also problems with regard to reporting. While Luddy claims that most cases were reported by the 'general public', this could very well be a small number of 'concerned citizens' in a community. It is highly unlikely that other families in a similar situation would report neighbours, unless fearing for the children's lives or to settle a rift or vendetta. In my opinion, the bulk of reporting was from those in the middle classes, as well as visits by the inspector to the same families. Most files demonstrate that the families were being visited from eight to fifteen times. Once they came to the attention of the inspector, they remained there. It is my contention that the work was undoubtedly a practice in class control.

INTEMPERANCE, POVERTY AND 'BEING A HABITUAL DRUNKARD'

The sharing of statistical information was not the only connection between the Irish and British Societies. Both financially and with regard to policy, the official reports demonstrate that the British ethos and model was influential in most Irish branches, especially the Dublin branch. Having examined British and Irish reports in the period, both the language and the offences being investigated are similar. A key difference was the greater focus on intemperance by the Irish Society. In the early years, discussions by the Society and most prosecutions were centred on 'drunkenness' or situations emerging from poverty. At a Dublin branch meeting in 1902 the chairman specifically addressed the connections between poverty and drink, arguing that 'poverty frequently engenders drink, and drink aggravates poverty'. In the first fifteen years of the Society, almost all sample cases cited in the surviving branch reports involved one or two parents who were 'addicted to drink'. Poverty in Dublin was also frequently discussed, with the Dublin branch in 1904 'driven to the conclusion that at least 100,000 of the people of Dublin are living in abject poverty, insufficiently supplied with even the barest necessities of life'.[22] Yet intemperance was used to differentiate the deserving from the undeserving poor. Intemperate mothers were seen as the most unnatural of mothers, pawning their children's clothes for drink, neglecting to maintain their homes and not caring adequately for their

22 AR Dublin Branch NSPCC, 1904 (ISPCC, Limerick), p. 14.

husbands. In 1903, two equally revealing and disapproving captions were contained in the Dublin report: 'INTEMPERANCE THE CHIEF CAUSE OF SUFFERING ... OFFENDING MOSTLY WAGE-EARNERS', while the 1904 report highlighted that 'the average wage of those offenders in work was 21/6'.[23] To spend money on drink when earning a wage was the most frowned-upon form of child neglect, and it was child neglect that became the focus of the Society from this period on.

In response to the issue of drunkenness, and the drinking habits of working-class parents in particular, temperance campaigners and the NSPCC in Britain succeeded in forcing legislation to deal with the 'habitual drunkard'. The result was the passing of the 1898 Inebriates Act and the opening of inebriate reformatories throughout Britain and to a much smaller extent Ireland. With regard to the reformatories, it is perhaps best to situate them in the discussion of other institutions at the time – from prisons, to reformatories and industrial schools, as institutionalization was used as a way to take care of any perceived social problem. The idea that the 'drunkard' could be rehabilitated and brought back to the middle-class ideal of a temperate, pious mother/father by being incarcerated for three years is interesting. Three years was a standard sentence in many of the cases investigated, and must have been seen as an appropriate period for reformation. That women constituted the greatest numbers sent to the reformatories is also worthy of further investigation. The use of the reformatories tied into the NSPCC's agenda, and its role in the placement of mothers in particular was significant as their absence would affect the entire family dramatically. Although in comparison to Scotland[24] and England removals in Ireland was on a much smaller scale, an examination of the reformatories is critical to this study as many of the women and some of the men placed there had been convicted of cruelty to or neglect of their children as well as for being an habitual drunkard. George Bretherton alludes to this connection and in particular a report from the governor at Ennis State Reformatory in 1914 which highlighted that in all these cases, such child neglect 'was a material factor leading to their trial and incarceration'.[25] While it is not possible to discuss the reformatories in detail here, the connection between them and the NSPCC is noteworthy, as in Ireland, the inspector's urging of a mother's placement often swayed the judge.

In Britain, support for the 1898 Act came from various groups including temperance advocates, local governing bodies (in particular poor law guardians) and members of the clerical and medical professions. Yet the temperance movement and support for the reformatories in Ireland never received the level of support the British movement did. Why? Was it that, as with other philanthropic campaigns in the period, religious sectarianism and the Catholic Church's fears of proselytism

---

23 Ibid.   **24** In his article on the Irish inebriate reformatories, George Bretherton cites a paper delivered by Patrick McLaughlin, 'Inebriate reformatories in Scotland, 1902–1: an institutional history', presented at the Social History of Alcohol conference, Berkley, CA, 4 Jan. 1984.   **25** George Bretherton, 'Irish Inebriate reformatories, 1899–1920' in I. O'Donnell and F. McAuley (eds) *Criminal justice history: themes and controversies from pre-independence Ireland* (Dublin, 2003).

suppressed support? In Britain, many of the reformatories were set up and run by religious orders. In Ireland, aside from the St John of God order in Waterford, religious orders from both the Protestant and Catholic denominations did not support the initiative. From 1899 to 1920 four institutions opened in Ireland – a Retreat in Belfast called 'The Lodge', the State Inebriate Reformatory, St Patrick's Reformatory in Wexford, and St Brigid's Reformatory in Waterford. 'The Lodge' was opened by the Irish Women's Temperance Union in 1902 and accepted 'only Protestant women of the better working-classes'; the State Reformatory was opened in Ennis in 1899; St Patrick's opened in 1906 and admitted only men; and St Brigid's opened in 1908 and admitted only women. Ironically, as Bretherton points out, the State Inebriate Reformatory in Ennis was the least restrictive and prison-like. On average, in the sample of cases of those sent for being an habitual drunkard as well as offences of cruelty to children, the sentence was two years. Three years appears to have been the maximum and was opted for in more severe cases.

In 1904, a woman was convicted of the wilful neglect of her two children by the Recorder of Dublin. She was also convicted of being an habitual drunkard and received a sentence of eighteen calendar months in Ennis State Inebriate Reformatory. In her memorial, her character is described as 'indifferent'. The file contains a deposition from Inspector Thomas O'Reilly of the NSPCC and her husband. The inspector's deposition states:

> Since 15th Dec 1903 I have had this lease under observation. Deft wasn't at home. I went to George's Quay to look for her and next morning she called to the offices and I arranged to meet her in her husband's place on the 17th Dec. I told her her husband's complaint against her and she said she wasn't as bad as he said. She was under Notice to Riot on account of her drunken misconduct. On 4th January 1904 I visited her at Cross Kevin St and found her under the influence of drink. The younger child was lying on the bed. On the 21st January 1904 I visited at 7p.m. and found the child in bed. Deft was absent and didn't know where his wife was. Later on in the month 22nd January 1904, I found her again under the influence of drink. I spoke to her several times tasked her to take the pledge. She said she would but didn't do so. The little boy is in a very helpless state and requires constant attendance which of course he doesn't get, he is now in hospital.[26]

Similarly, her husband gave evidence supporting the inspector's observations:

> Deft is my wife. She has two children living to me under 16 year's age. I have been 20 years in Guinness's and earn £1-6-0 per week out of which I give her £1-3-0. My wife is of very drunken habits and has been so for the past

26 The deposition of Thomas O'Reilly, NSPCC, 20 Molesworth Street, Dublin City, taken 22/01/1904 at Kevin Street, cited in CRF/1905/D8 (NAI, Dublin).

six or seven years. She took the pledge once and kept it for a day. Latterly she is drunk almost every day in the week. I have had to wash my own clothes many a time. She had taken away the Children's Clothes and the furniture and bedding and pawned them for drink. I have often had to cook dinner both for myself and the children. On the 9th Dec 1903 I found my little boy with her in George's Quay and I had to take him to the hospital. On the 21st January I came home at 6p.m. and found her drunk. She had been drunk all the previous week. She has neglected the children badly. I have washed the little fellow who is unable to walk. The children often told me they were hungry when I came home in the evening. My wife is unfit from her drunken habits to look after my house and my children.[27]

In the reports from the reformatory in Ennis, it was argued that it would be better to leave her for longer than the eighteen months, as 'she is not reformed enough and does not have the willpower to not drink'.[28] The fact that the courts and the system in general actually believed there was a time period for 'reformation' was probably based on observations of other institutions. .

In June 1909, a 47-year-old woman from Belfast was released a year early on licence to her husband. In 1907 she had received a conviction of three years in the reformatory from the Belfast Recorder for neglect of her three children and for being an habitual drunkard. The licence was granted due mostly to a letter from the NSPCC inspector involved in the case:

I would say that upon your strong recommendation of the conduct of this woman and having satisfied myself she is likely to receive real encouragement in her home, then I think this a case which may be dealt with by licensing without placing this woman's future in unnecessary jeopardy ... I presume, of course, provision is made for her immediate return to the Reformatory should she in the slightest degree begin to take intoxicating liquor.[29]

What this demonstrates is that the inspector could influence both the committal and release of prisoners. In a similar case in Dublin in 1906, a woman was convicted of neglecting her three children and being an habitual drunkard and was sentenced to eighteen months in Ennis. Her character was described as 'indifferent'. The file states she had been 'addicted to drink since her marriage and for the year before her committal ... She took the clothes of the children and pawned them for drink'.[30] The report goes on to state that 'chiefly owing to her drunken habits her family are in poor circumstances. She has served but nine months of her sentence which is too short a time to eradicate the drink craving.'[31] As these cases demonstrate, sociological or psychological explanations were not considered.

27 Ibid. 28 Ibid. 29 CRF/1909/M35 (NAI, Dublin). 30 CRF/1907/B3 (NAI, Dublin). 31 Ibid.

In some cases, the reformatory was used as a last resort. In a case before the Recorder of Cork in 1914, the judge looked 'very unfavourably' on the defendant's previous convictions, of which she had forty-four for larceny, assault, drunkenness, malicious damage and obscene language. She was given two years in Ennis. The reformatory's report stated the woman was: 'bad ... married about 19 years ago, she commenced to drink 2 years later through bad companionship and gradually drifted until she became a confirmed drunkard. Thirteen years ago she commenced an immoral course and has since led a deplorable life ... she is a mischief maker.'[32] All memorials were unsuccessful and the file does not state what happened to the woman after her release.

Aside from the NSPCC, the focus on women and drunkenness was also a concern of the poor law guardians. In Cork city during the First World War, numerous articles were published in the local press regarding the drunken habits of separation women,[33] and a brief look at the Circuit Court indexes for Cork from 1914 to 1920 does demonstrate an unusually large number of cases of neglect and cruelty to children. In 1914, Margaret Healy was sentenced to two years in Ennis Reformatory for the neglect of her four children and being an habitual drunkard; in 1915, Anne Creedon was also committed to Ennis for one year for neglect of one child; in 1916 there were numerous cases of neglect in the Cork borough, many resulting in transfers to Ennis and, finally, in a case in 1917, Hannah Walsh received eighteen months with hard labour for the neglect of her eight children. Yet in 1914 the RIC issued a report after an investigation into the 'Misuse of Separation Allowance to Wives of Soldiers', stating that 'there are no grounds for thinking that any marked increase has recently taken place in the drinking habits of wives of soldiers'.[34] For Cork East the report states: 'No increase in drinking habits. On the contrary the women and children are better clothed and fed and many are saving money'. Similarly, in relation to Cork West the report states: 'Generally the money is spent wisely. One case of drunkenness was adjourned by Magistrates and the woman is now saving money'.[35] Throughout the period, Belfast also had a very high number of committals to Ennis. In 1901, a woman pleaded guilty to ill-treatment and being an habitual drunkard and was sentenced to twelve months by the Recorder. The file states that she had three previous convictions for 'threatening her husband', 'drunken habits' and 'cruelty to children'. She is described as the wife of an ex-RIC constable with a pension of £42 a year. The file also contains a note stating that one of her brothers 'had for some years past been a religious maniac in Mullingar Asylum', while another was a clergyman of the Protestant Episcopal Church in Australia. The charge was initially brought after the NSPCC inspector called to the house and found her drunk. Interestingly, the file contains a letter from her husband asking for her release

---

32 CRF/1916/H16 (NAI, Dublin).   **33** See CSORP/1914/22394 on the 'Misuse of Separation Allowances to Wives of Soldiers' (NAI, Dublin).   **34** 'Misuse of Separation Allowances to Wives of Soldiers', 17 Dec. 1914, CSORP/1914/22394 (NAI, Dublin). **35** Ibid.

'on the ground that if he did not do so, she would make matters unpleasant for him on expiration of her sentence'.[36]

What were individual inspector's opinions on the reformatories? In a chapter entitled 'A Habitual Drunkard' in *The cruelty man*, Robert Parr tells the story of a mother 'who sold and pawned everything the family had'. She was sent to an inebriate reformatory for three years after a conviction of child neglect and for being an habitual drunkard. He describes the circumstances for the family as he saw them, and perhaps gives an insight into why the Society felt it preferable to send mothers to the reformatories, as they would usually not be the principal wage-earners in the home:

> It is not within my knowledge how the experiment of reforming the inebriate acted in this particular case, but I am concerned to point out that the removal of this, for the time being, useless and dangerous element from the Roy family group brought about an immediate change for the better. The money the woman had hitherto wasted could now be spent on food and clothing; the home, under kind and helpful supervision, became a place of moderate comfort; and the children, the chief concern of the Society, although bereft of 'parent' were, for the three years at least, allowed to live a tolerable existence.[37]

However, this mentality did not last long and the process of coercive 'reformation and rehabilitation' in the reformatories was set aside during the First World War in Britain, probably due to the fact that women were needed in the home and at work. In Ireland, the last reformatory closed in 1920. This is a significant marker in the context of the NSPCC in Ireland, as from this period onwards the Society attempted to adjust its role in post-independence Ireland and the issue of intemperance was replaced with other concerns.

CHILDREN'S SHELTERS AND THE INDUSTRIAL SCHOOL QUESTION

One of the few pictures published in the annual reports of the Irish branches in the early years was a photograph of a group of children in the Society's shelter in Dublin in 1894. This photograph was taken by a M. Glover, who appears to have taken all of the Irish Society's photographs in the early period. The shelter, at 20 Molesworth Street, was utilized by the Society in the early years, and also contained the offices of the Dublin branch. Interestingly, 19 Molesworth Street contained the offices of the Inspector of Industrial and Reformatory Schools, Dublin Castle. The shelter appears to have taken in, on average, 40 children per year. In 1896, for example, 44 children passed through the shelter and 29 were recorded as being sent to industrial schools.[38]

36 CRF/1901/D66 (NAI, Dublin).   37 Robert J. Parr, *Cruelty man* (NSPCC, 1912), p. 45.
38 In the same year, of the 368 serious cases, seventy-seven persons were convicted for

Although much more research is needed, in Britain it appears that shelters opened across the country's major cities, yet this was not the case in Ireland. Why? From the documentation it is not possible to provide a definitive answer, but a few observations and speculations can be made.

Initially the Society did attempt to develop the Dublin shelter and open shelters in other cities. The following appeal was included in the first report of the Dublin Aid Committee:

> The great drawback to the working of this Society in Dublin is the want of a Shelter. Shelters are not Homes, but places of safety. They provide temporary relief for the children of parents who are charged, pending trial, under the clauses of the Prevention of Cruelty to Children Act, 1889. They are to meet the requirements of the magistrates under this New Law, which provides for the keeping of injured and neglected children, until such time as their cases are determined, out of the custody of those who injured, ill-treated, or neglected them; and to shelter children, when one or both parents are sent for short periods to prison for offences committed against them ... At the Inaugural Meeting of this Society in Dublin, the necessity for such a Shelter was recognized. The Committee now appeal for such funds ...The cost of the house, fittings, etc., would be about £800, towards which your valuable assistance is desired.

In the first subscription list, £47 3*s*. 2*d*. was collected. However, although collections continued over the coming years, the shelter was never opened. It is probable that the system would have been in conflict with industrial and reformatory schools, orphanages and mother-and-baby homes, all now run principally by the Catholic Church. This issue appears to be the first of many compromises and concessions made by the Society when it came to potential conflict with the religious orders, as can be seen more prominently after 1922. Although the relationship between the industrial schools and the NSPCC cannot be fully addressed here, it is worth noting that in its early years the Society was completely opposed to their operation. However, it was forced to roll back on this once it became apparent that the shelters would not be supported, and if it was going to prosecute parents who could then be imprisoned, children would need to be placed. Aside from the conflict with other institutions, shelters would need to have been staffed and maintained around the clock, and perhaps in areas outside of Dublin the resources, both financial and voluntary, were not available. Either way, the fact that they did not develop is significant, as to have had a temporary facility for children that was not the workhouse or an industrial school would have been a considerable achievement. Internationally, crit-

offences against children, amounting to nineteen years imprisonment cumulatively. As the report recorded, four months per case was the average sentence, as opposed to two months in the previous year.

icisms of institutions had mounted in the second half of the nineteenth century, with the result that specialist homes and fostering were increasingly chosen. In 1886, W.P. Letchworth in the United States referred to children becoming 'institutionalized',[39] yet in Ireland this option would be repeatedly chosen. The NSPCC's inability to set up the shelters, therefore, represented a missed opportunity.

CONCLUSION: 'SAVER OF THE CHILDREN'

The NSPCC undoubtedly holds a prominent place in the history of child protection in Ireland. In contrast to religiously motivated philanthropic and charitable organizations, the NSPCC, as the first established, secular, child-protection agency, suffered less from the effects of sectarianism and fears of proselytizing forces than other groups. In this sense it thrived in a period of instability for other philanthropic societies. With connections to a highly motivated, upper-middle-class British organization, and broader connections with an international 'child-saving' movement, the Society in Ireland gained support from the Ascendancy and other influential members of Irish society. This can be seen in its rapid expansion, increasing financial returns and in the number of children and families investigated by inspectors. From its foundation, the Society's inspectors entered the homes of thousands of working-class and poor families, identifying intemperate mothers, fathers failing to provide for their families, children on the streets and not in schools, and others who fell short of meeting the ideals of the middle-class home. The Society was part of a distinctive social movement, one in which children were the focal point, and the family the means to nurture the future citizens of Britain, Ireland, the United States and many other western societies. Its objective was the prevention of cruelty to children and the creation of safer environments in which childhood could be nurtured. However, its methods often had a detrimental effect. Where parents are being threatened with prosecutions, fines, imprisonment or institutionalization, the environment for children rarely improves.

39 Robert H. Bremner, *Children and youth in America, 1866–1932, Vol. 2* (Cambridge, MA, 1971), p. 296.

From lace making to social activism: the resourcefulness of campaigning women philanthropists

MARY PIERSE

The names of Mrs Meredith and Susanne Day are relatively unknown in this century but yet their considerable philanthropic contributions to Irish society of their time deserve notice, not just for the economic and social aspects of their endeavours but also for the contrasting literary styles in which their records are rendered. Ellice Pilkington's description of the United Irishwomen's work provides evidence of further variety in philanthropic approach and scope,[1] as do the press reports of the Women's Watching the Courts Committee. Even a brief examination of the disparate involvements by these women will yield up interesting contrast in individual attitudes; moreover, it will demonstrate that, as they strove to highlight state deficiencies, or to compensate for the paucity of societal supports, these activists shared more than benevolence and determination.

Making forceful print contributions in newspapers, or founding lace schools or countrywomen's associations have not been traditionally or automatically identified as philanthropic pursuits. However, it will be one of the arguments of this contribution that the concept of philanthropy must be definitively expanded to include the work carried out by such pioneers, and that their particular philanthropy had some distinct qualities: in diverging markedly from the bountiful lady image, their methods and philosophies are intrinsically constructive and progressive in economic and social ambition, rather than being conservative and thereby facilitating maintenance of class-based poverty and ignorance. Furthermore, it can be contended that among the important ingredients in their campaigns were both a shrewd political awareness of potential resistance and a tactical excellence in circumventing opposition.

While 'Mrs Meredith' is a name that deserves to be inscribed on any list of remarkable Irish women philanthropists, she is a still a woman who needs some introduction. Susanna Lloyd, daughter of the governor of Cork Gaol, was born in 1823. She founded a successful lace-making school in the city, subsequently married a doctor and became Mrs Meredith, the authorial name that appears on the title page of *The lacemakers: sketches of Irish character, with some account of the effort to establish lace-making in Ireland; & The redeemed estate* (1865).[2] The absence of first name would seem

1 Ellice Pilkington, 'The United Irishwomen, part II: their work', *The United Irishwomen: their place, work and ideals* (Dublin, 1911). 2 Mrs Meredith, *The lacemakers: sketches of Irish*

to indicate the writer was somewhat accepting of 'feme covert' status, even that she was a passive, conventional type. The records tell a different tale. The lace industry, established by herself and others in the wake of the Great Famine, had practically died off by the time Mrs Meredith wrote her account but that history brings alive the dynamism of its main players and underscores the lively commitment of its author to ongoing progress and to unceasing involvement in philanthropy.

Detail of the industry apart, there are notable features of Meredith's approach in which one can perceive a philanthropy that differs from a common understanding of that word at the time. The dedication of her book opens with the words that it records 'the efforts of Irishwomen to help themselves' – a commitment that is hardly descriptive of a top-down, lady bountiful approach. In addition, the book makes 'suggestions' concerning provision for 'industrial instruction for the female poor of Ireland'. It is quite clear from the introduction to the account that the lace school she founded, the Adelaide school, moved rapidly from being a school to being an industrial concern with, at its earliest period, 120 people providing lacework for home and export. By 1857, when the lace industry began to decline, there were 22 ladies attached to the Adelaide school and Meredith quotes figures of 320,000 altogether in Ireland who worked in lace or crochet or sewed muslin, with a monetary value of one-quarter of the linen trade.[3] In her analysis of the industry's decline, Meredith identifies a lack of state training for Irish women workers, and she castigates the emphasis that is placed on a programme that 'seeks solely to induce them to become domestic, and suggests nothing but training them to foreign household habits'.[4] She recognizes that, for Irish women, domestic 'work has no ascertained value. It gives no promise of social elevation. No labour is worse paid for in Ireland than this'.[5] In her eyes, the educational system provides no information or help concerning industrial employment.

From such opinions, and from Meredith's own record of providing training and employment, it can be seen that her philanthropy is an empowering one, a programme that sets out to provide the poor with the educational and training tools that will allow them to rise above destitution and have a better life – and she is proud to furnish examples of little girls who worked to earn money that rescued their entire families from the workhouse and set them on the road to relative prosperity. Her philanthropic approach also advocates the employment of female inspectors of industrial schools. When Mrs Meredith moved to London in 1860, her attitude had not changed, merely her spheres of engagement. She edited a magazine (*The Alexandra*) that foregrounded women's rights and campaigned for women's employment; she became involved in prisoner reform and set up refuges both for released prisoners and for their families. If the impetus and the cultural capital for such endeavours derived from her superior educational status, the thrust of her philanthropic efforts was to encourage education and so to allow survival and upward mobility – not to copper-fasten inferior social status or to limit opportunity.

character, with some account of the effort to establish lacemaking in Ireland; & The redeemed estate (London, 1865). **3** Ibid., pp 17, 37. **4** Ibid., p. 29. **5** Ibid., p. 34.

Mrs Meredith's novella *The redeemed estate*, published in the same volume as her history of the lace industry, serves to confirm the atypical nature of Meredith's philanthropic philosophy and deeds when they are set alongside other examples of nineteenth-century philanthropic activity. Not alone does the story portray the various complexities of societal structures in rural Ireland, its depiction of the Encumbered Estates Court highlights the inadequacy of legal provisions to protect poor and wealth alike at that period, and the venality of court officers. In addition to spotlighting the failings of institutions, the tale promotes – albeit in a rather didactic fashion – the value of thrift, the importance of sensitivity towards others in the matter of displaying wealth, the worth of the 'bastard' child, and it decries snobbery and disparages sectarianism. The ostensibly serious description of 'an Irish gentleman of the old school' demolishes grounds for pretension by neatly summarizing key economic realities of manorial existence: 'The debts of an Irish gentleman of the old school were never encumbrances to himself, whatever they may have been to his creditors. He inherited some, and he created others.' The creation of additional debt, and the path to ultimate collapse of a manorial class, had its roots in the perception that 'he conceived that he owed it to posterity to endow it, as he had been endowed'.[6] In no case will any conventionally accepted status of lord or lady be allowed to equate with a degree of superiority in this story. The message and the lessons of *The redeemed estate* are quite different in tone from the century's 'improvement literature' and also from the self-righteous certainty of many who dispensed advice and assistance to those they saw as beneath them socially, educationally and economically. Could their purpose of creating a more secure and equitable society be anything other than philanthropic?

In 1916, a half-century after the appearance of Mrs Meredith's book, Susanne Rouviere Day published a mock-humorous account of the experiences of a female poor law guardian in Munster, under the title *The amazing philanthropists. Being extracts from the letters of LESTER MARTIN, P.L.G.*[7] In Day's epistolary novel, the names may be fictitious but the state of affairs is eminently plausible and realistic. As she notes in the preface, it is a record of her personal experience as one of the first women to hold such office. What is recounted by the new poor law guardian includes, as might be expected, descriptions of social deprivation; it is equally revelatory of considerable self-interest, rank discrimination, bias and bigotry on the part of entrenched office holders. In setting out to remedy each and all of those situations, 'Lester Martin's' areas of philanthropic activity centre on cleaning up jobbery, eliminating gender and sectarian prejudice, as well as working on the issues that women sought to make their own areas of expertise at the time: the care of children, women and families. With a humorous touch but a very sharp eye and pen, Day mercilessly condemns abuse of office, ridicules pretensions, and makes it impossible for the reader to condone any of the instances of neglect and exploitation that are uncov-

---

6 Ibid., p. 156.   7 Susanne R. Day, *The amazing philanthropists: beings extracts from the letters of Lester Martin, P.L.G.* (London, 1916).

ered. In Day's case, philanthropy means working to better conditions in the work-house, to improve the health of families in their homes, but, importantly, it is also public education for the ultimate benefit of the health and welfare of the community, and especially the poor. This work requires a whistle-blower because it demands that the cat be let out of the bag concerning committee men and so-called pillars of society who might consider themselves to be philanthropists. In laying bare their inactivity, their plots and venality, Day's exposés inform the public and make it more difficult for such abuse to continue unchallenged.

Day's literary offering is a significant contribution towards education of the public at several levels, and she can thus be considered as playing as valuable a philanthropic role in writing as she may have done as a poor law guardian. Her novel is more than a functional record, it is remarkably clever, frequently entertaining and persuasive in tone. There are several examples of how a light touch can render prejudice totally ludicrous, and simultaneously convey the speaker's own confidence and her competence to counter the indefensible – the following is typical:

> We met Sir Albert Franklin, who raised a frigid eyelid, and would have cut me but his courage failed him. He told Mary Longfield yesterday that no NICE woman would become a poor law guardian. And when Mary asked him why not, answered chastely: 'Things are discussed in a Board room which it is not fit for a woman to hear about'. And what do you think the things were? Sanitation and BABIES! These men![8]

However, any droll humour is abandoned when Day describes the inmates of the Workhouse:

> men saddened with drink, coarse, vicious, brutalized. Women like some awful curse-ridden witch, jibbering and leering, their vacant eyes and slobbering mouths disgusting to see, little children – in the lunatic wards – their hands rolled in bandages to prevent them from tearing and injuring their clothing, scratching, or maiming one another.[9]

She is far from accepting the conditions or their rationale or the impossibility of change and improvement: 'How can anyone imagine that it is good to mass hundreds of human beings together in such conditions of squalor and degradation?' The blame belongs in various places but Day particularly targets the appointments system: 'The chief qualification for a job under the poor law seems to be a capacity for shirking as much work as possible. Busy idleness is the motto. Look busy and earn your salary.'[10] Success in ameliorating many of the worst conditions is later recorded, a clear tribute to the philanthropic combination of interest, analysis, action, and publicity via epistolary novel.

8 Ibid., p. 11.   **9** Ibid., p. 46.   **10** Ibid., p. 50.

Yet another woman whose name is not well known, but whose work should also
be classed as philanthropic, is Ellice Pilkington. Even allowing for the difference
between Day's campaigning and entertaining novel on the one hand, and on the
other, a pamphlet concerning the organization of rural women, it is abundantly
obvious that both authors share a desire to empower people and thereby to allow
improvement in their lives, the alleged aim of philanthropy generally. Pilkington was
deeply involved in the United Irishwomen, a society that started in 1909–10.[11] Her
crusading spirit emerges in the account she published in 1911:'It is essential to Ireland
that her rural population should be strong, healthy, active. It must remain on the land,
happily occupied, well employed, socially and intellectually developed. Here is
permanent work for women to do'.[12] While Pilkington herself would have been
considered privileged in terms of education and economic status, her starting point
in rural organization is not to prescribe but rather to work with others:

> Now it may be as well to consider what our qualifications were for under-
> taking such work. We had no experience beyond that which is gained in the
> ordinary every day life of women. We had no special training for doing what
> we intended to do, and we, none of us aspired to reform society or preach any
> gospel but that of domestic economy, good comradeship and truth.[13]

This is surely the expression of a philanthropy that understands and embraces a
degree of egalitarianism; it is clearly not a top-down dictatorial prescription for lesser
beings. As Pilkington writes:

> Whatever our lack of skill might be we all knew what we intended to do, and
> were determined to do it, and therefore we never doubted but that we should
> find the way, and secure the willing services of those who possessed the
> training that we lacked.[14]

As Pilkington's account makes clear, the United Irishwomen's Association sought
to provide the economic and social framework that would enable people to stay
happily and profitably in rural Ireland. With eminent practicality, they divided their
work under three headings: agriculture and industries, domestic economy, and social
and intellectual development. The support framework they designed to facilitate
some of their aims included provision of district nurses and instructresses in domestic
economy. Under agriculture, two of their specialties were poultry and pig rearing;
interestingly and persuasively, they sought to organize both activities 'in the most effi-
cient and least uncomfortable and unattractive way'.[15] In industry, there was a fairly
wide range of possible pursuits which included knitting, spinning, and making mats.
Perhaps one of their most significant industrial aims was to substitute agencies that

---

11 Pilkington, 'The United Irishwomen, part II: their work'.   12 Ibid., p. 12.   13 Ibid., pp
12–13.   14 Ibid., p. 13.   15 Ibid., p. 15.

would be controlled by women's associations for those run by outside traders. Under the heading of social and intellectual, Pilkington is nothing if not blunt: 'exodus from the country ... is greatly due to the monotony and dullness of country life'.[16] To remedy this, the United Irishwomen planned usage of village halls for classes, concerts, plays, debates and opening libraries, running flower shows. They also aimed to have more women as poor law guardians and to encourage them to participate in local government. Two years after Pilkington's pamphlet, and three years after the association started, it is interesting to read an appeal from its officers for five-year funding, a document that underlines their understanding of philanthropy as a concept that was wider than its common, traditional meaning. The officers describe the society as follows: 'They are, of course, a philanthropic society, but not what is usually understood as a charitable institution. Their watchword is "Self-help" and their working method, to make self-help effective through organization.'[17] One of the early leaders of the association was a Mrs Harold Lett, a substantial farmer in Co. Wexford, and the make-up of her committee is described thus: 'the county families, the farmers' wives and the labourers' wives were represented'. With that scope and appeal, the United Irishwomen must be seen as a wide-ranging philanthropic movement that had obvious gains for its members and similarly clear advances for the communities in which they lived – seeking to improve quality of life for all falls well within any definition of philanthropy. Even to construe their aims thus is to under-value what they planned and what they achieved because when the existing organs of state had singularly failed to do so, the women set up and ran social operations in industry, agriculture, health, culture and education.

Campaigning journalism is yet another strand of altruistic and humanitarian activity that departs from the more traditional nineteenth-century model but yet justifies recognition as philanthropy. Long before the recent media exposés of wrong-doing and injustice, a reporter identified only as 'B' set out to highlight some odd legal provisions and equally dubious legal decisions. In August 1912, the *Irish Citizen* published B's report concerning a six-month sentence for a repeat offender who had sixty-two previous convictions. This time, the guilty party had broken a window valued at £7 8s. The Judge actually apologized to the man for the heavy sentence he had imposed but said he had no choice because 'the offence was so rife'. In contrast to that case, B cited a similar six-month sentence for two suffrage campaigners who had no previous convictions, about whom the Court Recorder said he was convinced their motive was a perfectly pure one, and whose crime was to break a window valued at £5 17s. 6d.[18] B also reported on a case heard in the previous week: a man who had assaulted his wife with a knife, seriously injuring her and causing her to be hospitalized for several weeks, did not get a prison sentence but was bound to the peace for twelve months, with the warning that any breach would result in a two-month custodial sentence. In delivering these very factual

16 Ibid., p. 17. **17** E. Fingall, M.E. Greene, Constance Pim & E.A. Stopford, *The United Irishwomen: an appeal* (Dublin, 1913), pp 2–3. **18** *Irish Citizen*, 10 Aug. 1912, p. 93.

reports, it can be argued that B's philanthropy consists in informing the public, in giving the information that allows increased awareness of unjust laws and inconsistent legal decisions, and that this knowledge will assist in fuelling campaigns for justice and equality.

There is similar motivation and philanthropic concern behind the court reports of M.E. Duggan, several of which also appeared in the *Irish Citizen*. In one article, Duggan records a case of bigamy brought against a twenty-four-year-old woman. Duggan's summary of the affair is pithy:

> marriage at fifteen; a quarrel with her husband; separation; an agreement to allow her 7s. 6d. weekly, not kept, and then another marriage; her only excuse being that she married the second lover because her 'protector' did not pay what he had promised.

The court decided to release her if she promised not to have anything to say to husband number two. A policeman objected to that decision and so it was then ordered that she should be detained in prison for a month until the next court sitting. As Duggan writes: 'Of course, adultery is wrong; bigamy is wrong; but what of marriage at 15? Do those who allowed it deserve no blame? And the husband?'[19] The newspaper article is very short but its very brevity delivers the case summary most effectively, and leaves the readers the points on which to ponder. The reporter's concern (and that of the newspaper) is to raise awareness and galvanize support for remedying the social conditions that make life all but impossible for some. Instead of moral condemnation of the woman, instead of recommending that she should be put into an institution, either penal or corrective or even charitable housing, the article refuses any unthinking acceptance of what had become custom and practice. In effect, that scrutiny of legal proceedings calls into question both the philosophical basis of laws and the method of their enforcement; in so doing, the article goes right to the root of several prevailing societal ills – family poverty, lack of education and training, gender bias and inequality, and judicial prejudice.

M.E. tackled some educational issues in a slightly different way. Under the heading 'Education and Sex', she provided the arguments that women would sorely need in their fight to gain entry to further education, making points with which to counter long-entrenched prejudice.[20] She mocks the ersatz psychology that avers 'highly educated women become sexless'; dripping sarcasm, she writes: 'Talent in a woman resembles a capacity for strong drink; if indulged it will lead to disaster.' Attacking 'this nonsense', she urges recognition of female talent, of economic pressures for women to earn a living, and she scoffs at the thesis that women are 'not mentally and physically strong enough to understand and endure politics'. She notes a widely voiced scare tactic that women's manners deteriorate when educated, and thus they risk alienating the opposite sex because 'men like amiable women'; she

---

19 Ibid., 3 Apr. 1915, p. 354.   **20** Ibid., 31 May 1913, p. 11.

demolishes the pleas that homes and housework would cease to exist: 'educated women use their brains to run their homes ... Do the dishes remain dirty? No, a machine is invented.' Impatience and angry disbelief leap from the page and they are both qualities that, in addition to specific arguments concerning Latin and Euclid, can transmit an increased confidence to those attempting to enter universities. In both legal and educational spheres, the conjunction of 'philos' and 'anthropos' underlies the author's concern for the betterment of humanity at several levels in society. The vital and central importance of those areas substantiates the case for emphasis on the true, wider understanding of philanthropy, both in the long nineteenth century and after it.

In today's world, there would seem to be a degree of difficulty in recognizing some philanthropists of the long nineteenth century. The main obstacle may lie in current usage of the term since 'philanthropy' now appears too often in connection with the concept of gain for the dispenser under the cloak of beneficence towards the needy.[21] At one extreme, one has only to think of the numerous papers written on philanthropy as a customer retention tool, or philanthropy as a benefit to corporate image (sometimes called strategic philanthropy), and the idea of 'for-profit philanthropy'. In addition, there are the innumerable university foundations that baldly state that their philanthropic aims include soliciting contributions from individuals, industry and other funding organizations. Trying to collect money is not philanthropic in itself and while the foundations' ultimate disbursement of the money is, presumably, directed towards a good educational cause, it would be more accurate and honest to exclude philanthropy from the blurb and just label the activity as necessary begging with tax advantages, available to donors who may, or may not, have pure philanthropic motivation. It has always been accepted that the idea underlying the term philanthropy has very often been tinged with some degree of self-interest, both in the nineteenth century and two centuries later. All of that is not to say that philanthropy in a purer sense has ceased to exist, because that would be absolutely untrue. It is important, however, to draw attention to a degree of possible confusion as to the current meaning of the word in some quarters. The website for the Ireland Fund provides ample proof of such misunderstanding: 'Philanthropy in Ireland, although it has grown rapidly in the last decade, is still in its infancy and will be facing severe headwinds in the next few years as the economy contracts and wealth evaporates.'[22] Further emphasis on the monetary emerges from the Fund's confident assertion that 'the non-profit sector is large and growing' and the claim that it gives employment to '63,000 people, nearly 9% of the workforce and makes up 8.4% of the Gross Domestic Product.'[23] Such focus and interpretation limit the

21 See, for example, Soma Hewa and Darwin H. Stapleton (eds), *Globalization, philanthropy and civil society: toward a new political culture in the twenty-first century* (New York, 2005); Robert Payton, 'Philanthropy in action' in Robert Payton et al. (eds), *Philanthropy: four views* (New Brunswick, NJ, 1988); Helmut K. Anheier and Diana Leat, *Creative philanthropy: towards a new philanthropy for the twenty-first century* (London & New York, 2006). 22 http://www. irlfunds.org/news/ffund/index. Accessed 31 Jan. 2011. 23 Ibid.

meaning of philanthropy just as much as does appropriation of the word for less than true philanthropic purposes; the result seems to be that viewing the nineteenth century through the prism of the twenty-first century occludes, to some extent, the variety of philanthropic activities and activists of the earlier time.

In the nineteenth century, as Maria Luddy has pointed out, it was the case that women philanthropists were convinced of their own moral and spiritual superiority.[24] (This certainty was surely shared by male philanthropists too.) It was that conviction, often combined with religious evangelism, which led to the establishment of many institutions that benefited the health and education of the populace. The self-same beliefs often resulted in construction of a top-down system where the dispensers of philanthropic assistance identified a problem and then prescribed their own solution, one that was to be applied to the lower orders, and very frequently restricted to the 'deserving' lower orders as they defined them. Although distinction may now be made between benevolent and reformist types of philanthropy, the identification, and the reality of later depictions of nineteenth-century philanthropy focus mainly on the so-called benevolent sector. This may be understandable but only so in terms of numbers engaged in two dominant spheres of activity. Certainly, priority in that century was more often accorded to moral reform rather than social reform, and egalitarianism would have been anathema to many. In much of nineteenth-century philanthropic thinking, the main focus was definitely *not* to galvanize a community and thus empower the people; rather it was to contain, to control, to 'civilize'.

The mind-set of some of the privileged who, armed with the security of their own moral and spiritual superiority, then sought to control those lower on the social scale, can often be discerned in the language used, in the limited expectations laid out, and in the generally conservative and conformist tone of their own lives. While ambitions may have been worthy, the values were less than democratic. There are records in which some of the careful and stilted language employed is reflective of class-based prejudice and suggestive of associated hide-bound societal structures. One such account is a posthumous tribute to Sarah Atkinson, written by Lady Gilbert in 1894.[25] Given the year of its composition, the idiom exudes a surprisingly dated stiltedness, all the more unexpected but revelatory since it was penned by a novelist. Gilbert's opening sentence lauds Sarah Atkinson as 'lovely as a rose between the leaves of a book'; the accepted gender roles are apparent in descriptions of Atkinson's parents with her mother 'a strong and noble character, hidden under a sweet and gentle exterior'. In contrast, her father's features included 'strength of mind, the largeness of his views'.[26] Atkinson was hurried 'into a bustle of helpfulness' for girls born in the workhouse, who were 'found in an almost savage state, looked on as untamable' (*sic*). However, in Gilbert's words, 'the wise tact and sweet solicitude

---

24 Maria Luddy, *Women and philanthropy in nineteenth-century Ireland* (Cambridge, 1995), p. 214.   **25** Rosa M. Gilbert, 'Memoir' in Sarah Atkinson, *Essays* (Dublin, 1895).   **26** Ibid., vii; viii.

expended on them individually' prevailed and she reports the successes with many who left for England, Australia and America and who 'went forth, after long training, having given proof of their trustworthiness'.[27] The few who remained in Ireland went in search of places in 'factories or households, where their antecedents were unknown to, or kept a secret by, their employers'.[28] There is absolute acceptance by Gilbert (and possibly by Atkinson) of the shame attached to being born in a work-house – and no evidence of any attempt to change discriminatory practices and outlooks. Neither does Gilbert consider any greater opportunity for the girls than domestic service or menial factory work: 'Under Sarah Atkinson's influence they slowly and gradually accepted the bondage and admitted the blessedness of labour'.[29]

To pay further tribute to Sarah Atkinson, Gilbert imports into her text a short paean by Katharine Tynan Hinkson. While she is most impressed by Atkinson's spirituality, Hinkson also finds it important to praise her house: 'I have never known anything like the purity of that house. It was so clean that the most vigilant sunbeam found no mote to float in it.'[30] The urge to eulogize by reference to a dust-free environment communicates an unparalleled approval of conformity to gender stereotype, and an equal understanding of its perceived desirability in the eyes of readers. The pattern of Atkinson's philanthropy included afternoons 'on her way to pay visits of charity and kindness, the pockets which lined her skirt and cloak well filled with a variety of articles for the comfort and use of the needy and sick'. To show her excellence as a 'lady', Gilbert portrays Atkinson as 'fond of society', interested in 'high-class music' and 'her taste in pictorial art was of the same fastidious order'; 'conversation was brilliant'. Her personal appearance is impeccable: 'luminous dark eyes … Her delicate mouth had a sweet curve of pure red, which gave value to the tender paleness of the oval face.'[31] Thus is set out the portrait of the gracious philanthropist. If the reality of Atkinson's work had less of the dilettante about it than appears in Gilbert's portrayal, if Atkinson's interest and involvement in Temple Street Hospital, in the Hospice for the Dying ('her favourite charity'), and in the Children of Mary Sodality in Gardiner Street were in any way reformist rather than palliative, there is not a hint of that motivation in Gilbert's 'Memoir'. On the contrary, there is an unspoken approval of charitable work that draws inspiration and strength from the spiritual and cultural capital of an attractive lady, 'the dignity, the sweetness, the winning attractiveness of her character'.[32]

Against that general backdrop, the practical interventions of Mrs Meredith in launching the lace school, her acknowledgment of the shared needs of all classes and creeds in the immediate post-Famine years, her multiple suggestions for societal improvements – all these things mark her out as an unusual and campaigning philanthropist but perhaps also as almost dangerously reformist where class and sectarian divisions were concerned. That judgment is reinforced by the values that were promoted in her novella *The redeemed estate*. While her factual account of the lace

27 Ibid., x.   **28** Ibid., xi.   **29** Ibid., xxi.   **30** Ibid., xii.   **31** Ibid., xiii; xv; viii.   **32** Ibid., xxii.

industry documented success and promoted paths out of poverty, the novella emphasized the qualities that underpinned such journeys. If her target audience was not
disposed to retain the more prosaic detail about the lace industry, it would have no
difficulty in receiving the subtler messages delivered in the novella. In that double-
pronged approach to life enhancement, Mrs Meredith displayed her ingenuity as well
as her experience.

Originality and inventiveness are also the qualities that distinguish Susanne Day's
strategy in her efforts to expose mismanagement and cruelty in the workhouse
system, and the lack of concern and inertia on the part of self-interested poor law
guardians. Her epistolary novel delivers the message that common sense can over-
turn bad practice and, while not understating the difficulties encountered by a sole
woman poor law guardian, it suggests that determination can expect to effect change.
Rather than thundering with statistics or lamenting any personal hardship, Day's use
of the novel form, her cheery tone, her almost naïve-sounding reproduction of
council proceedings, and her evident empathy with sufferers are disarming, and their
net result is to effectively promote her philanthropic concerns. The literary novel as
humanitarian tool is novel in more senses than one.

The straightforward language used by Ellice Pilkington in her report mirrored
her direct approach to helping others to make life better for themselves and the rural
communities. Is it possible that the broad scope of ambition of the United
Irishwomen has somehow militated against Pilkington being viewed as a philanthropist? Is it equally likely that the association's emphasis on assisting women in the
home to make a living could somehow skew judgement on what philanthropy is?
Has Pilkington's joint focus on ills and remedies touched raw nerves, especially when
the ills of rural Ireland are listed? Could her interesting remarks on patriotism –
'Patriotism for women is a thing of deeds, not words'[33] – have conveyed a preoccu-
pation with politics, whether nationalist or unionist, which was somehow deemed to
separate the association's work from charitable benevolence? Is a philanthropic label
never to be applicable to an agenda with some degree of democratic purpose? Those
are questions that must be asked when the nature of philanthropy is being re-assessed
and when the title of philanthropist is to be bestowed. The classical interpretation of
philanthropy unquestionably admits Pilkington and her like into the fold; the political concerns of past and present may well be the barriers that tend to refuse
admittance.

In the case of M.E. Duggan, her special interest in suffrage affairs was firmly
intertwined with her anxiety to highlight, in her articles, the multiple problems faced
by women in the early years of the twentieth century. The underlying values are
apparent in her question: 'Do we want to see workingwomen free and independent,
or humbly receiving the legislative bounty of the better-off sisters?'[34] Marion
Duggan may have been feared for her public crystallization of issues that many would
have swept under the carpet, prostitution and its clients being a case in point; she has

33 Pilkington, *United Irishwomen*, p. 18. **34** *Irish Citizen*, 8 Aug. 1914.

been described as a journalist, as a suffragist, as a woman barrister, as a woman denied professional work on account of her sex. It must be asked why she, too, has never been lauded as a philanthropist. Perhaps the rationale is similar for the exclusion of Maud Gonne in connection with her work for school meals for the poor? And for Constance Markievicz's help with soup kitchens during the 1913 Lockout? And for Kathleen Lynn's efforts at St Ultan's Hospital? Rocking the boat, defying stereotype, confronting sectarian and class prejudice, identifying with particular political colour – all facilitate the labelling of individuals primarily as characters, as malcontents, as unusual, as politicians, as medical pioneers, or as self-serving publicists, rather than as philanthropists.

The examples of Mrs Meredith, Susanne Rouviere Day, Ellice Pilkington, 'B', M.E. Duggan and others, strongly suggest that they shared certain qualities. Obviously, each was concerned for the welfare of others, a commitment that should always be at the heart of philanthropy. Equally clearly, and this is where their modes of engagement differed from the traditional concepts of charitable benevolence, each of those mentioned sought to bring people with them rather than impose or dictate. They set out to generate thought and argument, they endeavoured to empower by providing example and by lending the authority of their own medium and of their own personal status. They were far from naïve when it came to assessing potential opposition and they countered antagonism, often by pre-emptive, strategic argument and action. Their campaigning tactics were shrewd and informed and varied. The scope of their application was wide in the cases of the United Irishwomen, and sharply focused when it came to law and legal process. In every case, it was progressive and aimed at filling the lacunae and remedying the defects of the state and social systems. The distinctive nature of their generous humanity is all the more unmistakable when it is compared with much philanthropic activity in both the nineteenth and twenty-first centuries, but most remarkable of all for the egalitarian spirit that was far from common in the long nineteenth century.

Cultural philanthropy in
mid-nineteenth-century Ireland

PHILIP McEVANSONEYA

We are used now to seeing or perhaps even participating in a variety of activities inspired by philanthropic motives and designed to publicize charitable endeavours and to generate funds for them. Sponsored walks, sporting and more outlandish events are common enough but the involvement of the cultural sphere in charitable works has a long history. For example, it is well known that Handel's *Messiah* received its first performance in Dublin in 1742 but it is less well known that it was written to be performed for the benefit of three city charities, the society for relieving prisoners, the Charitable Infirmary and Mercer's Hospital, raising £400 in the process.[1] There were numerous other occasions on which organizations and philanthropically minded individuals employed the appeal of various artistic forms – music and drama most commonly – to the material and cultural benefit of Irish society.

Musical performances remained very important during the eighteenth and nineteenth centuries in raising both cash and consciousness. They were frequently social performances too: events benefited from the patronage, even if only in name, of the socially estimable and powerful. Those types in society may have been charitable out of conviction, or a sense of *noblesse oblige* (or perhaps *bourgeoisie oblige*), but it did harm to no one's reputation to be so connected. As is still the case, the greater the number and the bigger the names, the better for the prestige of the event and the likelier it is that large sums will be raised. The most famous example in Dublin of the connection between charity and culture is the Rotunda which was built in the 1750s as an entertainment venue with attached pleasure gardens to raise funds for the adjacent lying-in hospital.[2] Theatrical performances were also a source of donations to various causes and it is perhaps into that category that the so-called charity sermon might also be placed. On the basis of the amounts he supposedly raised, the chief of the charity sermonizers may have been the Revd Walter Blake Kirwan, whose forceful and emotional performances made him into something of a celebrity and whose pulpit turns were annual events, becoming part of the social calendar. His status led to the production of a painting by the leading artist of the time, Hugh Douglas Hamilton, although the authenticity of his idealized image of Kirwan in full flow may be questioned. Be that as it may, the painting was something of a group portrait

---

1 Donald Burrows, *Handel. Messiah* (Cambridge, 1991), pp 17–18; Laurence M. Geary, *Medicine and charity in Ireland, 1718–1851* (Dublin, 2004).   2 Brian Boydell, *Rotunda music in eighteenth-century Dublin* (Dublin, 1992).

too as various members of the congregation, such as the duke of Leinster, the earl of Moira and Elizabeth La Touche, are identifiable, adding to the respectability and cachet of the event and giving prestige by association.[3] Although the painting is now lost it had an afterlife as an engraving which was published in both Dublin and London, presumably as an entrepreneurial ploy to cash in on Kirwan's fame. This image may also have served to perpetuate his activity and perhaps even to encourage emulation: it was at least a model of how such sermonizing might effectively be shown, if not actually conducted.

This essay assesses three episodes from the middle of the nineteenth century related to exhibitions which indicate some of the ways in which art was employed to the combined ends of the material and cultural benefit of Irish society. In the mid-1840s, and at intervals subsequently, the Royal Hibernian Academy (RHA), which was the principal artists' organization in the country at the time, began to experiment with cut-price entry days to encourage attendance by the 'operative classes' at its annual exhibitions. In 1847 the Royal Irish Art-Union combined the earlier sporadic efforts of the Royal Irish Institution for the Promotion of the Fine Arts (RII) to bring old master art to the general public with a charitable aim when it mounted a loan exhibition intended to raise both funds for famine relief and public consciousness of the history of art. In 1853 the organizing committee of the Irish Industrial Exhibition sought to maximize attendance and pursue social aims by applying a scale of entrance charges according to the phase of the exhibition or the day of the week, with the ambition of encouraging not just numbers but numbers from amongst the working class. The motives and operations of each of these events will be set out, in the light of which some wider issues regarding philanthropy and culture will be discussed. There is an overlap to be found among the personnel involved in these events, each of which contributed momentum towards the establishment of the National Gallery of Ireland (NGI) which opened in 1864. This can be seen as the ultimate, albeit indirect, outcome of this series of philanthropic-cultural efforts.

THE ROYAL HIBERNIAN ACADEMY AND THE 'OPERATIVE CLASSES'

In 1845 the RHA decided on an experiment. It was hoping to increase attendance at its annual exhibition and to show a more embracing social usefulness not least in an attempt to help justify the annual government grant it had received since 1832, although it was not a condition of the grant that it did so. The RHA was founded in 1823 to promote the fine arts in Ireland by training young artists and mounting an exhibition of the work of its members and outsiders. The fact that the RHA had its own premises in Abbey Street, Dublin, comprising exhibition space, teaching rooms and offices, was due to an act of great philanthropy as the site and building

---

3 Fintan Cullen, *The Irish face: redefining the Irish portrait* (London, 2004), pp 123–6.

were donated by a founder-member, the architect Francis Johnston. Its exhibitions had had mixed success since the first, held in 1826. Initial enthusiasm among both artists and audience tailed off and certain ploys were decided on to assert the Academy. Members of the sister organization, the Royal Academy of Arts (RA) in London, were encouraged to bolster the exhibitions in both quantity and quality and they, like others who submitted to the shows from Ireland or Britain, had their despatch and return carriage costs paid.[4] The early financial fortunes of the Academy fluctuated and it sought and was awarded support from the state in the form of a grant of £300. Although this helped to secure its existence, its annual budget up to about 1900 was tiny, rarely amounting to more than £1,000. Attendance at the exhibitions remained low and a nadir was reached in 1839 when no exhibition was held. But the establishment of the Royal Irish Art-Union (RIAU) in that year gave it a great boost in the early 1840s in both audience numbers and income through entry fees and commission on sales. The RIAU was founded to promote the economic interests of Irish artists and to foster an Irish public audience for art. It also had an unmistakable mission to promote Irish subject matter. Subscribers of one guinea (21s.) to the Union were entered into a lottery for paintings purchased at Irish exhibitions, principally the RHA; they also received each year a specially commissioned engraving, which was sometimes after an earlier prize, or some other reproduction.[5] The improvement in fortunes took an unexpected dip in 1844 when exhibition income nearly halved. The need to increase numbers became an economic imperative, but the satisfaction of the need was presented as socially progressive, hence the experiment.

Immediately after the main period of its next exhibition the show was reopened with the daily admission charge reduced from 1s. (12d.) to 1d. This was designed to encourage attendance by the 'operative classes', that is the working classes, to whom newspaper advertisements for the penny exhibition were specifically addressed. The experiment was promoted in various ways, for example, as an exercise in democracy allowing 'artisans' and 'workmen' to see 'the best collection of Irish art in Ireland ... heretofore ... almost exclusively confined to the wealthier classes' or as an occasion to allow the natural Irish appreciation of art, 'which feels and admires without being able to analyse or explain the sources of the pleasure felt'.[6] This assertion of inarticulate sensitivity is something of a leitmotif in Irish art journalism when working-class viewers are concerned. Despite some scepticism, this gesture of cultural philanthropy was very successful as daily attendance rates of nearly 4,000 were reported.[7] By the end of the nine-day penny period, 7–16 August, 34,629 people had attended and generated an additional £144 from fees plus over £40 from the sale of catalogues

---

4 Philip McEvansoneya, 'John Constable and the Royal Hibernian Academy in 1834, with an unpublished letter to Martin Cregan PRHA', *Burlington Magazine*, 149:1255 (Oct. 2007), pp 685–9. 5 Eileen Black, 'Practical patriots and true Irishmen. Royal Irish Art Union 1839–59', *Irish Arts Review Yearbook 1998*, 14 (1997), pp 140–6. 6 E.g., *Saunders's News-Letter*, 8 Aug. 1845; *Freeman's Journal*, 7, 8 and 9 Aug. 1845. A season ticket costing 2s. 6d. was also available. 7 *Dublin Evening Post*, 9 Aug. 1845.

which were reduced in price to 4*d*. from the usual 6*d*.[8] That may not sound like a large sum in itself, but in terms of the RHA's annual budget it was significant, being nearly 30 per cent of the exhibition income (£644 8*s*. 7*d*.) that year and nearly 20 per cent of total income (£949 0*s*. 8*d*.). Unaccountably, the RHA council failed to trim its expenditure while seeking to increase its income: for example, the 1845 exhibition cost £361 8*s*. 6*d*. to mount.[9]

The widening of access to the RHA garnered high praise from much of the Dublin press which saw it as a welcome development. The *Freeman's Journal* helpfully listed some of the notable exhibits that visitors would encounter, including sculptures by Christopher Moore, a marble bust of the Countess of Charlemont, and J.H. Foley, *A youth at a stream*, as well as paintings by Francis Danby, *The two Marys at the tomb of Christ*, Daniel Maclise, *The actor's reception of the author* (a scene from *Gil Blas*) and Frederic William Burton, *Portraits of the lady and daughters of Sir Robert Gore Booth, Bt*. Many comments were made regarding the 'propriety of demeanour' and 'order and decorum' of the 'humble but intelligent crowds' and the fact that no damage was done to the exhibits.[10] George F. Mulvany, who was keeper of the RHA, the member charged with the conduct of art teaching within the organization, thought that this successful policy would 'confute for ever the idle calumny that the people at large cannot with safety be admitted to galleries of art'. He claimed that 'Art-taste, both in the appreciative and operative sense, is characteristic of the Irish temperament'.[11]

However, the praise was not universal and opinions were divided on the policy of encouraging working-class access to an exhibition such as the RHA's. On the one hand there was a strong belief that exposure to art was automatically beneficial. On the other hand the fears of the age regarding the potential lawlessness of the working class, and the doubt as to whether it could be expected to benefit from cultural events or be trusted to behave properly in cultural confines, were yet to be fully dispelled in Ireland. This was asserted in the *Irish Quarterly Review* by an anonymous writer who, ignoring any capacity for self-education or self-improvement, doubted that the exhibition had any real appeal to the 'operative classes'. It was argued that the 'great mass of our population' lacked the education and experience to benefit from the 'beautiful and refined', a supply of which had been created in the exhibitions, academies and schools of art without a supporting knowledgeable demand. That writer dismissed the RHA's 'unfortunate philanthropy and yielding to an absurd furor about spreading a taste for Art amongst the masses'.[12]

---

8 *Kew Gardens, &c. Report on the Royal Botanic Gardens, &c. at Kew; also, reports from scientific and charitable institutions receiving grants from parliament*, Parliamentary Paper 1845 (PP No. 345), p. 6. **9** Kew, the National Archives [TNA], Audit Office [AO], 19/57/20, abstract of RHA accounts for the year ending 31 Mar. 1846. **10** *Freeman's Journal*, 7 Aug. 1845; *Saunders's News-Letter*, 9 Aug. 1845; *Dublin Evening Post*, 12 and 21 Aug. 1845. See also *The Times* (London), 16 and 19 Aug. 1845. **11** G.F. Mulvany, *Thoughts and facts concerning the fine arts in Ireland and schools of design* (Dublin, 1847), pp 26, 46–7. **12** *Dublin Evening Mail*, 6 Aug. 1845; Anon, 'Art in our metropolis – an Irish National Gallery', *Irish Quarterly Review*,

There are echoes in this of the debate regarding the ability of the homogenous 'working class' to appreciate such cultural provision that had been conducted in England since the National Gallery (NG) was set up in London in 1824. The comments made in Dublin echo the two antiphonal positions that were apparent in the English situation and which might be summed up in a pair of contrasting quotations from Sir Robert Peel. Speaking against the background of the debate over the Great Reform Bill in 1832 he thought that expenditure on the NG would:

> confer advantage on those classes which had but little leisure to enjoy the most refined species of pleasure ... [the NG] would not only contribute to the cultivation of the arts, but also to the cementing of the bonds of union between the richer and poorer orders of state.

But in 1850 Peel described his misgivings about allowing unrestricted access to the Gallery, placed as it was 'in the greatest thoroughfare of London, the greatest confluence of the idle and unwashed'.[13]

Although access to art was widely thought to be beneficial to society as a whole, it was not in the 1840s promoted in Ireland as a means to foster social cohesion in the enthusiastic way Peel had once stated. A different belief regarding the social power of art had circulated when the RHA was set up in the 1820s. Thomas J. Mulvany (the father of the George Mulvany mentioned above, whom he preceded as keeper of the RHA), writing to Sir Thomas Lawrence, the president of the RA in London, found it remarkable that the organization had been born:

> in a country torn asunder as [Ireland] is, by the most furious and unmeaning party feuds – at a time too when few, even of the informed classes of society, have wholly escaped the infectious contagion of religious or political rancour.[14]

When its first exhibition opened in 1826 the RHA was identified as a place of respite from the strife in Irish society to which people could 'turn from the brawling and heart-burnings of politics to the cultivation of the fine arts'.[15] These comments suggest the power of art to help overcome sectarian rather than economic divisions, if the two are ever completely separate, that the exhibition venue can be neutral ground where contrasting outlooks can be set aside in favour of a shared belief in the authority of artistic values. This comment on the wider social situation was echoed

3:11 (Sept. 1853), pp 791–816, at 792–3, 814.   **13** *Hansard's Parliamentary Debates*, third series, 14 (1832), col. 645, 23 July; Peel, letter of 20 May 1850, quoted by William Russell, a trustee of the NG, in *Report of the select committee on the National Gallery ...*, HC 1852–3 (PP No. 867), para. 8186.   **14** [A. Mulvany, ed.], *Letters from Professor Thomas J. Mulvany, RHA., to his eldest son W.T. Mulvany, Esqre., Royal Commissioner of Public Works, Ireland, 1825–1845, and appendix containing correspondence with Sir T. Lawrence, and obituaries*, (n.p., c.1908), p. 91, 30 Apr. 1824.   **15** *Freeman's Journal*, 24 May 1826.

in a reference to the 'distresses of Ireland' in the preface to the catalogue of the first exhibition.

The RHA experiment was, at least initially, a great success and it was proudly claimed to be the first time that such a reduced charge had been applied anywhere in the Empire.[16] Some in England were quick to suggest that the RA should do the same thing there (it didn't). The income from entry fees, however small, was very useful but the short-term rise was followed by a decline. The fall in numbers and income was attributed to two causes: that 'those of the unwashed, who saw the show once, cared not, apparently, to see it again' and the 'numbers who heretofore paid a shilling ... waited until they could gain admittance as the operative classes'.[17] The former claim is partly right as the number of penny entries fluctuated, but the latter is accurate. That the reduced entry rate was exploited by those who could afford to pay the normal 1s. fee is supported by the evidence of the RHA returns to the Audit Office which show that by 1854 the number of shilling entries had fallen to 624, bringing in £31 4s., but 37,497 pennies raised £156 4s. 9d.[18]

Although it is not possible to say confidently who proposed the experiment, it is hinted very strongly by his biographer that the polymath, George Petrie, who was the secretary of the RHA at the time, played the leading role and it is certain that Petrie later felt he was being blamed when a decline in the Academy's finances was attributed to this policy.[19] Petrie was supported by George Mulvany who firmly believed that the exhibitions would provide the public with 'instructive enjoyment', surely a synonym for the Victorian concept of rational recreation. He described the introduction of the 'penny system' as the 'first great step in an intellectual movement', believing that artists would benefit from having to appeal to a broader audience and no longer be 'limited within a compass by the exaction of a shilling fee'.[20] The financial irresponsibility mentioned above and the decline in the institutional fortunes of the RHA in and after the Famine period caused a deal of controversy and frustration within the organization. This led to a crisis and a schism towards the end of the 1850s that was only resolved, after a government investigation, by the reorganization of the Academy.

THE ROYAL IRISH ART-UNION AND FAMINE RELIEF

Petrie's ambition was an educational one, the 'improvement', as it was then frequently termed, of all ranks, but the timing of the experiment suggests that the stimulation

---

16 William Stokes, *The life and labours in art and archaeology of George Petrie, LL.D., M.R.I.A.* (London, 1868), p. 382. **17** 'Art in our metropolis', p. 814. **18** TNA, AO, 19/57/20, abstract of accounts for the year ending 31 Mar. 1855. The reduced rate was abolished in 1856 (when a rate of 6d. for members of mechanics' institutes was tried but produced only twenty-four admissions), reintroduced in 1858, raised to 3d. in 1862 and returned to 1d. in 1863. The penny admission policy is discussed by Peter Murray, 'Petrie and the Royal Hibernian Academy' in Peter Murray (ed.), *George Petrie (1790–1866): the rediscovery of Ireland's past* (Kinsale, 2004), pp 108–11; 108–9, but without reference to the documents in TNA. **19** Stokes, *George Petrie*, pp 382–3. **20** Mulvany, *Thoughts and facts*, pp 46–7.

of an interest in the Irish school of art was also intended. Although that aim was fundamental to the RHA at the time of its establishment the pursuit of it had been more active following the advent of the RIAU because of the growth in the market it created. With its connection with the RHA, by 1844 the RIAU had become quite a prominent organization. Petrie and his friends such as Burton, who was also a close colleague in the RHA, certainly supported the RIAU's 'national' intentions (of which both were also beneficiaries).[21] But by 1847 the RIAU was in decline, and soon to fall into abeyance as a consequence of the generally deteriorating Famine situation. Nevertheless, it sought to play a part in the response to that crisis.[22] The RIAU was founded and led by Stewart Blacker (1813–81), a non-practising lawyer from Portadown who resided in Dublin until about 1862; he was also a considerable figure in the Orange Order. He received various proposals as to how the RIAU could help alleviate the situation but the most practicable, put forward by a member, Joseph M'Carthy Meadows, who was installed as an assistant honorary secretary of the Union for the occasion, was to mount a loan exhibition of old master paintings to generate funds for Famine relief from entrance fees.[23] This was quickly organized alongside the normal business of the RIAU. The exhibition was promoted as having two complementary aims:

> The exhibition will be in the highest degree attractive, as well as valuable in promoting a taste for art in the country, as the nobility and gentry amongst us, who are possessed of such treasures, have evinced the utmost willingness to aid in the benevolent as well as useful object.[24]

Loans came from the most prestigious sources, the lord lieutenant, the earl of Bessborough, the lord mayor of Dublin, the provost and fellows of Trinity College, the under secretary for Ireland, Thomas Redington, and from the private collections of Irish peers, the marquis of Drogheda, the earls of Arran, Charlemont and Milltown, Viscount Harberton and Lord Talbot de Malahide, the Cork MP Alexander McCarthy, as well as Sir Compton Domville, John La Touche and other, less prominent, individuals. Many of the lenders were members of the RIAU committee of management some of whom, such as Charlemont, would have been well acquainted with the effects of the Famine from other roles such as county lieu-tenancies, or its impact on their own estates.[25]

21 Philip McEvansoneya, 'New light on the artistic and personal aspects of the second version of The Last Circuit of the Pilgrims at Clonmacnoise by George Petrie', *Irish Architectural and Decorative Studies, Journal of the Irish Georgian Society*, 12 (2009), pp 24–37. **22** Christine Kinealy, 'Potatoes, providence and philanthropy: the role of private charity during the Irish Famine' in Patrick O'Sullivan (ed.), *The meaning of the Famine* (The Irish World Wide, vol. 6, London, 1997), pp 140–71. Kinealy is the only modern writer to touch on the role of the exhibition in Famine fund-raising, but the £200 she mentions (p. 152) was an installment, not the total sum. **23** *Freeman's Journal*, 18 Jan. 1847. **24** Ibid., 12 Feb. 1847. **25** *Royal Irish Art-Union. 1847. The first exhibition of the paintings of ancient & celebrated deceased masters … improved and full edition* (Dublin, 1847), pp [2], 5–8, copy in the Centre for

In total more than 200 works were lent, among them many authentic works of high artistic merit and historical importance, but it must be admitted that some loans were of dubious authenticity and those paintings have subsequently disappeared. More works were offered than could be accommodated, and for reasons of time and convenience the selection was made from collections in Dublin and the immediate vicinity.[26] For example, from the Milltown collection, then at Russborough House in Co. Wicklow but later bequeathed to the NGI, came such works as as the *Holy Family* (1649) by Poussin, *Rome, the Campo Vaccino* after Claude Lorraine and Panini's *capriccio* of the Colosseum (1744). Amongst Charlemont's loans was one of the greatest masterpieces ever to be found in an Irish collection, an early Rembrandt, *Judas returning the thirty pieces of silver* (1629, Private Collection). This was reported to be the principal work in the exhibition by *Art-Union*, the leading British art journal.[27] The two works lent from the vice-regal lodge, *David's dying charge to Solomon* (1643) by Ferdinand Bol and *The entry into the Ark* (*c.*1650–74) by Hondecoeter and Weenix, now attributed to Pieter Boel, were donated by a later lord lieutenant, the earl of St Germans, to be part of the nucleus of the NGI. Other loans included canvases attributed to significant names in the history of art such as Cuyp, Dou, Rubens, Snyders, Canaletto, Titian, Reni, Zuccarelli, Reynolds and Hogarth, all being artists whose work had long had a high status among collectors. Thus we find works of the various Italian schools, as well as the French, Dutch, Flemish and British (including Irish) schools. Irish artists were comparatively few in number: *Landscape – Sunset* by George Barret was one of several works lent by Eliza West, the widow of the lawyer and former Dublin MP, John Beatty West, whilst the transport entrepreneur, Charles Bianconi, contributed the *Death of Cordelia* (i.e., *King Lear weeping over the body of Cordelia, c.*1774, John Jefferson Smurfit Foundation) by James Barry. From an art-historical point of view the make-up of the exhibition managed, despite its limitations, to give a good cross-section of periods, schools and genres. However the overall composition was dictated by the availability of works rather than their correspondence to a plan. It would not be easy, for example, to argue that particular sorts of subject matter – such as scenes or allegories of charity – were chosen for their suitability to the exhibition's charitable aim or social context. Nevertheless, religious subjects were prominent among the loans, hanging alongside the many landscapes and genre paintings, and were often commented on by journalists. Works attributed to well known and historically significant artists were secured, which would have boosted the popular appeal and cultural lustre of the event.

The normal exhibitions of the RIAU were devoted to contemporary works by Irish artists selected from the annual exhibitions (with a good number of British ones

the Study of Irish Art, National Gallery of Ireland, Dublin. The considerable interest of this catalogue lies beyond the scope of the present essay. James Grant, 'The Famine in County Tyrone' in Christine Kinealy and Trevor Parkhill (eds), *The Famine in Ulster, the regional impact* (Belfast, 1997), pp 197–222; 207–10. **26** *Royal Irish Art-Union. 1847,* pp 4–6. **27** 'Royal Irish Art-Union', *Art-Union* 10 (May 1847), p. 162. The *Art-Union* was unconnected with the RIAU.

too, but that is another story). The few loan exhibitions of old master paintings that had been held in Dublin up to 1847 were organized by another body, the RII, which was set up in 1813 to do precisely that, but it had succeeded in holding only eight such shows between 1814 and 1832. It was in the gallery built for this organization in College Street, Dublin, that the RIAU held its exhibitions. Thus in 1847 continental old master work may have been less well known among the general public than contemporary Irish painting and therefore had the allure of unfamiliarity attached to it. The fact that the exhibition was restricted to old masters may have been designed to exploit that interest, and also to avoid any suggestion of the sombre event being directly to the advantage of living artists. The private view took place on 4 March and was attended by the lord lieutenant, the earl of Bessborough, the archbishop of Dublin and the lord mayor of Dublin as well as the officers and members of the RHA. Thus the exhibition was endorsed as a thoroughly respectable event by the conjoined hierachies of the state, the established church and the fine arts. The social and moral propriety of the exercise is evident from some of the newspaper reports. For example, on Wednesday 24 March the *Freeman's Journal* noted that the exhibition would be open only after the hours of Divine service, i.e., that it would not tempt people away from their religious observance on that national day of humiliation and prayer. It continued:

> As the whole proceeds go to the relief of the awful calamity which it is our object not merely to mourn over, but to do our best to relieve, what opportunity or what channel can be more suitable for the handing in of? contributions? Many of the principal works are illustrative of scriptural subjects, and of a serious character: while the mind is gratified and instructed, it is delightful to think that the suffering and the hungry are being relieved.[28]

The writer evidently sought to reconcile the enjoyment of the exhibition with the seriousness of its purpose by asserting the appropriateness of some of the works displayed. The exhibition ran until 18 May, admission costing either £1 for a family, season or subscriber ticket which was also valid on 'the three private days reserved for the Court Circle', 2s. 6d. for a season ticket, or 1s. for daily admission.[29] From 3 May the two latter prices were lowered to 1s. 6d. including catalogue, and 6d. respectively, and the price of the catalogue was cut from 6d. to 4d., the Gallery owner having reduced the rent and given two additional weeks free as his contribution.[30] The entry fee was never lowered to a penny which would surely have deprived some of the chance to attend and contribute. Within a month £200 had been raised and sent to the Central Committee for Famine Relief and another £200 had accumulated a week or so later. It was reported then that 1,400 season tickets had been sold

28 'Exhibition of the works of the ancient masters for the relief of the general destitution', *Freeman's Journal,* 24 Mar. 1847; Peter Gray, 'National humiliation and the Great Hunger: fast and famine in 1847', *Irish Historical Studies,* 32:126 (Nov. 2000), pp 193–216. 29 *Nation,* 6 Mar. 1847. 30 *Freeman's Journal,* 4 May 1847.

raising £175; no figure was given for the number of £1 tickets, meaning that up to 4,500 shilling entries, totalling £225, had been made. In all, a total of £500 was raised and various donations were received to cover the costs of £250. To put this into context, the Central Committee had received over £59,439 by 1 July 1847.[31] On one occasion the exhibition was visited by the deaf and dumb pupils of the Claremont Institution, an intriguing superimposition of charitable endeavours.[32]

The preface to the exhibition catalogue stated that the Union was instrumental in making 'the highest enjoyments and luxuries of civilized life minister to the relief of the perishing and destitute of our native land'. Not only were there aesthetic pleasures and charitable benefits, but the event was also made use of on a practical level. Soon after the exhibition opened a 'morning academy' was established and run by George Sharp and other members of the RHA who supervised the artists, numbering from twenty-five to forty, who attended daily between 6 and 10a.m. for the 'free and exclusive' study of the works in the exhibition. This meant copying from the works in accordance with long-standing academic practice as had been facilitated in the earlier loan exhibitions organized by the RII. As a consequence, the exhibition was called the 'most successful undertaking as far as both charity and art are concerned'.[33] In the words of Stewart Blacker, speaking immediately after the closure of the exhibition, the event had been made to serve 'the main purpose' of the RIAU, 'the advancement of correct feeling and taste for art in Ireland'.[34] This would have been especially satisfactory to George Mulvany who, in addition to being the keeper of the RHA, was also a member of the RIAU committee.

At exactly that time Mulvany was promoting the idea that a national gallery should be established in Ireland as part of a general expansion of the social role of art, be it utilitarian, educational or aesthetic. He had no choice but to acknowledge that the prevailing circumstances were hardly conducive to his aims:

> It may be said, with famine stalking through the land, desolation and death piling corpses on our shores, society almost shaken to its centre, and each man asking his neighbour – what is next to happen ? – how can any sane man expect attention to abstract theories of Fine Arts, and plans for Schools of Design?

But he made a virtue of this problem, the answer to his own question being:

> Simply because the Arts are amongst the highest elements of regeneration. Art-knowledge is essential to manufacturing or commercial wealth.
>
> Broken in fortune, but not in spirit, as we nationally may be, we should remember that, as citizens of the State, we hold our places only in sacred trust for our successors; that we must work if we would advance; and that the

31 Ibid., 2 Apr., 28 May, 18 June, 2 July 1847.   **32** *Saunders's News-Letter*, 18 May 1847.
33 *Freeman's Journal*, 2 and 24 Apr., 28 May 1847.   **34** Ibid., 28 May 1847.

generation which lays the foundation of ultimate national prosperity is perhaps even more to be honoured than the happier generation which reaps the profit in enjoyment.[35]

This is an interesting argument. Mulvany accepted and repeated the nineteenth-century belief that art is ennobling – automatically and inevitably – and that knowledge of art is to the general good and should be universal. Because this was so widely believed its precise mechanisms never had to be explained. In his opinion, people needed to think to the future as well as act in the present. Art may have a role in even the direst of circumstances, as a source of solace or 'regeneration' at least. In that respect the RIAU's loan exhibition of old masters may have had an additional value. The exhibition raised money, it delighted the eye and it facilitated artistic training; but it also suggested the continuity and durability of cultural values in a time of crisis and provided hope for the future. The charitable purpose of the enterprise and the religious subject matter of many of the paintings may also have assuaged the consciences of exhibition-goers.

PHILANTHROPY AND CULTURE AT THE IRISH
INDUSTRIAL EXHIBITION IN 1853

In 1853 the organizing committee of the Irish International Exhibition varied its entrance charges to maximize attendance with the particular ambition of encouraging numbers from among the working class. This event was one of huge contemporary significance and substantial and wide-ranging impact, especially in the cultural sphere.[36] The exhibition had a strong educational underpinning but its aims might be summed up as the desire to re-position post-Famine Ireland on the international stage as a country of economic potential, at home with international trends in industrialization and technology. The country was shown to be eager to embrace the cosmopolitanism of mainstream European culture as manifest in the loan exhibition of works of art by Irish, British and continental artists which was a substantial part of the event. Simultaneously Irish pride in historic, local artistic traditions was proved by the inclusion of real and facsimile high crosses in the main atrium of the exhibition building and an area dedicated to Irish antiquities including most of the

---

35 Mulvany, *Thoughts and facts*, p. 26.   **36** The exhibition and its effects have inspired much discussion, see, for example: Leon Litvak, 'Exhibiting Ireland, 1851–3: colonial mimicry in London, Cork and Dublin', and A. Jamie Saris, 'Imagining Ireland in the Great Exhibition of 1853', both in Glen Hooper & Leon Litvak (eds), *Ireland in the nineteenth century: regional identity* (Dublin, 2000), pp 15–57; 66–86; Maggie Williams, 'The "temple of industry": Dublin's industrial exhibition of 1853' in Colum Hourihane (ed.), *Irish art historical studies in honour of Peter Harbison* (Dublin, 2004), pp 261–75, and Stephanie Rains, 'Here be monsters: the Irish Industrial Exhibition of 1853 and the growth of Dublin department stores', *Irish Studies Review*, 16:4 (Nov. 2008), pp 487–506.

collection of the Royal Irish Academy as well as the 'Tara' brooch. The occasion was seen as one of collective social and cultural enterprise within a framework to which no sectarian associations were attached. This multifaceted event was all the more important in the era before the foundation of the National Museum or the National Gallery. Indeed, it marked a substantial step towards the establishment of public institutions such as the Natural History Museum (1857), the NGI (1864), the Dublin Museum of Science and Art (1890, the forerunner of the National Museum of Ireland) and the National Library of Ireland (1890), which are all on or very close to the site of the exhibition.

The educational motive meant that as inclusive an audience as possible was required but the financial demands of the exhibition, which was mounted entirely by private enterprise under the aegis of the entrepreneur and industrialist, William Dargan, meant that income maximization was essential. Nevertheless, the exhibition lost just under £20,000 which Dargan paid. The entry tariff was initially set at 5s. standard admission (five times the 1s. rate that had long been the norm at most Dublin events and entertainments), season tickets were provided at two guineas (42s.) for gentlemen and one guinea for ladies and boys – girls were not specified. There were also excursion tickets that combined the railway fare to Dublin and the admission fee. After two weeks the standard admission price was cut to 2s. 6d. and after two more weeks the price was reduced to 1s. although Wednesdays (until 29 June) and Saturdays (until 10 September) were kept at the higher rate. For the final three weeks from 10 October the price was further reduced to 6d. but the price rose again to 2s. 6d. on the final day. The effect on attendance was dramatic: at 5s. the weekly average was about 1,100; at 2s. 6d. it was 16,000; at 1s. it was 23,500 and at 6d., 44,000. The total attendance of daily entrants (589,372) and season ticket holders (366,923) was 956,295; of the former category, 132,457 (22.47 per cent by number, 11.43 per cent by value) paid 6d.; 422,968 (71.78 per cent by number, 72.97 per cent by value) paid 1s.; 31,722 (5.38 per cent by number, 13.68 per cent by value) paid 2s. 6d., and 2,225 (0.37 per cent by number, 1.92 per cent by value) paid 5s.[37]

For some the reduction to 6d. was a welcome gesture, albeit one that came too late to be fully useful, especially given that the Sabbatarian proscription of Sunday opening was observed. The Exhibition closed on 31 October 1853 despite numerous calls for its prolongation specifically to permit 'working men ... to reap the full advantages designed for them'. It was pointed out that as country people would not be able to visit Dublin until after the harvest was in, they would be denied the opportunity to see the Exhibition. In an editorial the *Freeman's Journal* resorted to a religious vocabulary in decrying the exhibition committee's unwillingness 'to open wide the Temple gates for the humble classes'.[38] The interpretation of the museum or exhibition visit as a pseudo-religious ritual was already long in circulation, being something of a cliché in mid-nineteenth-century thought. For example, it is

37 Calculated from the figures given by John Sproule (ed.), *The Irish Industrial Exhibition of 1853* (Dublin, 1854), pp 23–5.   **38** *Freeman's Journal* 9, 29 Sept., 6, 13, 28 Oct. and 1 Nov. 1853.

commonly found in discussions of the Great Exhibition, held in London in 1851, which was the model for the Dublin exhibition.[39]

CULTURE AND PHILANTHROPY

The policy of artists generally to avoid the Famine as a subject for representation has often been noted. There were some exceptions, a few of which, such as Daniel MacDonald's *The discovery of the potato blight in Ireland* (c.1847, Delargy Centre for Irish Folklore, University College Dublin), are well known.[40] Other examples include a panorama by Philip Phillips depicting scenes from Queen Victoria's visit to Ireland in 1849, which was shown in London the following year. Then, it was stated that in addition to scenes of Queenstown (Cobh), Cork and the lake and mountain scenery of Killarney, some of the venues of the royal visit, the panorama depicted the 'half-ruined and half-deserted Irish village … it would not have been historically true without it'.[41]

While it was beyond the means or inclinations of most contemporary artists to depict the Famine, those within the broader sphere of art did not stand idle. The RIAU Famine fund-raiser can be seen as one of several attempts by individuals and organizations to make a contribution to Famine relief by using particular knowledge or abilities in the absence of other resources. Kinealy has listed some of the auctions (including a papal autograph supplied for the occasion), bazaars, knitting circles, theatrical performances and so on that took place, but the RIAU exhibition seems to have been unique in Ireland. The chef, Alexis Soyer, established successful soup-kitchens in Dublin simultaneously with others in London in 1847. To fund this work in London he mounted an exhibition there in 1848 of the work of his late wife, the artist Emma Jones, possibly under the influence of what he saw in Dublin. This collection of 140 works, shown at the Prince of Wales's Bazaar, Regent Street, was known as Soyer's Philanthropic Gallery. He raised £260, which is said to have come from fewer than 300 visitors. This may partly be explained by the fact that such benefit exhibitions were as uncommon and unfamiliar in nineteenth-century London as they were in Dublin.[42]

The events discussed here manifest different philanthropic uses of culture. On the one hand there is the RHA's provision of an economic incentive to encourage attendance at a socially endorsed event in an attempt to stimulate a form of education, or rather self-education. The attempt to develop a working-class audience for the RHA exhibitions was an unprecedented act of cultural outreach. On the other hand, there

39 Geoffrey Cantor, *Religion and the Great Exhibition of 1851* (Oxford, 2011). **40** See the entry by Tom Dunne in Peter Murray (ed.), *Whipping the herring, survival and celebration in nineteenth-century Irish art* (Kinsale, 2006), p. 122. **41** 'Minor topics of the month', *Art Journal* 12 (Apr. and June 1850), 129, 201. **42** 'Minor topics of the month', *Art-Union* 10 (June 1848), p. 202; F. Volant and J. Warren, *Memoirs of Alexis Soyer...* (London, 1859), pp 128–88; Richard Altick, *The shows of London* (Cambridge, MA and London, 1978), pp 410–11.

was the use of a specific cultural form, the RIAU's temporary loan exhibition of old master art, one that was infrequently seen in Ireland at the time, for charitable fund-raising. Both events were opportunities simultaneously to promote the belief in the social value and unifying power of art alongside the interests of the organizations responsible.

The critic in the *Irish Quarterly Review* argued that there was not in the 1840s a working-class audience for art in Ireland due to a lack of education and there were others who agreed,[43] although the number of people who attended the penny exhibition might suggest that this opinion was questionable, if not mistaken. Be that as it may, when it came to visual enjoyment it was the commercial panorama that had the greatest popular appeal. It had a long track-record of success in Dublin which can be traced back to at least to 1801 and it continued to thrive in the 1840s. For example, the single-painting exhibition at the Rotunda in 1821 of *The raft of the Medusa* (1819, Louvre, Paris), a large canvas by the French painter, Théodore Géricault, was a commercial failure owing to the the direct competition posed by Marshalls' 'Marine Peristrephic Panorama' in Abbey Street nearby, on the same subject. In six scenes covering a total of nearly 10,000 square feet of canvas that unrolled across the stage to musical accompaniment, it narrated the voyage and loss of the Medusa and the rescue of the survivors on the raft.[44] Between 1846 and 1848 Dublin enjoyed a 'colossal panorama' on the war in India said to contain upwards of 100,000 figures, and a panorama 'of the Heavens, comprising Seven Thousand objects of Stellar Creation', which also toured to Belfast, Limerick, Cork and Waterford.[45]

The RHA was essentially a middle-class institution, being a chartered body intended, in the first place, to promote and safeguard the interests of its small membership and the values of mainstream European art as embodied in the academic practices and formulae that developed in the seventeenth and eighteenth centuries. To say the least, nineteenth-century Ireland was not entirely conducive to the pursuit of those classically derived values. The RHA's exhibitions were of a somewhat-intro-spective composition, although by the mid-1840s the proportion of works by non-resident artists to be found there was increasing dramatically, from 7 per cent in 1841 to 30 per cent in 1846, as artists sought to benefit from the patronage of the RIAU.[46] The rise in numbers also served to foster the reputation of the RHA exhibition. Paradoxically, in order to secure its longevity, pursue its goals and give exhibiting opportunities to its members and other Irish artists, the RHA had to allow non-residents to participate.

The RIAU exhibition and the fine art section of the Industrial Exhibition were expressive of a more cosmopolitan and more elite cultural identity. The loan exhibition of old master paintings, which usually consisted of works borrowed from the

43 Michael Angelo Hayes, *The Royal Hibernian Academy. A glance at its former management and recent proceedings* (Dublin, 1857), p. 48. **44** Philip McEvansoneya, 'The exhibition in Dublin of Géricault's *Raft of the Medusa*', *Burlington Magazine,* 150 (May 2008), 325–6. **45** *Nation,* 14 Nov. 1846 and 29 Jan. 1848. **46** These statistics are calculated from the addresses of artists as listed in the RHA exhibition catalogues.

private collections of the aristocracy and gentry, had developed rapidly in London at the very beginning of the nineteenth century, where it was fostered by the British Institution from 1805. Its precepts were soon followed in Dublin by the RII. The failure of the RII after 1832 left a space in Irish cultural life that was eventually filled by the establishment of a permanent collection in the NGI, complemented by the loan art sections of subsequent industrial and other exhibitions in Dublin and elsewhere. But between 1832 and 1853 the RIAU exhibition was the only one of its type to be held in Dublin. It was therefore notable as a cultural enterprise as well as a philanthropic one. The key officers of the RIAU were the secretary, Blacker, and one of the two treasurers, Walter Sweetman, a barrister who had many connections with Irish civic life and the Royal Dublin Society in particular. In 1847 three artists served on the committee of twenty-eight running the RIAU: Martin Cregan, the president of the RHA, Petrie and George Mulvany. The first of these seems to have been ex-officio and may not have contributed much to the day-to-day affairs of the Union or to its public promotion. But as for the two others, it would seem that they had ideas about what might be termed the moral, or perhaps even ideological, contribution that art could make to society, Petrie as the prime mover of the penny admission policy and Mulvany as his supporter and the holder of a distinct vision of how art, in both 'the appreciative and operative sense', could have a social value on a national scale and therefore perform truly philanthropic work.

Doing good and being bad in Victorian Ireland: some literary and evolutionary perspectives

JOHN WILSON FOSTER

SOME CULTURAL ORIGINS OF PHILANTHROPY

The Ireland of the Victorian English and Anglo-Irish novel bears unsurprising traces of the Ireland of previous literature, be that fiction or the literature of colonial exploration and survey, commercial advertisement and 'civilizing' mission. These two broad kinds of literature, fictional and nonfictional, were not always distinct. To interest prospective undertakers, developers and investors, Ireland was cried up to the edge of romance, in order to peddle beauty and abundance of woodland and wildlife (an exploitable abundance, of course). Like the New World, Ireland through Elizabethan and Jacobean eyes was often depicted as pristine and inviting. At the same time, and from the opposing perspective, its dense, tory-sheltering forests and 'infamous' bogs could also suggest a Nature sullied and unregenerate, like the native inhabitants themselves.[1] Against these natives, stern measures must be taken if this fallen and wasted, even if bountiful, land were to be redeemed, reclaimed and radically improved in obedience to a biblical as well as colonial imperative. Happily for the English, the 'civilizing' mission (an oblique and harsh philanthropy of a kind) was at the same time profitable, with forests felled for shipbuilding, minerals sought, land cleared for English elbow room.

As familiar natural resources were depleted, or ways of exploiting them grew ineffectual, new natural resources or new methods of exploitation of the familiar were sought. Over time, the colonial Irish economic structure grew complex enough to sustain an examination of how priorities should be rearranged. To the English, however, it must have seemed from the beginning that all was not right with Ireland or the Irish. All of these – the evident natural resources, methods of accessing, developing and utilizing them, negotiating the unease in this sometimes unsafe land, and to which can be added military considerations – were the motivations behind the innumerable modern surveys and reports that in part were descendants of such

1 William King (later archbishop of Dublin) called Irish bogs 'infamous' and equated them with barbarity: 'Of the bogs and loughs of Ireland', *Philosophical transactions* (1685). I discuss early English readings of the Irish and Irish landscape in 'Encountering traditions' in J.W. Foster and Helen Chesney (eds), *Nature in Ireland: a scientific and cultural history* (Dublin, 1997), pp 25–30.

colonial texts as Spenser's *A view of the present state of Ireland* (1596) and Sir John
Davies' *A discovery of the true causes why Ireland was never entirely subdued* (1612). But in
part, the surveys and reports were reflections of a new source of concern: how to
remedy or at least improve rather than how merely to exploit, and how to advocate
or teach improvement on the basis of information gathered in the field in a more
comprehensive way than hitherto, the itinerary being one obvious form of compre-
hensiveness. I am thinking of such notable works as Arthur Young's *A tour in Ireland:
with general observations on the present state of that kingdom* (1780) and Henry Inglis'
Ireland in 1834: a journey throughout Ireland (1835) in which the investigator replaces the
explorer or planter, suggestion supplants recrimination, warning or polemic, and
practicality (an oblique but more benign philanthropy) supplants moralism.

Of course, apparently clear-eyed (if not truly scientific) surveys could falter and
relapse when the Irish themselves are in vision, when the surveyor yields to impatience, contempt or Irish-directed misanthropy. From the beginning, the *difference* of
the Irish (a difference of inferiority) was deplored, a difference in custom and appearance sometimes recorded as so sharp as to cause the natives to seem bizarre, terrible,
otherworldly. (To this I will return.) While the difference was often held to be
endemic and chronic (a matter for anthropology or even zoology even before the
words were coined), at times the circumstances of poverty, starvation and ill-health
were seen as causing an estranging transformation in the people. I am thinking of the
native Irish Spenser saw in post-war Munster and described as 'anatomies of death',
and the descriptions of Dublin's appalling daily poverty in Richard Head's novel, *The
English rogue described in the life of Meriton Latroon* (1665), which are Swiftian before
the fact of Swift's own early eighteenth-century magnifying glass held up to the
disfigurement caused by disease.

But the difference, albeit on fewer occasions, could also be celebrated. Sir Philip
Sidney was enviously approving in his *Apology for poetry* (1595) of the high Irish regard
for the poet. (The literary appreciation of the Irish by the English has remained as a
thin but important countervailing strand in Anglo-Irish cultural relations.) Then, to
enlarge the canvas, there was the early nineteenth-century Anglo-Irish novelists'
rosier perception of select (or wholly imagined) Irish as embodiments of ancient
Gaelic culture in fictions which at once promoted a romantic and distinctive
Irishness and the desirability of English-Irish understanding, even union (indeed, an
undeclared political union, some contemporary literary critics would say), pre-
enacted in the romantic marriages between the English visitor and the Irish native,
or between the native Irish and the Anglo-Irish. *The wild Irish girl* (1806) by Sydney
Owenson (Lady Morgan), the subtitle of which gave a subgenre its name, the
'National Tale', is in some respects the fictionalized or narrativized version of those
contemporary and often print-illustrated books of travel to Irish picturesque places
in the later eighteenth century and after. The wilder and more natively Irish those
places were the better, in which the picturesque, even sublime, landscape (always
improved by ancient Irish ruins) induced a more favourable impression of the Irish
(at least of the ancient Irish) whereas the dark forests and bogs had cast grim shadows

over their fugitive or impoverished inhabitants from the perspective of the Elizabethan and Jacobean Pale.

The pervading pro-Irish benevolence of the National Tales seems to me to be almost a literary form of passive philanthropy. And I see it too in the National Tales' diverse progeny: popular romances that are also problem novels, the chief problem being English-Irish relations (later, the decline of the Big House). These progeny survived through the nineteenth century and into the first few decades of the twentieth, and they were mostly from the pens of women novelists. They offered a reading of Anglo-Irish relations that was its own kind of relief from hostile English perceptions. (Presumably a survey of English reviews of the novels could measure the success of these relief efforts carried out in the realm of the literary imagination.) Relief in its more literal sense of benign practical intervention in the real world was often an acute necessity in Ireland, and often thwarted. In Inglis' experience, for example in Kilkenny, relief was often resisted by middle-men in control of the land. As for the landlords themselves, only resident landlords who practised philanthropy would cure the malady of absenteeism, he claimed.[2] But some of the biggest landlords themselves opposed philanthropic projects. In Callan, a town of between 4,000 and 5,000, 1,000 were without regular employment, 600 or 700 were destitute, upwards of 200 were mendicants. 'An attempt was made by some philanthropic persons to have the common enclosed and cultivated, which would have given some employment', Inglis tells us, 'but the project was unsuccessful. The great resisted it ...'[3]

And some eminent social philosophers, too, resisted the recommendation of organized relief at the expense of the state. Having found 1,800 starving inhabitants in Mitchelstown, a town of around 5,000 people, as well as 1,200 unemployed, and in one side of one street 570 people requiring relief, Inglis sniffs: 'I should like to know how Dr Chalmers' "*sympathies*" would have permanently provided for the six hundred aged and infirm'.[4] This is an unexplained reference to the influential Thomas Chalmers, Scottish mathematician and leader of the Free Church of Scotland, who, Robert M. Young tells us, saw his life's work as the unification of religious doctrine and laissez-faire economic theory. 'Since at least 1808 he had been arguing in particular against state charity on Malthusian grounds.'[5] As an idea and a philosophy, relief was for some an alternative to, and for others a makeshift precursor of, serious practical improvement and reform of the kinds advocated or implied by Young, Inglis, Thomas Carlyle (who sprinted round Ireland in July 1849) through other investigators until, much later, Young's namesake, Filson Young (Antrim-born

---

2 Henry Inglis, *Ireland in 1834: a journey throughout Ireland* (London, 1835), vol. 1, pp 84–5. 3 Ibid., pp 98–100. Inglis angrily held Lord Clifden and Lord Dysart to account. He generalizes: 'As a body, the landlords of Ireland have not been towards their tenantry what they ought to have been ... the condition of the Irish poor is immeasurably worse than that of the West India slave', pp 101–2. 4 Ibid., p. 143. 5 Robert M. Young, *Darwin's metaphor: nature's place in Victorian culture* (Cambridge, 1985), p. 33. See also Thomas Chalmers, Wikipedia entry.

and London-domiciled) in his book, *Ireland at the cross roads*, the product of a two-months' tour in 1903.

One problem for the improvers and reformers was that their prescriptions often involved them in an attack, from English or Protestant perspectives, on indigenous Irish institutions and customs that aroused the hostility and resistance of the Irish themselves. Moreover, reform (be it in agriculture, technology, economics or politics) was often too late, inadequate or non-existent when it was needed. It could not prevent a fatal collective resignation in the case of the Great Famine, or rebellion (or at least agitation) in the case of the land issue in the late nineteenth century, or revolution in the case of Easter 1916. During these failures, the mechanisms of relief were either started up or, if they were already in function, were diverted to the calamity at hand. Amidst the criminal dereliction of authority during the Famine, relief *was* given to the Famine sufferers but not enough to prevent scenes of human misery that Edmund Spenser, Richard Head and Jonathan Swift would have been at home in describing. Nor did relief rock the edifice. I assume (and it *is* only an untested assumption) that the catastrophe of the Great Famine provided an impetus to the culture of philanthropy that was already in place and which, as well as providing delivery systems of relief, also provided (since it *was* a culture) a way of seeing and representing Ireland, not only in fact (in reports and statistics), but also in Irish imaginative literature, particularly novels.

A CASE FOR PHILANTHROPY

After all, to the charitably inclined, and as soon as the charitably inclined appeared, Ireland was a clear and present case for both improvised and schematic philanthropy. Certainly after 1838, when the Irish poor law was introduced (the first national system of poor relief on the island),[6] the state (or its local subsets) was a philanthropist of sorts, but before that the churches were in the business of benefaction. (I use the word 'business' to suggest the seriousness of the clerical agenda that included attempts at the retrieval of backsliders and the conversion of those beyond the faith.) One early Victorian example among many can suffice: Sean Farrell has recently shown the breadth of philanthropic endeavour in south and west Belfast between 1833 and 1852 by one Anglican church facing foursquare the challenges mounted by the almost pituitary growth of an industrial city – the acute problems of poverty, drunkenness, domestic violence, homelessness and illiteracy amidst overcrowding –

---

6 Olwen Purdue, '"A den of drunkenness, immorality and vice": public representation of the workhouse and the poor in late nineteenth-century Belfast', a paper delivered to the Institute of Irish Studies, Queen's University Belfast, 22 Feb. 2010. The novelist Thackeray in 1842 reported that the Irish poor law report identified 1,200,000 Irish as having no means of livelihood but charity 'and whom the State, or individual members of it, must maintain. How *can* the State support such an enormous burden?', William Makepeace Thackeray, *An Irish sketch-book* (1843; London, 1857), p. 40.

and doing so through the information gathered in its own census of its huge parochial hinterland. Christ Church in Durham Street brought charity of various kinds to working-class families; it provided loans and alms to the needy, it engaged in home missions (Farrell refers to a 'visitation culture'), and created outreach centres for the poor, including 'prayer houses' and Sunday schools, all adding up to what another historian (Mark Smith) calls a 'pragmatic evangelicalism'.[7] This is a reminder that philanthropy could and can take many forms, including donating, organizing relief in hard times, employing, fund-raising, financially assisting, founding trusts and charitable schemes, ministering materially or spiritually.

The intensely religious, Kilkenny-born novelist Deborah Alcock, author of, among other historical fictions, *The Spanish brothers* (1870), *Crushed yet conquering* (1894) and *By far Euphrates* (1897), the daughter of a Church of Ireland curate, claimed that 'the early Evangelicals were the pioneers of all the great philanthropic movements of the nineteenth century, and we in Ireland were not far behind them ...'.[8] The late Victorian period was indeed characterized by a plethora of charitable projects in Britain and Ireland, carried out at home and abroad. Indeed, a wealthy and exasperated rack-renting landlord in London's East End tells the heroine of the Cork novelist L.T. Meade's slum novel, *A princess of the gutter* (1896), that 'The craze for colleges for women, and all that sort of nonsense, is just as objectionable as the philanthropic craze of the age'.[9]

As well as the state and the churches, the universities had philanthropic urges and they established so-called 'Settlements' among the poor (there was one in Belfast), both denominational and non-denominational. There were also voluntary philanthropic associations, such as the Charity Organization Society, all displaying a variety of approaches and philosophies. And there was even scope for charity as private enterprise, as the heroine of *A princess of the gutter* demonstrates. According to one of the tireless Victorian philanthropic organizers in the United Kingdom, Baroness Burdett-Coutts, the English manor-house was, after the Napoleonic wars, the original source of organized philanthropy.[10] (She disagrees, therefore, with Alcock.) In Ireland, obviously, the Big House was a different animal, yet the Irish country house could be, fitfully, a hub with radiating spokes of concern and bred some women, at least, who often engaged in what we would call outreach work. (Lady Gregory was one of these before she met Yeats and became involved in the Irish literary revival.)[11]

7 Sean Farrell, 'The sectarian dilemma: Christ Church and the making of Sandy Row', paper presented to the Institute of Irish Studies, Queen's University, Belfast, 1 Mar. 2010. Farrell quotes Mark Smith on evangelicalism.   8 Elisabeth Boyd Bayly, *The author of 'The Spanish brothers' (Deborah Alcock): her life and works* (London, [1914]), p. 41. Martyrdom (the ultimate form of philanthropy) is Alcock's chief fictional theme.   9 L.T. Meade, *A princess of the gutter* (New York, 1896), p. 162. A lawyer in May Crommelin's novel, *A woman-derelict*, is sure that 'the philanthropic craze shows a mind slightly off its balance': *A woman-derelict* (London, 1901), p. 43.   10 Baroness Angela Burdett-Coutts (ed.), *Woman's mission: a series of congress papers on the philanthropic work of women by eminent writers* (London, 1893), p. xv.   11 Lady Gregory is praised by Mrs John T. Gilbert (see below) as an improver of the red

'Women' is the operative word. Victorian benefactors were as often women as men, indeed probably *more* often, perhaps because intelligent and energetic women, being through custom or law barred from the professions, found in organized charity an outlet for their energy and organizational ability.[12] Burdett-Coutts claimed in 1893 that 'The beautiful word "Philanthropy"' combines piety and charity and that 'women have always had a full, perhaps an unrecognized, share in maintaining and continuing works of mercy'.[13] The claim was made in her Introduction to *Woman's mission: a series of congress papers on the philanthropic work of women by eminent writers* (1893) which has an epigraph by Mrs Cecil Alexander, celebrated hymnist, wife of the archbishop of Armagh and mother of Eleanor Alexander the Irish novelist. One Congress paper is 'On philanthropic work of women in Ireland' by Mrs John T. Gilbert, later Lady Gilbert. The author can serve to remind us of the overarching non-sectarian philosophy of philanthropy in Ireland (even if the delivery was often denominational) and the extent to which novelists (particularly women novelists) were either involved as citizens in it and/or wrote novels with philanthropic themes. Lady Gilbert, for example, was also Rosa Mulholland, an upper-middle-class Catholic from Belfast whose novels are often set among the poor, including *Father Tim*, a 1910 novel whose quite graphic depictions of Dublin slum life off Cuffe Street predate those in James Stephens' *The charwoman's daughter* (1912), the slum scenes in which were once thought to be ground-breaking.

Mulholland as Lady Gilbert moved in upper-class philanthropic circles in Dublin in which her friend and co-religionist, the novelist and poet, Katharine Tynan, also moved. Mulholland wrote the fascinating memoir which prefaces the *Essays* (1896) of the formidable Dubliner, Sarah Atkinson (1823–93), the Catholic philanthropist, critic, historian, traveller and translator who supervised the Children's Hospital in Upper Temple Street, managed the Sodality of the Children of Mary in Gardiner Street and patronized the Hospice for the Dying, as well as being active in social science, including the Social Science Congress in Dublin in 1861, championing the Catholic Truth Society, and writing a biography of the foundress of the Irish Sisters of Charity, Mary Aikenhead.[14]

flannel made by the local people in her Galway neighbourhood. **12** One woman who perhaps embodies the truth of my speculation is Lady Pirrie, wife of Lord Pirrie, the eminent Belfast shipbuilder (Chairman of Harland & Wolff and begetter of *Titanic* and other giant liners) who carried out effective charitable work in Belfast (including the financing through donation and fund-raising of the Royal Victoria Hospital at the end of the nineteenth century) and then, when her husband died in 1924, became president of Harland & Wolff in what seems not to have been an honorary position since it was well-known that she had assisted Lord Pirrie as a shipbuilder in a very practical and knowledgeable way. See Herbert Jefferson, *Viscount Pirrie of Belfast* (Belfast, [1947]), pp 84–97. **13** Burdett-Coutts, Introduction to *Woman's mission*, p. xx. **14** I discuss Atkinson, Mulholland, Alcock and Meade in *Irish novels, 1890–1940: new bearings in culture and fiction* (Oxford, 2008). Atkinson and Aikenhead are huge figures in the landscape of nineteenth-century Irish philanthropy. They are joined by Vere Foster (1819–1900), philanthropist and educator (a reminder that education had its philanthropic impulses and patterns); he had a special interest in assisting

Mulholland herself was hardly idle, publishing forty-three volumes of novels and stories.[15] The image of Dublin in *Father Tim* is one that would tax both the charity-worker and the 'problem-novelist': among the social ills the novel diagnoses are illegitimacy, emigration (and the plight of exploited Irish workers abroad, especially in Brazil), suicide, wife-beating, unwise financial speculation, poverty, unhealthy living conditions, the decline in marriage, and, of course, the 'drink plague' (on which Mulholland is enlightened). Mulholland's solutions to these terrible problems that she has taken pains to recite are *piety* and *ministration*. The philanthropist will do what she can, going down among the destitute with spiritual and material provisions (though never apportioning blame to the government, the Church, or the Big House, and rarely betraying anger) but while she does, the Irish poor should embrace their poverty and pain as evidence of their spiritual superiority and wealth. In a sermon, the activist priest Father Tim tells his flock that 'it might be God's special loving intention to keep Ireland always poor',[16] and there is no textual reason to believe Rosa Mulholland thought differently. It is a reminder that this kind of organized philanthropy could be an underlying conservative instinct and top-down programme that supported the status quo and tacitly opposed serious systemic reform. For example, the poverty in the County Cork of the 1880s in Mulholland's novel *Norah of Waterford* (1915) is the fault of gombeenism (the polar opposite of philanthropy) and perhaps of 'The Organization' (the Land League or the National League in disguise), but not of the government, nor of the gentry bar the latter's asking rent that is a little too high.

Still, it would be a mistake to underestimate the kind of women Father Tim calls for to work in the slums: intensely pious but vigorous, independent, 'not bound by the rules of the convent' (nuns were apparently displacing lay women in charitable institutions), witness to the daily struggle for existence, demonstrating organizational power and energetic adaptability and initiative – yet withal, accepting of an incorrigible Church-orchestrated social containment. A similar case for what was then called 'slumming' is made in the novel, *Her Irish heritage* (1917), by Annie M.P. Smithson (like Atkinson, a convert to Rome), in which an English cousin of the heroine is initiated into Irish culture, including destitution in the Coombe neighbourhood of Dublin. The victims of this neighbourhood serve to impress the visitor with their patience and piety and whose Catholic faith is depicted as one of the three

female emigration to the United States. There are convenient summaries of Foster's large and diverse achievements by Desmond McCabe (*Dictionary of Irish biography*) and Peter Gray (*Oxford dictionary of national biography*), both available online. **15** A literature on Irish women's philanthropy of the nineteenth century has recently sprung up, which includes Alison Jordan's *Who cared? Charity in Victorian and Edwardian Belfast* (Belfast, 1992), Maria Luddy's *Women and philanthropy in nineteenth-century Ireland* (Cambridge, 1995) and Margaret Preston's *Charitable words: women, philanthropy and the language of charity in nineteenth-century Dublin* (Westport CT, 2004). My own modest contribution (in *Irish novels, 1890–1940*, passim), has been to show the role of philanthropy in late Victorian and Edwardian novels written by Irish women. **16** Rosa Mulholland, *Father Tim* (London, 1910), p. 160.

pillars of Irish nationhood, the others being Gaelicism and republicanism. The dynamic is an interesting one, whereby the novelist, on behalf of the poor, makes poverty (and indeed, its companion, philanthropy) a fourth pillar, making a virtue out of what was seen as a necessity (not a remediable ill) and one that the novelist (or philanthropist) could accede to in some virtual or vicarious way. Incidentally, the young Catholic historian Mary Hayden also 'slummed' in the Coombe and in her diary mentions the various societies that took part in this philanthropic enterprise.[17]

Novels like this, written as late as the second decade of the twentieth century, differed rarely *qua* novels from those of the 1880s and 1890s. Perhaps a little more open-endedness can be found in the novels of Protestant Irish women novelists than in Catholic women novelists. For both, philanthropy provides setting, certain kinds of characters and a framing philosophy, but it may be that the marginally more sceptical intelligence at work in the novels by Protestant women creates the illusion that philanthropy is constructive, even reformist.[18] Also, Protestant women were more likely to set their novels in London than their Catholic fellow-writers. In the event, this serves to suggest certain differences between English and Irish societies at the levels of poverty and its attempted schematic alleviation (though the philanthropic culture clearly straddled the Irish Sea), yet also reminds us that London-set novels by Irish writers are contributions to the English as well as Irish novel: they include Ella MacMahon's *A pitiful passion* (1895, known in the United States as *A pitiless passion*), Mrs J.H. (Charlotte) Riddell's *A rich man's daughter* (1895), L.T. Meade's *A princess of the gutter* (1896), May Crommelin's *A woman-derelict* (1901), W.M. (Winifred) Letts' *The rough way* (1912). The novels by MacMahon, Meade and Letts are portrayals of Anglo-Catholicism, a problem-faith at the time, suspended between Catholicism and Protestantism; MacMahon was another convert to Rome. And in *The rough way* it is the Anglo-Catholic hero, not heroine, who is the slum-worker.

But what most of these share with the Catholic novels is a linkage between this kind of philanthropy and femininity, Christian piety, and self-sacrifice. Elinor Grey, the young middle-class amnesiac of Crommelin's title, for example, has become a vagrant or derelict, quite literally losing (or mislaying) herself, and after being taken in by a kindly doctor, she devotes herself through philanthropy to 'a life of renunci-

---

17 Conan Kennedy (ed.), *The diaries of Mary Hayden, 1878–1903* (Killala, Mayo, 2005), vol. 4, p. 2045; vol. 5, pp 2116, 2120, 2150, 2151, 2155, 2197.   18 As it often was when the goal of the philanthropy was improvement. Helen O'Connell has shown that nineteenth-century 'improvement' tracts and pamphlets fed into fiction proper and encouraged didacticism (Carleton's novels were influenced by them) while the novels in turn (for example, those of Maria Edgeworth) influenced the tracts and pamphlets and encouraged narrative and dialogue; some of these tracts composed what O'Connell calls 'fiction of improvement'. ('Improvement', she notes, emerged as schemes of agricultural reform.) This fiction-tract interaction mirrors that between fiction and exploration-survey-commercial advertisement that I mentioned earlier. See Helen O'Connell, 'Fiction of improvement' in Jacqueline Belanger (ed.), *The Irish novel in the nineteenth century: facts and fictions* (Dublin, 2005), pp 110–22.

ation and unselfishness', denying herself the sexual and romantic desire she briefly feels for her rescuer: she congratulates herself that she had 'truly forgotten Self for the sake of others'.[19] In selflessness she paradoxically finds her true self.

There were women writers, of course, who demurred, qualified or bridled. Alcock was a powerhouse of active self-sacrifice but despised self-pity; she made self-sacrifice sound like the most muscular activity imaginable. May Crommelin was aware of the faddish element of charitable work, while a social worker in Smithson's *Her Irish heritage* asks the English visitor: 'Well! Are *you* suffering from the slumming craze too? . . .it's becoming so fashionable just now amongst the "quality" that really we poor workers may soon have to take a back seat'.[20] This was a token demurral, but Sarah Grand's opposition to the priority of female philanthropy was the real thing. 'I see that the world is not a bit the better for centuries of self-sacrifice on the woman's part', says a character in Grand's novel, *The heavenly twins* (1893), 'and therefore I think it is time we tried a more effectual plan. And I propose now to sacrifice the man instead of the woman'.[21] In Grand (born in Donaghadee, County Down), we have the aggressive instincts of the reformer and campaigner, not philanthropist.

In using the novel as her vehicle, Grand was confirming what the idealist philosopher T.H. Green had said in his valuable paper of 1862, *An estimate of the value and influence of works of fiction in modern times*: the novel, though inferior to epic and poetry by giving us only the real world, avoiding idealized passion and sentimentalizing the life around us, nonetheless by finding its material everywhere and discouraging us from seeing ourselves and our experiences as central, allows the novelist to be 'a great expander of sympathies', thereby aiding social reform. 'From Defoe to Kingsley [the novel's] history boasts of a noble army of social reformers.'[22] We might wish, of course, to distinguish the over-sentimentalizing philanthropic Irish novel from the angrier reformist novel, but in Green's terms self-demotion in the cause of idealism could take reformist *or* philanthropic shape.

In Dubliner Ella MacMahon's novel about alcoholism, *A pitiless passion*, an elderly aristocratic lady complains that 'The world has gone crazy over this altruism, or whatever you call it . . . this mad, mawkish sentimentality over the happiness of *others*'. She finds tiresome 'Sensible persons who seem to feel it their duty to place their own good sense at the service of others' foolishness'.[23] Lady Halliday is holding the word 'altruism' at arm's length as though with tongs. According to Thomas Dixon, the word was coined as late as 1852 and the coinage seems to have stimulated even more philanthropic activity than there had been before it. Dixon defines altruism trebly as

19 Crommelin, *A woman-derelict*, pp 251, 187. **20** Annie M.P. Smithson, *Her Irish heritage* (1917; Cork, 1988), p. 63. **21** Madame Sarah Grand, *The heavenly twins* (New York, 1893), p. 80. **22** T.H. Green, *An estimate of the value and influence of works of fiction in modern times*, ed. Fred Newton Scott (Ann Arbor, 1911), pp 61–2. This book is available online at Project Gutenberg. **23** Ella MacMahon, *A pitiless passion* (New York, 1895), pp 316, 317. By 1917, H.G. Wells could observe that '"Philanthropist", like "respectable person", is, in English, a mere term of abuse. It implies a petting condescension . . .', letter to the *Times Literary Supplement*, 24 May 1917.

instinct or emotion; as action; and as doctrine or ideology; it was a kind of humanist religiosity inside or outside the churches. It was not until the 1890s that the word was fully accepted (though reluctantly by Lady Halliday) and according to Dixon the previous decade, the 1880s, was a pivotal one in Victorian moral thought, when a 'new wave of awareness of the plight of the urban poor was expressed in a range of both practical and intellectual activities'.[24] These activities included writing novels and it may be no coincidence that a case, I think, can be made for the emergence, in a critical mass, of the mainstream and popular Irish novel, dominated by women authors, in the 1880s and 1890s.

EVOLUTION AND PHILANTHROPY

Philanthropy in all its guises would seem to have flown in the face, implicitly or explicitly, of the other great contemporary idea that challenged Victorian moral thought: organic evolution with its seemingly core, and morally neutral, components (and as seen as natural) of struggle, competition, supersession or extinction (with the organism's striving to adapt the only alternative to the latter two). While this is true, Dixon reminds us that altruism in action was compatible with Darwinism, that sympathy, love and cooperation were observable in nature, and that both Darwin and Herbert Spencer foresaw greater altruism among human beings.[25] Recently, the zoologist Matt Ridley has analysed in *The origins of virtue* (1996) the extent to which altruism, as effect rather than motivation, is a genetic and instinctual matter.[26] Clearly, in any case, philanthropy could have complicated human motivations, and apparent altruism might even have been in some cases disguised egotism. (Ridley uncovers the depth of the complexity.) The earnestness of philanthropists came in for some guying. That peculiar Belfast novelist, Herbert Moore Pim, has a character in his novel, *The pessimist: a confession* (1914) observe in Wildean fashion that 'Charity covers a multitude of sins! That's what makes philanthropists so contented as a class'.[27] I have already mentioned the possibility that philanthropic activists might have been seeking vicarious thrills; there might have been an element of the prurient and the self-

---

24 Thomas Dixon, *The invention of altruism: making moral meanings in Victorian Britain* (Oxford, 2008), p. 8. 25 Ibid., p. 7 and chapters 4 and 5. See also A.J. Lustig, 'Darwin's difficulties', *Cambridge companion to the 'Origin of species'* (Cambridge, 2009), pp 126–8. It is doubtful, however, that sociality, cooperation and sympathy were seen in late Victorian times as important Darwinian ideas. 26 A recent study by Oren Harman, *The price of altruism: George Price and the search for the origins of kindness* (New York and London, 2010), recounts twentieth-century attempts by biologists and game theorists to square Darwinism with altruism, in part through the mechanisms of kin selection and intra-individual cooperation. In other words, Victorian philanthropy, often seen as sentimental and unscientific in motive and approach (Oscar Wilde saw it as such), can now be re-evaluated without the entirety of our previous condescension. 27 Herbert Moore Pim, *The pessimist: a confession* (London, 1914), p. 212.

serving. Seth Koven goes farther and sees slumming in Victorian London as sexual and class politics. One of his case-studies is L.T. Meade's *A princess of the gutter* whose heroine seeks 'happiness in self-denial' (p. 110) but whom Koven sees as following lesbian urges among poor but vital East End women.[28]

I would question Koven's sexual interpretation of certain scenes in Meade's novel but accept his thesis that there was sometimes a sexual dimension to slumming to which we could attach socio-biological meanings. Certainly it seems that the most practical philanthropist, the slum-worker, could be responding to personal circumstances through what the behaviourist calls displacement. Mrs J.H. (Charlotte) Riddell (from Co. Antrim) depicted poverty, drunkenness and wife-beating in London's East End in *A rich man's daughter* (1895) but does so without real sympathy for the poor or a sense that a remedy must be advocated. Her heroine rejects one young man's overtures, telling him she wishes to become a 'Sister of Charity'. A worldly baron, when told of this, remarks: 'she is in love with somebody else. That is always the meaning of the Sister of Charity business'.[29] In her short story, 'A Friend of Little Sisters', in *Cousins and others* (1909), Katharine Tynan shows the tangled motives of her heroine, daughter of a peer, when offered the competing attractions of marriage, romantic love, the Little Sister convent in London's East End, and the Carmelite order of nuns.

It remains the case, however, that Irish poverty, like London's, could be seen quite deliberately in socio-biological terms, and we might hazard a guess that the author who did so was more likely to be a man. A colloquial anthropological vocabulary (in which certain peoples were 'savages' or 'primitives' and a colloquial zoological vocabulary (in which certain peoples resembled animals) were ready at hand. Swift used such language satirically but with such intensity that satire doesn't always redeem it. Early English travellers reached uncharitably for animal metaphors when describing the Irish. Edward Ward thought in his *A trip to Ireland* (1699) that the natives were 'lively Portraitures of the Prodigal Lad in his most Swinish Condition'. They bred prolifically in part to keep together for warmth: 'they engender as thick as *Fly-blows*, each little *Hutt* being as full of *Children*, as a *Conney-Burrough* in a well-stock'd *Warren* is of Rabbits'. Of Irish women: '*Amorous* they are as *Doves*, but not altogether so chast as *Turtles*'; 'meer *Scare-Crows*' whose '*Phisiognomies*' are 'a refrigeratory against the flames of *Lust*', and so on.[30]

When recreating a scene in Galway as late as 1841, J.A. Froude noted 'the rags insufficient to cover the children and boys of twelve running about absolutely naked … The inhabitants, except where they had been taken in hand and metamorphosed into police, seemed more like tribes of squalid apes than human beings.'[31] In his

28 Seth Koven, *Slumming: sexual and social politics in Victorian London* (Princeton, 2004), pp 219, 295. **29** *A rich man's daughter* (New York, 1895), p. 161. **30** Edward Ward, *A trip to Ireland* (1699) in *five travel scripts commonly attributed to Edward Ward* (New York, 1933). Howard William Troyer in his Bibliographic Note does not believe Ward was the author of this travel script. **31** James Anthony Froude, *The English in Ireland in the eighteenth century* (1872–4), quoted (from Froude's biographer, Waldo Hilary Dunn) in A.N. Wilson, *The*

Reminiscences of my Irish journey in 1849, Carlyle draws time and again on a simple reflex anthropology and zoology. Even when embarking on his Thames steamer he notes 'Canaille of various kinds, Irish by look' and before long has identified 'five or six type-physiognomies' (Ward's word before him) of the Irish rabble, while before his tour is over he has imagined a nightmarish 'black howling Babel of superstitious savagery'. Scarecrow figures haunt Glendalough (this metaphor that Ward used before him is repeated often by Carlyle), and Youghal has a 'semi-savage population'. A swarm of beggars are like 'ravenous dogs round carrion'. One woman is a squirrel; a shopkeeper is 'ferrety'; an elderly traveller is '*horse*-faced'; Isaac Butt displays a visible animalism: his 'big bison-head, black' is 'not quite unbrutal'.[32] Carlyle didn't want to go to Ireland but felt obliged because he reckoned Ireland was 'the breaking point of the huge suppuration which all British and all European society now is' (p. v). He was also sleep-deprived during most of this travels which might explain some of, but of course not all of, his impatience and irritation with much of what he saw and who he met (Gavan Duffy was his fitful guide). He visited workhouses; the Killarney workhouse with 3,000 inmates he saw as a 'human swinery' (p. 133; the metaphor is extended on pp 191, 202, 211); in the Westport Union, with *thirty-thousand* paupers (the workhouse constructed to hold only three or four thousand), is reached 'the acme of human swinery' (p. 201). He is losing faith in philanthropy; 'Can it be a *charity* to keep men alive on these terms?' (p. 202) Yet Carlyle objected to the brutalism of the workhouses. One subsidiary workhouse had 'continents' of young women waiting to be fed when he arrived and his reaction is disgust not just with the scene but with the system and to some extent, of course, with the Irish as the human occasions for disgust. (But he had little time for the 'shamlords', as he called them.)

After Darwin, and despite the emergence of the term 'altruism' and its compatibility with evolutionism, epithets from these counter-philanthropic vocabularies suggested that certain peoples were unevolved and thus inferior in a way seemingly ratified by science; such peoples might be undeserving of charitable relief and methods of improvement because incorrigible. In 1860 (one year after publication of *The origin of species*), Charles Kingsley, the English naturalist and writer, stayed at Markree Castle, County Sligo, and having in a letter home complimented the castle and loveliness of its grounds, confessed:

Victorians (London, 2003), p. 79. **32** Thomas Carlyle, *Reminiscences of my Irish journey in 1849* (London, 1882), pp 3, 16, 160, 72, 111, 130, 73, 181, 68, 54. Froude provided a Preface to this edition. The instincts of Carlyle and Froude were hardly philanthropic; rather they derived culturally from a harsh (judgmental) Christianity and a (proto) Darwinianism that could lapse into misanthropy. Thackeray was not quite of their group. But it must be remembered that the exasperation or even despair caused by enormity and the apparently insoluble can sometimes translate itself into misanthropy as a self-protective psychological device.

> But I am haunted by the human chimpanzees I saw along that hundred miles
> of horrible country. I don't believe they are our fault. I believe here are not
> only many more of them than of old, but that they are happier, better, more
> comfortably fed and lodged under our rule than they ever were. But to see
> white chimpanzees is dreadful; if they were black, one would not feel it so
> much, but their skins, except where tanned by exposure, are as white as ours.[33]

It is hard to believe from that passage but Kingsley was not ill-disposed towards the
Irish and probably assumed he was being almost scientifically neutral with his references to apes, not as explicit metaphor but as something close to literalism. To this
extent, I think his white chimpanzees are to be distinguished from the simian Irish
of the later *Punch* caricatures during the agrarian 'outrages' and from the earlier Irish
who were believed, like the Scythians, to turn into wolves once a year, a belief
Spenser's character Irenius recalls in *A view of the present state of Ireland* and that
William Camden thought was a disease called 'lycanthropia'.[34]

A view of animal and human life that saw the struggle for existence and survival
of the fittest, and witnessed (or remembered) catastrophes such as the Great Famine,
and calamities such as failed rebellions, was one that had to have influenced drama
and novels. The widely promulgated ideas of Darwin's bulldogs, evolutionists T.H.
Huxley and County Carlow-born John Tyndall, and of H.G. Wells in his fiction and
nonfiction, helped create a mentality that affected imaginative writers. At the far
edge of this mentality (yet hugely popular) were, for example, Oscar Wilde's *The
picture of Dorian Gray* (1890) and Bram Stoker's *Dracula* (1897). These novels depict a
darker dimension of evolution: monstrosity and degeneration in human nature. Both
are drenched in contemporary race-consciousness and fascinated by pathology and
by the roles of heredity and environment. Lord Henry Wotton first hears Dorian
Gray's name at his Aunt Agatha's house in London when she wishes Dorian to help
her in her charitable efforts in the East End. Lord Henry is cynical about the kind
of empathetic philanthropy fictionalized by the women novelists and preaches instead
a new hedonism and a new individualism; he discourages the attempt to improve the
hopeless failure and finds 'something terribly morbid in the modern sympathy with
pain'.[35] Philanthropy is a useless attempt to interfere with scientific laws (he means
Darwinism) and so it is for the scientist, not the philanthropist, to solve the problems
of the East End.[36]

The premise of the struggle for existence is one shared by Wilde and Stoker with
the fiction of philanthropy but in the latter, relief and assuagement through fellow-
feeling and charitable provision are sufficient if the human objects of charity retain
their spirituality. In the absence of the spiritual compensation, the evolutionary

33 *Charles Kingsley: his letters and memories of his life*, ed. Mrs Kingsley (London, 1877), vol.
2, p. 107. Kingsley stayed with Froude on his visit to Ireland in the summer of 1860.
34 See my chapter, 'Encountering traditions' in *Nature in Ireland*, p. 26. **35** Oscar Wilde,
The picture of Dorian Gray (London, 1985), pp 36, 46, 64. **36** Ibid., p. 65.

perspective could encourage a laissez-faire approach to social ills which could contemplate individuals and groups going under, perhaps in hopes of the better human qualities among the survivors being inherited. Or it could encourage scientifically-based interventions, of the kind socialists of the time considered – perhaps even root-and-branch reform that would alleviate and then eradicate poverty and inequality. Lord Henry implies the former yet gestures, as Wilde (the author of *The soul of man under socialism*) did too, towards the latter. Meanwhile, Lord Henry's concern for himself was the mirror-image of the disguised self-gratification of the philanthropic who when doing good *felt* good. Perhaps the poor can afford only self-denial, but for the rest of us, Lord Henry says, self-development is the goal, 'to realize one's nature perfectly'.[37] When Dorian does descend into the social abyss of the East End, it is as a drug-addict, a degenerate habitué. He is slumming for ill, not for good. Dorian ends badly, of course, which seems to throw doubt on Lord Henry's anti-philanthropy, but Dorian's end does not validate the Aunt Agathas of the world. Wilde's Darwinism – which he learned as a student at Oxford – remains pervasive and enduring and he is able to derive individuality, self-realization and creative imagination from its principles, not only in *The picture of Dorian Gray* but throughout his works, notably including 'The critic as artist'.[38]

Like *The picture of Dorian Gray*, *Dracula* takes the base material (the settings, the characters, the social exchanges) of philanthropic fiction and turns human degeneration into something truly horrifying and all but intractable, with its origins in poisonous heredity that long predates industrialization and urbanization. The Count's pursuer, Van Helsing, is convinced that the medieval Dracula Voivode and the present Count Dracula are one and the same creature. Here the ancientness of aristocracy, whose seat, Castle Dracula, is the ultimate, degenerated Big House, is terrifying rather than reassuring, and it inverts the venerable *noblesse oblige* that sometimes could inspire philanthropy. Dracula *takes*, indeed *sucks and drains*, rather than gives. He is a selfishness so pure he casts no reflection: he is almost abstract. Yet in a perverted way he *does* give: he offers the promise, even the guarantee, of life beyond the grave, of a quasi-immortality. He even loves in his own terrible way. Philanthropy often professed to draw its inspiration from Christ, and Dracula for his part is a perverse or reverse Christ, drinking the blood of others instead of shedding his blood *for* others, though it still remains a blood transaction.

Dracula's horror is deepened by the guise of the English gentleman he assumes, the better to infiltrate and poison British society. He resembles outwardly those who went among the poor, not as social workers but as those socially slumming, dispensing relief and assurance. Yet he is, underneath, bestial, just as under the civilized surface of the city (Dublin or London) lay the abyss, the underclass, the so-called submerged tenth who posed an insuperable problem for philanthropy. In another

---

37 Ibid., p. 41. **38** See my article, 'Against nature? Science and Oscar Wilde', *University of Toronto Quarterly*, 63 (1993/4), 328–46, reprinted in John Wilson Foster, *Between shadows: modern Irish writing and culture* (Dublin, 2009).

sense, Dracula swings between the cultivated and the animal, according to the sun and moon indeed, by turns embodying the retrogression and progression of evolutionary movement. In doing so, he resembles his near contemporaries, Robert Louis Stevenson's Dr Jeykll, Oscar Wilde's Dorian Gray, Wells' Dr Moreau. A distant implication might be that the cultivated (not the ragged trousered) philanthropist might actually harbor within murderous misanthropic instincts.[39]

We might say fancifully that in *Dracula* and *The picture of Dorian Gray*, Victorian philanthropy makes its last stand. (Count Dracula is beaten, but by business and applied science, not by philanthropy, by anyone's being good or doing good.) Ahead in the new century lay forces and events that would reshape, redirect and shrink the culture of philanthropy – the rise of organized labour, the rise of state welfarism, and, in independent, Catholic Ireland, the rise to predominance of a Church that took social custody of its adherents and succeeded for decades in minimizing and overseeing state welfarism while practising its own virtually monopolistic 'philanthropy'.

---

39 Lord Henry tells Dorian Gray about a philanthropist who, having attained his life's goal of redressing some social grievance, was thereafter plunged into disappointment and became a misanthropist, Wilde, *The picture of Dorian Gray*, pp 139–40.

Index

Page numbers in italic refer to illustrations.